# RESTRUCTURING THE COUNTRYSIDE: ENVIRONMENTAL POLICY IN PRACTICE

To all those who made it happen on the day,
many thanks from Crans-Montana

Restructuring the Countryside: Environmental Policy in Practice

edited by

ANDREW W. GILG

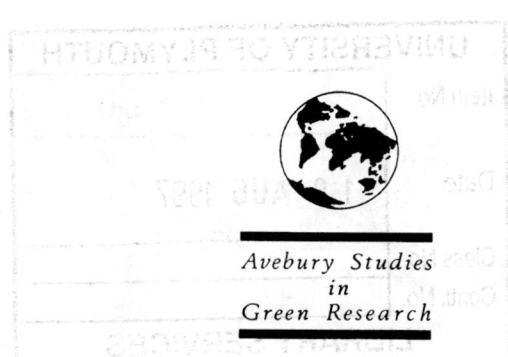

Aldershot · Brookfield USA · Hong Kong · Singapore · Sydney

© A. Gilg 1992

All rights reserved. No part of this publication may be reproduced, stored in a retrieval system, or transmitted in any form or by any means, electronic, mechanical, photocopying, or otherwise without the prior permission of the publisher.

Published by
Avebury
Ashgate Publishing Limited
Gower House
Croft Road
Aldershot
Hants GU11 3HR
England

Ashgate Publishing Company
Old Post Road
Brookfield
Vermont 05036
USA

A CIP catalogue record for this book is available from the British Library and the US Library of Congress.

Reprinted 1997

ISBN 1 85628 248 1

Printed and bound in Great Britain by Intype, London.

Contents

Foreword ... vii

List of contributors ... xiv

SECTION 1 : SOME UNDERLYING ISSUES AND CONCEPTS

1. Restructuring the countryside : An introductory essay Andrew W. Gilg ... 3

2. The modern food system and the environment David Goodman and Michael Redclift ... 19

3. Rural restructuring : Mechanisation and the agricultural workforce Nigel Walford ... 37

4. Elderly farmers as countryside managers Clive Potter and Matt Lobley ... 54

5. "All winds and weathers": Uncertainty, debt and the subsumption of the family farm Steve Pile ... 69

SECTION 2 : CASE STUDIES

6. Patterns and implications of policy-induced agricultural adjustments in the European Community David J Briggs and Elaine Kerrell ... 85

7	The success of set-aside and similar schemes Ian Brotherton	103
8	Soil characteristics of reverted farmland in upland mid-Wales John Gerrard	117
9	Britain's new forests : Public dependence on Private Interest? Kevin Bishop	138
10	Countryside in revolt : Rural response to a proposed hazardous waste facility Owen Furuseth	159
11	Nitrates in water : The politics of pollution regulation Susanne Seymour and Graham Cox	178
12	Water protection zones : A valid management strategy? Ian Foster and Brian Ilbery	203
13	Conservation, conversations and countryside change Ken Willis	221
14	Ecology and land use in Britain R.G.H. Bunce	230

Foreword

This book is the result of many people's ideas and much work by many people whose names do not all appear on the Contents list. The book began its life in 1990, when the AGM of the Rural Geography Study Group of the Institute of British Geographers volunteered me, in my absence, to organise a one day session at the 1991 Annual Conference of the Institute on the Conference theme of 'Environmental Policy in Practice'.

On my return to Exeter I was naturally delighted to undertake this task, and decided to superimpose the theme of 'Restructuring the Countryside', in order to attract the political economy section of the Institute to the session.

Work then began in earnest on organising the day, and in February I wrote round to members of the Committee and other prominent rural geographers to seek ideas for the day, and to solicit contributors. It soon became obvious that the theme was going to attract a good deal of interest. The decision was thus taken to limit the paper sessions to 12 or 13 short, twenty minute position papers, of the type given at the Annual Conference of the Association of American Geographers, and to use these to stimulate a final discussion period attended by non-academics working in the environmental field.

The lack of traditional papers for people to take away with them, then led me to think about the need for a permanent record of the day's proceedings, and so I approached Gower/Avebury to see if they would be prepared to publish the papers from the day. This they gladly agreed to do and so by early summer 1990 plans for this book were being laid.

In May I attended a pre-planning day at Sheffield, a tiresome necessity in this day of slick presentation and media attention on academic conferences, and soon after this the session began to take its final shape as shown on page viii and ix.

INSTITUTE OF BRITISH GEOGRAPHERS ANNUAL CONFERENCE 1991
UNIVERSITY OF SHEFFIELD - THURSDAY 3 JANUARY 1991

Programme for Rural Geography Study Group Session: Convenor: Andrew W Gilg
Restructuring the Countryside: Environmental Policy in Practice

Module 1 Chairman - John Gerrard (University of Birmingham)

Bunce, B (Institute of Terrestrial Ecology)	The ecological consequences of land use change in Britain
Brotherton, I (University of Sheffield)	The success of set-aside and similar schemes
Munton, R and Willis, K (University College London) University of Newcastle upon Tyne)	Progress reports on ESRC countryside change projects

                10.45-11.15   **COFFEE**

Module 2: Chairman - Brian Ilbery (Coventry Polytechnic)

Gerrard, J (University of Birmingham)	Soil changes associated with the reversion of improved farmland to moorland. An example from mid-Wales
Tarrant, J R and Cobb, R (University of East Anglia)	Agricultural extensification and landscape change in East Anglia
Briggs, D (Huddersfield Polytechnic)	Agricultural policy extensification and environment in the European Community
Furuseth, O (University of North Carolina)	The hazardous waste disposal planning process and rural areas
Cox, G (University of Bath)	The PATCH programme

12.45-14.15   **LUNCH**

Module 3: Chairman - John Tarrant (University of East Anglia)

Ilbery, B and Foster, I (Coventry Polytechnic)	Water Protection Zones: a valid management strategy?
Cox, G and Seymour, S (University of Bath)	Nitrates in water: the politics of pollution regulation
Walford, N and Ward, N (Kingston Polytechnic and University College London)	Agriculture and the environment; identifying farmers' responses
Potter, C (Wye College)	Ageing, succession and inheritance on family farms - the environmental implications

15.45-16.15   **TEA**

Module 4: Discussion session led by discussants: Chairman - Ian Bowler

<u>Discussants</u>
Peter Nash, Head of Environmental Protection, MAFF
Roger Clarke, Countryside Commission
William de Salis, Country Landowners Association
Fiona Reynolds, Council for the Protection of Rural England
David Baldock, Institute for European Environmental Policy
H Currie, Regional Manager, MAFF.

In attendance:
K Parker, Peak District National Park

Between May and December many minor hiccups intervened but thanks to all the people involved in the pre-planning period the day itself as reported in Area went off very well.

The report that appeared in Area, (1991), Vol. 23, pp. 169-170

> The restructuring of the countryside is a key area in current rural research and Andrew Gilg (Exeter) convened the Rural Geography Study Group's session on this theme, bringing together 13 papers and 7 policy makers as discussants. Some of the papers had a strong

environmental theme - Bunce (Institute of Terrestrial Ecology) on the ecological effects of land-use changes, Gerrard (Birmingham) on the pedological consequences of moorland improvement, and the two papers on nitrates in water (Ilbery and Foster, Coventry Polytechnic; Cox and Seymour, Bath). Several of the papers were progress reports on research in hand, particularly that under the aegis of the various countryside initiatives from the ESRC - for example the papers by Munton (University College, London), Willis (Newcastle), Cox (Bath), Walford and Ward (University College, London) and Potter (Wye College).

The preliminary nature of the reports (most were only 20 minutes long) and the lack of printed papers limited the extent to which the audience could glean 'results' from the session. What was clear, however, were the common threads to the research agenda today in many of the sub-fields of rural geography. The first point echoes the familiar tag that 'all geography is historical geography'. There is an increasing realisation that a full understanding of processes of rural change requires one to consider long-term issues which work themselves out over decades (such as family life histories or changes in political ideology) as well as more quickly acting processes. The papers by Potter (Wye College), Furuseth (UNC, Charlotte) and Munton (University College London) stressed this dimension of *longue durée*. A related theme is that of geographical scale, both literally and rather more metaphorically. Many of the authors stressed how essential it was to link small scale and large scale processes. Issues such as post-modernism, the service economy and the working of the CAP or GATT can be understood only in relation to the grass-roots forces which nourish them. Equally their working out in practice will be uneven and this can be fully explained only when it is related to the distinctive mix of conditions found in each locality. Briggs (Huddersfield Polytechnic), Tarrant (UEA) and Brotherton (Sheffield) showed how patchy the uptake of extensification and set aside has been, while explaining farmers' responses to new technology was the prime focus of the paper by Walford and Ward (University College, London). Equally valid is the need to ground locality studies in strong policy and theoretical frameworks which allow for the interplay of 'internal' and 'external' factors, themselves scale-dependent terms.

While the importance of these issues of historical and geographical scale has been recognised for some time, a more recent perspective is that of 'discourse'. The UCL group has adopted land development as a focus for their research and they model this as a contest between conflicting groups each seeking to extend its influence, power and property rights by moulding the discussion along its lines. The groups seek to set an agenda, prioritise issues, use scientific evidence or even use words in such a way as to make more likely an outcome favourable to their interests. This was neatly illustrated by the panel of outside speakers from the Ministry of Agriculture, Fisheries and Food, the Countryside Commission, the Council for the Protection of Rural England, the Country Landowners' Association, the Peak District National Park and the Institute for European Environmental Policy. Their commentaries on our work not only added a policy dimension missing from some of the academic papers but demonstrated how their sectoral interest controlled their use of language, their choice of issues to highlight and their attitudes to certain evidence. The importance of the social construction of knowledge was amply demonstrated by these policymakers.

The session was very well attended - up to 70 in the audience - and the Rural Geography Study Group would like to thank most warmly the convenor, Andrew Gilg and the chairpersons (Drs Gerrard, Ilbery, Tarrant and Bowler) for an excellent programme.

Gordon Clark
Lancaster University

I should at this stage also like to thank the speakers, the chairmen, the discussants, and most of all Ian Bowler the then chairman of the Study Group who took over the running of the day from me after mid December, while I was absent in Switzerland.

Following the conference I wrote around asking contributors for the longer versions of their papers for this book. At this stage several people who had earlier expressed reservations decided to drop out, mainly because their research was still at an early stage and they didn't want to rush into print too soon. Reluctantly at this stage we lost Richard Munton's contribution on his ESRC team's major research effort into changing rural Britain; John Tarrant's study of 'Agricultural Extensification in East Anglia; Graham Cox's review of the multi-academic PATCH programme including Walford and Ward's contribution to the programme on identifying farmer responses to pollution.

However, this proved to be a double blessing in disguise. First, it allowed the speakers to prepare more considered, updated and polished papers than they would otherwise had time for and, second, it allowed me to widen the breadth of topics and authors to those who couldn't make the Conference or wouldn't normally attend a Geography conference.

At this stage therefore, David Goodman, Michael Redclift, Steve Pile and Kevin Bishop joined the project, while Nigel Walford and Susanne Seymour rejoined the project with different papers. Therefore the project became much more than a series of conference papers, but a commissioned set of papers on various aspects of current environmental change and the planning response to this. The book is thus a very good reflection of the current research effort in this field.

The delay caused while new authors were commissioned also allowed the editor time to write a considered personal review of environmental change in the early 1990s, rather than as planned merely write a precis of the book.

Such a precis is presented here instead, mainly as an attempt to explain the logic behind the order of the Chapters. The book begins with an introductory essay by myself which makes some cautionary comments about the concept of 'restructuring'. No attempt is made to examine the concept of environmental policy and how this can be assessed because this has been discussed elsewhere by the editor in great depth in his 'Countryside Planning Policies for the 1990s' published by CAB International in 1991. Suffice it to say at this stage that environmental policies can range from voluntary exhortation at one extreme, and to land nationalisation at the other. The trend in recent years has been to try voluntary methods, and if these fail, to move to controls often backed up with financial inducements. In the wider rural policy arena, there has also been a shift from production orientated grants to conservation payments. The reaction of farmers and other rural land users is of course the acid test of changing policies, and Section 2 of the book discusses these reactions in some detail, and finds not surprisingly some big gaps between policy expectations and implementation on the ground.

Returning to Section 1, Goodman and Redclift update their well known and useful analysis of the wider context in which countryside land users operate. Walford provides some useful background data, Pile introduces people into the scene, and Potter and Lobley consider the growing impact that elderly farmers will have on the changing countryside. Section 1 thus sets the parameters within which policies have to operate, the perceived world of decision makers.

Section 2 then provides 9 case studies or research programmes which are attempting to link policy with practice. The section begins with Briggs and Kerrell discussing the evolution of environmentally centred policies within a European dimension. This discussion is then continued by Brotherton in the British context, and it is suggested that much of the programme is so far failing to be accepted by farmers, notably Set-Aside. If Set-Aside does take off Gerrard's analysis of upland land reversion provides some interesting clues as to what might happen in the lowlands. It is more likely however that lowland land will be afforested rather than abandoned, and so Bishop's chapter on the current explosion in afforestation schemes, is particularly timely.

Abandoned land could however also be used to solve the growing problem of what to do with waste, now most existing holes have been filled up. Furuseth's story of resistance to waste disposal in the USA indicates that this may not be an acceptable use. Existing pollution from waste products in agriculture, notably nitrate is the subject of two contrasting papers by Seymour and Cox, and Foster and Ilbery. Finally, two major research projects into the changing countryside are described by Willis and Bunce.

It is thus hoped that this book is much more than a set of conference papers, and is also more than a series of essays. However, there are gaps, both in conceptual issues as well as in practical issues on the ground. Nonetheless, it is hoped that this book in presenting a number of contemporary case studies by both established and emerging experts will fill as many gaps in our knowledge of the changing countryside as any book of 70,000 words or so can do.

Andrew W. Gilg
Moorview Lodge, Exeter, 1 August 1991.

List of contributors

Kevin Bishop is with the Department of City and Regional Planning at the University of Wales at Cardiff.

David Briggs is with the Department of Geographical and Environmental Sciences at Huddersfield Polytechnic.

Ian Brotherton is with the Department of Landscape Architecture at the University of Sheffield.

R.G.B. Bunce is with the Institute of Terrestrial Ecology at Merlewood, Cumbria.

Graham Cox is with the School of Social Sciences at the University of Bath

Ian Foster is with the Centre for Environmental Science Research and Consultancy at Coventry Polytechnic.

Owen Furuseth is with the Department of Geography at the University of North Carolina at Charlotte.

John Gerrard is with the Department of Geography at the University of Birmingham.

Andrew W. Gilg is with the Department of Geography at the University of Exeter.

David Goodman is with the Department of Environmental Studies at the University of California at Santa Cruz.

Brian Ilbery is with the Department of Geography at Coventry Polytechnic.

Elaine Kerrell works with David Briggs at Huddersfield Polytechnic.

Matt Lobley works with Clive Potter at Wye College.

Steve Pile is with the Department of Geography at Middlesex Polytechnic.

Clive Potter is with the Environment Section of Wye College (University of London).

Michael Redclift is a Reader in Rural Sociology at Wye College (University of London).

Susanne Seymour works with Graham Cox at the University of Bath.

Nigel Walford is with the Department of Geography at Kingston Polytechnic.

Ken Willis is with the Department of Town and Country Planning at the University of Newcastle upon Tyne.

SECTION 1
SOME UNDERLYING ISSUES AND CONCEPTS

1 Restructuring the countryside: An introductory essay

ANDREW W. GILG

It is traditional for editors to write an overview chapter in a book of this type, partly culled from conference papers. However, it is also traditional for reviewers of such books to criticise them for being disjointed collections, which no one overview chapter, however brilliant, can overcome. Perhaps reviewers are at fault - myself included - for expecting any book, let alone a series of papers, to be comprehensive, and in this era of post-modernism, maybe we should expect less general order and seek instead a view of reality based on ad hoc case studies. In such a context, this book which includes contributions from most of the active researchers in the field should be viewed as a 'State of the Art' statement, rather than a textbook. Nonetheless, for those seeking a textbook overview this introductory essay does provide some brief references to some of the contributions of the other workers in this field - including some paper givers at the conference - albeit in the context of the essay, rather than as a card index inspired piece of comprehensiveness.

The purpose of this essay is thus not to provide a summary of the papers (see the foreword for this) or any overarching theory. In contrast its purpose is to provide some cautionary comments about overambitious claims made by some theoreticians concerning the processes involved in restructuring the countryside. The underlying theme is that no one theory can be used to illuminate the chaos of day to day change, and indeed Chaos Theory which supports this contention is briefly discussed at the end of the essay. Hopefully, this essay will thus provide a cautionary perspective from which to view each chapter.

Three key points about restructuring

There are three key points to consider. First, the difficulties involved in providing concepts of the process. Second, the different strategies that farmers may adopt and, third, the crucial point that there may be more inertia in the countryside than many people care to admit because of a vested interest in hyping up the process.

Problems with the concept itself

The main problem with the concept lies with the very phrase itself, for axiomatically, 'restructuring the countryside' implies the existence of an underlying system of control, whether this be: the hidden hand of Adam Smith's market; the grand design of capital accumulators; a conspiracy of Zionists/Europeans/or other groups; a grand strategy masterminded by Whitehall mandarins, or any other fanciful ideas dreamed up by those deluded enough to seek out conspiracy theories.

The currently fashionable delusion is, of course, so-called Marxist Political Economy which, although it contains a good deal of valid assumptions, contains at its very heart a fundamental flaw, notably the assumption that Capital Accumulation drives the world in its search for industries to 'penetrate'. The difficulty with this position lies in the total failure to explain how capital, an inanimate concept, can act as a sentient being in the world of human affairs. It also ignores the fact that constant research into the decision making processes of those people employed to manage capital, shows that their main motivation is to preserve their jobs and their organisations, even if this does not always maximise profits or capital growth.

Steve Pile in his excellent chapter indeed reminds his fellow travellers of Marx's dictum that it is people who make history, albeit not in circumstances of their own choosing. Pile cautions Marxist political economists that, even when they have considered farmers' beliefs and motivations, they have treated people as the bearers of the 'logic' of capital, and failed to appreciate that it is people who do things, not capital.

Unfortunately, the prime mover of the 'Restructuring Thesis', Terry Marsden (1990), while accepting that the initial 1980s reformulation of Marxist agrarian theory now needs to be modified to incorporate diversity over and above the unilinearity of the initial model, still places capital accumulation at the centre of the process, as the following passage demonstrates:

> 'Pluriactivity of farm households confronts some of the inadequacies of political economy in general, and Marxist agrarian theory in particular. Through a re-

conceptualisation of the process of commoditisation and uneven development, we are now developing a more flexible political economy *without abandoning* our previous emphasis on political and economic structures or the centrality of the capital accumulation process. Such a development involves....focussing upon the variable sets of interactions which occur between external capitals, farm households and labour processes' (p. 381).

If we strip away the jargon, Marsden's last sentence does in fact provide a valuable tool for analysing how in an ad hoc and accidental world, farming and capital interact, by viewing the process within the context of Steve Pile's observation that farmers welcome some of the possibilities that capitalism offers, while rejecting others.

This still leaves the problem of how 'capital en masse' is supposed to be attempting to penetrate agriculture and so restructure the countryside. The literature here is very silent, and there are few, if any, studies of how managers of capital design the great penetration exercise, how battle plans are drawn up, how different strategies are evaluated, let alone of how the takeover is consummated. Richard Munton's (1980) study of how the financial institutions decided to invest in farmland in the 1970s is a rare example, and is limited to one aspect of the process. There are though studies of the food processing and other industries in terms of how the food chain has been altered, see for example, Goodman and Redclift's chapter. However, these do not answer the questions of why, if at all, these industries should have restructuring the countryside on their agenda. For example, there are few worked examples of how financiers and entrepreneurs have appraised the economics of countryside investment, apart from Munton's earlier work. All too often it is assumed that capital is not only animate, but clever, risk free and possessed of a perpetual winning streak. If more of these 'experts' on capital accumulation had ever contemplated running a business and stared into the dark abyss of actually losing everything, they would realise the dilemmas and uncertainties that plague any capital investment. Those who can, do. Those who can't, theorise.

More fundamentally, we need to ask why capital should want to be involved in penetrating a declining industry, agriculture. In contrast most recent evidence shows firms leaving the agricultural scene, for example, ICI's flight out of loss making fertilisers. Nonetheless, the farming industry remains as important a part of the economy as any other single industry, and will continue to control at least 60 to 70 per cent of rural land use, and thus the environment.

If we wish to understand how the countryside is being restructured we thus need to know how farmers are reacting to the changed economic and political situation of the 1980s and 1990s.

Different strategies employed by farmers and their households

The key point here is that most farmers want to remain farmers. This is shown by virtually every survey of farming. For example, Harrison and Tranter (1989) in a study of 1276 farmers have examined nine possible strategies for farmers to follow in response to falling incomes. The most popular response, favoured by 58% was perversely to increase output. More sensibly, 40% cut inputs, 34% cut machinery, 33% cut labour costs; 21% cut out an unprofitable enterprise; 21% took financial advice' 13% carried on regardless; 8% diversified; and 6% paid off debts by selling land.

Marsden, Whatmore, Munton and Little (1986) in a more analytical approach have divided farmers up into four groups: full time agriculturalists (34%); survivalists (32%); accumulators (26%); and hobby farmers (9%). They have used these categories to examine the degree to which farmers are more or less willing to be subsumed, in their words, or in mine, to seek help from outside sources of finance or expertise, e.g. growing crops under contract. The degree to which independence of decision making has been surrendered has then been developed by the same team (Whatmore, Munton, Marsden and Little, 1987) in a typology with at one extreme, 'closed enterprises' run by owner occupier families completely independently, to at the other extreme 'open enterprises' run by tenant farmers deep in debt, and subject to marketing contracts for their produce. The team has found some evidence, though not consistent, that farms are losing independence.

Elsewhere, however, Shucksmith and Winter (1990) report that a majority of farm households see no need to diversify or restructure their holding. They observe that restructuring is an all or nothing decision, usually related to a complete sale of the farm or transfer of its assets to another family member. Where alternative income or capital is sought, it is found either in off-farm employment, or by selling off buildings for barn or similar conversions. The core business is perceived to be the farm, and even if this is an economic fiction, it remains a psychologically important fact which helps to explain why inertia rather than restructuring may be the order of the decade to come.

Inertia

According to Marxist theory farming should have become an industry dominated by large farms several decades ago, in line with, for example, the car industry. This of course ignores the unique facts of the farm economy and its way of life. First, farming is an extensive form of production, and even with large machines, few economies of scale are achievable once a farm extends to 500 hectares. Attempts to do otherwise as in the Soviet Union have manifestly failed because no one manager can oversee thousands of hectares closely enough. Nonetheless, where production can be intensified, as in the case of indoor poultry units, production has become concentrated in very few hands. It is arguable however whether such activities can be considered to be farming.

Although farms of 500 hectares may be the desirable compromise between economies of scale and satisfactory supervision, even in Britain these farms are the exception rather than the norm. This is because few farms come onto the market in any one year, since farmers have every disincentive not to sell. First, in many cases they would be selling their livelihood. Second, they would be selling not just a farm, but in most cases their home too, and third, if they have heirs they would be selling their inheritance. Even where farms are sold, more likely than not the farm will not be sold to a neighbour but to a farmer new to the area. The adventitious nature of the land market thus makes farm expansion, except in separated, difficult to manage holdings problematic. Significantly, most really large farms - over 1,000 hectares - are run as corporate units scattered across the countryside, though in recent years many of these have run into management difficulties. Ironically, the largest farms are those estates of the landed gentry which escaped the break up necessitated by death duties.

A final reason for inertia is provided by agricultural policy which has engendered a belief among farmers that they are a protected species. This has been reinforced in 1991 by the McSharry proposals which, incredibly, actually plan to increase farm policy spending. Significantly, the plan proposes to divert EC agricultural spending from production to farmer support, notably small farmers. Farmers thus have every incentive to stay in farming and in Steve Pile's words:

> the *real* subsumption of the labour process may be restricted by the availability of land, diminishing returns on investment in land, site specificity, and the immobility of capital in land and property relations.

Two case studies are now provided in order to illuminate some of the comments so far made.

TWO CASE STUDIES

Case Study One: Oliver Walston

Oliver Walston is a well known journalist and farms 800 hectares at Thriplow in Cambridgeshire. In 1991 he bared his soul in his column in Farmers Weekly (5 July 1991, p.13) concerning his attitudes to farming since the 1970s. The following paragraphs are an abridged version of his article.

> 'I sold some land the other day. It was the most difficult decision I have ever made. Don't listen to anyone who says that it is the occupation rather than the

ownership of land which matters. They may be right in hard economics, but they fail to understand human nature.

I had always assumed that the possession of land is the second most basic desire of the human race. The pleasure of owning the soil on which you grow crops, raise animals, walk, and hunt is indescribable. Today as I pass my 50th birthday, I must admit that the desire to procreate wanes while the need for more acres increases.

A decision to sell land should, in theory, be a straightforward one based on a rational assessment of the facts and an intelligent guess about the future. In practice, nothing could be further from the case. To hell with budgets, cash flows and my fears about the CAP. What did I actually think about? I became obsessed with the pleasures of ownership. That was bad enough, but there were other unpleasant sensations which lingered in what I laughingly call my brain. What would the neighbours think? Would everyone assume I was going bust? Would local merchants stop giving me credit? Did this mean I was a failure as a farmer? Or a failure as a member of the human race?

Walston then considers doing nothing and reflects on the 1970s and 1980s.

My farm, like so many others in Britain, had flourished mightily during the 1970s and early 1980s. In those days my biggest single problem had been knowing what to do with the profits which kept pouring in as both yields and prices moved steadily upwards. For a few years I solved the dilemma by buying gigantic quantities of shiny new machinery. But it soon became clear that was not sufficient. Brussels kept throwing money at me ....

So I looked around for a quicker and more efficient way of getting rid of my money. The solution was not hard to find. I bought land whenever it came up for sale on the boundary of the farm. I felt as if I had died and gone to heaven. Each year the farm got bigger ...

The capital value of my land rose even faster than my profits, and within five years my investment had doubled. There were a few minor irritations, like the fact that my rent went up embarrassingly fast too, but I could live with that.

And then things began to turn sour. Prices went down, costs continued to rise and yields remained static. As if this were not bad enough, interest rates crept higher and higher. Nobody ...could fail to notice that the whole political climate in the EC was changing profoundly. This was no minor hiccup....It was a profound seismic change which meant that once again British agriculture was entering a period of depression we had not known since the 1930s...

One vision kept pushing itself to the front of my

> mind...Back in 1984 I had spent some time in Nebraska visiting bankrupt farmers; I was amazed to learn that bankrupt farmers were not necessarily bad farmers. Indeed the opposite was more often the case. The bankrupt farmers of Nebraska all had one thing in common, they had borrowed more money than they could afford to repay. Thus the realisation dawned on me that being a good farmer would not inevitably enable me to survive the 1990s. No. To survive I would have to be a low-cost farmer. And a low-cost farmer is a man who does not owe any money.
>
> That of course was not a comfortable realisation. Thanks to my land purchases, I was saddled with substantial debts. And so over a period of five months I found myself spending more and more time talking to every expert I could find...

These experts informed Walston that he could survive but with a drastic change in lifestyle if everything that could go wrong did so.

> So after months of indecision during which I changed my mind every couple of days, I squeezed my guts into a knot and decided to sell one third of the farm. My objective was clear. I should end up owing no money whatsoever, and having a bit of cash in the bank with which to take advantage of any opportunities which might appear in the next few years. I would become a farmer who can survive in the real market place in the real world and not be dependent on subsidies.
>
> If wheat falls to £85/t I shall still be in business. But I shall be a smaller farmer, with only two thirds of the acres I used to occupy last year.

What does Walston's story tell us? Basically, it tells us that we live in a chaotic world in which individuals make decisions with imperfect knowledge, and not always for rational reasons. It shows us too that capital is a key factor, as are politics. These two factors can then be combined with people to give us a trinity on which to base our interpretation of restructuring in the countryside: *People, politics and capital*. This is of course not too far removed from the classical economic trinity of: Land, labour and capital. All I have done is to combine land into capital, substitute people for labour, and introduce politics into the equation. It is my belief that this composite concept is a useful base from which to evaluate the contents of this book, and thus the process of restructuring the countryside. To this end a second case study is now presented.

Case Study Two: Mrs Fraser, the Gilgs and the Tickners

Mrs Fraser is in her seventies. In 1945 she inherited the Westhide estate in Herefordshire from her grandfather. In order to avoid death duties the estate bypassed her mother who was a wealthy woman in her own right. Death duties had in fact been the prime reason why the estate came into the family in the first place. In the early years of the century the Stoke Edith estate comprising over 6,400 hectares had been sold off into smaller estates of around 480 hectares in order to pay duty. Mrs Fraser's grandfather, Mr Jenkins a wealthy coal mine owner from South Wales, purchased the Westhide section of the estate and left Wales, following the well worn path of Victorian entrepreneurs out of industry and into the squirearchy.

Mrs Fraser thus grew up as a highly eligible landed lady and it was no surprise in 1945 when she married a Cambridge Athletic Blue. The happy couple then looked around for a personal secretary to manage their affairs. One unfortunate applicant was my father who, in his letter of employment, was given what now look like feudal conditions of service. But, as a victim of the Wall Street crash when the cotton trading business left in trust to him by his father on his death in 1924 failed, he had known the experience of riches to rags only too well. To live in the Court, a Georgian farmhouse – albeit a tied cottage in the eyes of the law – and to serve wealthy people was one way of living out a genteel if relatively poor life. Coming down to earth after service in the RAF, and beginning his marriage to my mother again was another consolation, which resulted in my birth as one of the post war bulge in 1946.

For a while things were good. The estate was run as two separate entities. The 'home farm' of 240 hectares was run by a bailiff, Bill Amos, as a typical mixed Herefordshire farm: pedigree Herefords; Hops; Orchards; and a 100 hectare wood. Incredibly the estate employed over forty workers, in the fields, in the gardens and in the 'big house', the Porch. The rest of the estate was run by three tenant farmers. The fields were small, the hedges high, and the meadows full of horses and butterflies. It was a countryside I now only see in parts of Mid Wales.

By the mid 1950s however things began to change. Mr Fraser began to be bored and sought new challenges. New farming techniques were coming in, and on visits to North America the Frasers had seen how big farming could work. Accordingly they looked for a young technocrat who could develop a new arm to the estate, a pedigree Jersey herd. They found him in Peter Clewes, an outrageously attractive graduate of the Royal College of Agriculture at Cirencester. The son of a small businessman from Birmingham he was in contrast to my father upwardly mobile. He was young, blond, clever (top in his year), and athletic (good enough to play top class Rugby for Gloucester). To Mrs Fraser he became a blue eyed boy.

To Mr Fraser, Bill Amos and my father, he was however a cuckoo in the nest. The cosy farm would never be the same again. Peter Clewes was soon promoted to run the whole estate and given the new role of Manager and he soon set about rationalising the farm in a vigorous way. The first victim was Bill Amos, and I shall never forget one breakfast when a tearful yeoman thrust a grubby envelope onto the table. 'This is it' he said. There were to be many more 'this is its' over the years, as people came and went in rapid succession. I soon learned that 'this is it' was a euphemism for handing in notice. For poor Bill Amos it was more than that. It was a betrayal of his whole life, and before long he died a broken man.

Mr Fraser too suffered from the change, since he was no longer Mrs Fraser's right hand man. For a time he found consolation in photography, painting and journalism, where he contributed an Oliver Walston type column for John Tickner, the then editor of a now defunct weekly 'Farm and Country'. The column titled 'Leaning on the Gate' had a Sunday evening deadline. Many a Sunday including village cricket on our lawn was spoiled by urgent requests for information from my father's office with which to embroider the column. Nonetheless these columns provide an interesting insight into how the estate was rapidly restructured between the mid 1950s and mid 1960s.

My father suffered too because he now had three bosses, and never really knew who was in charge. This was meant to be sorted out at daily conferences over coffee in the 'big house' which brooded over ours in a sort of threatening way. It was the seat of power and authority, from which my father would often return in despair and rage. Gradually however it became clear that Clewes would prevail.

He brought in fellow Cirencester graduates to develop a crack dairy herd of 200 Jersey milking cows. He replaced traditional farm workers with agricultural students and graduates from around the world, including George Orwell's adopted son. As the tenant farmers retired he brought their land into the farm. He simplified the economy of the farm into three core areas: hops, which trebled in size with the acquisition of the tenant farms; the dairy herd; and cereal production. Other enterprises were run down: the pedigree Herefords were kept as an expensive showpiece hobby for the Frasers; the traditional orchards were grubbed up, and on one of the tenant farms pasture land was replaced by 40 hectares of contract dwarf cider trees. Horticulture was also abandoned. This enterprise had once provided work for my mother and had helped provide the income to send me and my elder brother to public school, albeit Hereford Cathedral School rather than the top ten school Haileybury, which my father wished he could have sent us to. How lucky we were!

The net result was a very simplified landscape. Hedges were ripped out; meadows were ploughed, drained and covered with chemicals; and large buildings erected. In employment terms the area of land to be covered doubled, but the amount of work fell, so that only twelve people were employed by the mid 1960s. Tied cottages were sold and bungalows put up for former tenant farmers.

For Peter Clewes all this was a great success. The farm became fabulously profitable, it was awarded prizes for modern husbandry, and visitors arrived in droves to marvel at the transformation. Mrs Fraser could do her daily tour in the Land Rover, stand on Poll Noddy and be Queen of most she surveyed.

There were however tensions, most notably in the area of field sports, a recreation strongly favoured by the Frasers – especially field trialling – but not by Peter Clewes. To those not familiar with field trials, Golden Retrievers or Labradors are trained to retrieve pheasants, ducks or partridges which have been shot by lines of tweed-suited 'guns', after they have been 'beaten' up into the air by lines of 'beaters'. The dogs then expound an inordinate amount of effort in a long-winded attempt to retrieve the often half-dead birds whose dying flaps are highly visible to all present, except for the dogs. The dog which is the least inefficient is deemed to be the winner. A good time is had by all, except for the victims who make tasty eating.

The rearing and raising of game birds however conflicts with commercial farming, since land has to be set aside for this purpose, and farming operations delayed so as to provide cover for the birds. The operation also involves the employment of two gamekeepers. It is therefore a hobby which demands big profits from the farm or outside capital to support it.

Field trialling is more though than a hobby. Indeed as with other field sports, the 'unspeakable' in pursuit of the, in this case highly eatable – to paraphrase Sassoon – allows entry into the upper echelons of the English class system. Mrs Fraser's grandfather had achieved the first step by acquiring land, Mrs Fraser took the next step by entering into the world of field trialling, which gained her access to a highly desirable prize, tea at Sandringham with the Royal Family who are also into field sports.

Ironically, it was on another visit to a field trial that Mr Fraser suffered a fatal heart attack.

Another death in the family occurred in this period. This time it was Mrs Fraser's mother, who apart from leaving much money also bequeathed one Rolls Royce and an Aston Martin DB5. In spite of the James Bond connotations, it was not only the time of Goldfinger but also of Harold Wilson. Threats to control the flow of capital out of the country, the fear of socialist taxation and other measures, encouraged Mrs Fraser to invest heavily in farmland in Australia. In particular, several thousand hectares of land released by Western Australia were purchased and transformed from rangeland to arable land. Peter Clewes was dispatched twice a year to dispatch snakes from his pied à terre, and to sow and harvest the crops. The resulting profits provided an Australian source of income for Mrs Fraser who took to spending her winters down under.

This period, the mid 1960s, was the zenith of the estate, and

I spent a very happy pre-Edinburgh year from Christmas 1964 to September 1965 working on what was a very well managed model estate. It also enabled me to see how the half dozen or so farm men thought and how they related to the middle class students and graduates who also formed the workforce. For example, Ginger Jones, a rough diamond who had succeeded Bill Amos as bailiff was an ardent Conservative, as were most of the men. In contrast Wally Reynolds the Herefords' stockman had seen a bit of Britain by travelling to livestock shows and realised the insecurity of his position. He saved avidly, and by literally furnishing his tied cottage with orange boxes he managed to buy his own house in the 1970s. The roughest man, Paddy McArthy an Irish Catholic with a brood of children baited George Orwell's son and his Loretto accent most cruelly. Personally, the year and two further summer vacations gave me a financial base to accumulate my own capital in the form of a flat in Edinburgh before my twenty-first birthday, but it also made me for a time a Socialist. I saw for the first time how the farm men worked for relatively poor rewards compared to the riches I had seen on many visits to the 'big house' where I had often been summoned to play with the children of visiting friends, some from the pages of the Gossip columns and the so-called County set. One particular incident while grain drying - a ninety hour a week job - remains in my memory.

Mrs Fraser appeared one evening about 6.30 and found a pile of grain that had fallen off the grain trailer and failed to enter the drying machine. She not only scooped it all up with her bare hands, but berated me soundly for wasting money. Her money of course, and that night I returned home singing the Red Flag. Like most of the farm men I knew that we could have run the farm not only as well as them, but better. A cooperative run by Clewes, and with shares for all, would have provided a very nice lifestyle. The only difficulty was that Mrs Fraser owned the resources, and creamed off what seemed an inordinate share of the profits in return for hardly risking only a proportion of her capital. Indeed the farm then was a licence to print money, a fact from which I benefitted with a crate of 'Veuve Cliquot Pousardin' champagne given to me to celebrate my engagement to Joyce, the daughter of a local farming family in June 1967.

Although farming continued to be prosperous the estate began to founder from the mid 1960s onwards. First Peter Clewes, once the cuckoo himself, found himself under threat. In 1965 towards the end of my pre Edinburgh year off I was aware of a violent new presence, announced first by a grain trailer driven with considerable panache, and then by the squealing acceleration of a Triumph Vitesse.

The new entrant was a pre Cirencester student, replacing the solid reliable Andrew Perrins, heir to the Worcester sauce empire immortalised by Harold Wilson. His name was Sir Alister Brook, son of Lord Brook and heir to much of the land north of the Great Glen in Scotland. Alister was a wild impetuous boy. Keen on racing, he helped convince Mrs Fraser that the estate should attempt to win the Grand National. Such an endeavour would have suited Oliver Walston's failed attempts to spend his farm profits, since all but a handful of National Hunt horses run at vast losses to their owners. In this regard Mrs Fraser's horses were spectacularly successful, even more so than falling at the first fence.

This might not have been a problem if the estate had remained under sole management. In the early 1970s Mrs Fraser was involved in a near fatal car crash and having been reminded of her mortality decided to divide the estate into two limited companies. Peter Clewes took over most of the former tenant farms including all the hops, the most wonderfully profitable crop in a good year, and one interestingly controlled by quotas and a Marketing Board since the 1930s. Alister Brook managed the home farm and some of its accretions. This he did badly. The estate suffered from neglect, and the unthinkable occurred, debts began to be incurred. After many rows Alister Brook was thrown out in a palace coup and Peter Clewes restored. By then, however, Peter Clewes had used the interregnum to set up his own management business and was now successfully managing thousands of hectares of land around the West Midlands as well as acquiring his own land.

The net result was that the estate was now run with minimal attention. The crops grew in fields managed according to formula husbandry carried out by a shiftless and shifting workforce of young cowboys on ever more monstrous machinery. On my sporadic visits to home I would wake to see only three long-haired youths assemble for work, compared to the fifteen cloth capped farm men of my teenage years and the forty of my birthday. My father struggled on in these miserable years in the 1970s, mainly to put my younger brother through public school. In a triumph of hope over experience he left school at eighteen, to enter farm college three days before my father died at the age of 69, leaving my mother and brother with virtually no assets at all.

This left my mother living alone in a Georgian farm house with an acre of garden, and a personal pension of £500 a year verbally promised by Mrs Fraser. As a widow she was entitled to live there for as long as she liked. However, two years before she had befriended a new entrant to the village, John Tickner, the famous sporting cartoonist and erstwhile editor for Mr Fraser's 'Leaning on the Gate' column in the 1960s. He too had experienced restructuring, this time in the magazine world, where IPC had rationalised his job some years before. Falling on relatively hard times Mrs Fraser had invited him and his wife to live in a grace and favour cottage, with no rent being payable. My mother became friendly with John when she helped nurse his blind wife through a terminal illness, and then helped John deal with his own illness. In due course John was a tower of strength when my own father became terminally ill in 1978. It was no surprise when they married in the summer of 1979.

This however meant that my mother lost her personal pension

and any legal right to stay in the Court. However it was always understood, mainly from precedent, that no former employee or their widowed spouses had ever been evicted from one of the estate's houses, although people had been asked to move from one house to another.

This uncertain but apparently stable tenure allowed my mother and stepfather to rebuild their lives, and for John to have an Indian summer as an author and cartoonist. The Court became a beacon of civilised lifestyle among a sea of unkempt and uncared for farmland as Mrs Fraser's few remaining minions and some seedy horses went through the motions of farming. Increasingly Mrs Fraser had led the life of a recluse in the 'big house' which became dirtier and dirtier, as all the old retainers retired or died. With fewer and fewer links with the past and no heirs - the nearest relative is a cousin who is married to another large landowner - Mrs Fraser also spent more time in Australia.

In 1989 she decided that the 'big house' was no longer for her and attempted to move to one of the farm cottages. The first move was easy. She descended on Mary Greenwood - one of her grace and favour non-rent paying tenants - one morning and gave her six months' notice to quit. The failure to pay rent, even though offered by Mary Greenwood - over the half dozen years of her occupation - meant of course that there was no legal right of tenure. The next move was to apply for planning permission to demolish the ramshackle cottage and to build a modern new bungalow. This was refused by the planners.

This precipitated the ultimate act of the Fraser era at Westhide. Rumours began to abound that the estate was to be sold, with all workers being sacked and everybody else - retired included - to be evicted. Without warning estate agents came to value my mother's house and unofficially told her that she had six months to find somewhere else, since the estate was to be sold and Mrs Fraser was moving to Australia.

During various discussions conducted between my mother's solicitor and Mrs Fraser's solicitor (my mother never met Mrs Fraser to discuss the matter, nor did Mrs Fraser even say goodbye after forty-five years), several options emerged:

First, to fight the threatened eviction in court without any hope of winning on legal grounds, but to deflect the attempt from even being made;

Second, to accept the offer of another much smaller and dilapidated tied cottage on the estate. This however was to be renovated at my mother's expense, albeit rent free; and

Third, for my mother and John to buy a small house, using the savings that John had earned from his retirement earnings and with my brothers and me helping out with the payments on the mortgage.

The third option was chosen and in April 1991 my mother and John moved into a 1980s two up, two down semi in a small village.

As for Mrs Fraser, she emigrated to Australia in the Spring of 1991. The estate however wasn't sold but all the working capital was. Some former workers however remained in estate cottages on a rent paying basis, while another widower who had not remarried remained legally in her tied cottage. As far as local rumour is correct, Peter Clewes now owns part of the farm and rents the remainder.

What does this tale of intrigue and change tell us about rural restructuring? First, it reminds us that restructuring isn't new, and has been going on all this century. Second, it tells us that it is people who make history, not capital. Third, it tells us that in the process, many people get hurt. Fourth, it tells us that there is no logical imperative to take up technical innovation, government policy, or to accept the blandishments of capital, as far as all the actors were concerned, they were masters of their own destiny, including the farm men. Some people may see them as only pawns in the capitalist's game, but they did not then, nor now does my younger brother, who is a happy as a sand boy thirty-two year old farm worker for a farmer who is a member of CND and a Quaker. Now there's a farmer stereotype. Fifth, it tells us that restructuring doesn't always lead to economically efficient solutions. Sixth, in terms of gender, it tells us that women are not always the subservient actors. Seventh, it demonstrates that outside capital can penetrate, as in the case of the contract cider orchards, but to mutual advantage. Eighth, it shows that politics do influence events, for example, the first move into Australia following the election of Harold Wilson in the mid 1960s. Ninth, it shows that personalities are crucial, in particular the different personalities of Peter Clewes the ambitious petit-bourgeois technocrat and Alister Brook, the dilettante bourgeoise. Tenth, as Gordon Clark has pointed out in the Foreword, it reminds us that change takes place over decades, and is the result of complex interactions between a whole host of forces. Eleventh, it confirms my view set out at the conclusion of the Walston case study that the key forces are people, politics and capital, and also confirms Marsden's assertion that restructuring is a result of interactions between external capitals, farm households and labour processes. But neither case study supports Marsden's theory that capital accumulation is the centre of the process. Finally, and most importantly it tells us that no one theory or explanation can cover even the history of one estate, even over only forty-five years. A combination of theories, based on the interaction of people, politics and capital can however allow us to make generalisations about a chaotic world.

A concluding thought about chaos theory

According to some commentators (Cartwright, 1991) chaos theory is arguably the most important scientific idea of this century, and could challenge theories and beliefs that have dominated science and philosophy for three centuries. The basic idea of chaos theory is indeed unsettling. In simple terms, chaos is order without predictability. Thus there are systems, both physical and social, that we are allowed to understand in the sense that they can be fully described by means of a finite set of conditions or rules. These systems are at the same time, however, fundamentally unpredictable.

Thus chaos is not anarchy or randomness. Chaos is order, but the order itself is 'invisible'. What chaos thus implies is a kind of inherent uncertainty principle, not just in how we perceive the world, but in how the world actually works.

What are the implications of this for theories about restructuring in the countryside? First, chaos theory may make it easier for us to understand the world, thus we need to build only very simple models or theories. Second, because our ability to understand each element of the world is limited by the assumptions of chaos theory we need to build an ensemble of models and theories and mix and match them as time and place changes. Third, because chaotic systems are predictable only on an incremental or local basis we need to build area and time specific models, rather than global ones which are subject to too much cumulative feedback.

In the final analysis we must all make up our own minds as to how we rationalise the chaotic world around us, and as such we will all be prisoners of our prejudices, and see what we want to find from the succeeding chapters in this book. I bid you good reading.

References

Cartwright, T.J. (1991), 'Planning and Chaos Theory', *Journal of the American Planning Association*, vol. 57. pp.44-56.

Harrison, A. and Tranter, R.B. (1989), *The Changing Financial Structure of Farming*, Centre for Agricultural Strategy, University of Reading.

Marsden, T. (1990), 'Towards the Political Economy of Pluriactivity',*Journal of Rural Studies*, vol. 6, pp. 375-82.

Marsden, T., Whatmore, S., Munton, R. and Little, J. (1986), 'The restructuring process and economic centrality in capitalist agriculture', *Journal of Rural Studies*, vol. 2,pp. 271-80.

Munton, R. (1977), 'Financial institutions: their ownership of agricultural land in Great Britain', *Area*, vol. 9, pp. 29-37.

Shucksmith, M. and Winter, M. (1990), 'The Politics of Pluriactivity in Britain', *Journal of Rural Studies*, vol. 6, pp. 429-35.

Whatmore, S., Munton, R., Marsden, T. and Little, J. (1987), 'Interpreting a regional typology of farm businesses in southern England', *Sociologia Ruralis*, vol, 27, pp. 103-22.

2 The modern food system and the environment

DAVID GOODMAN AND MICHAEL REDCLIFT

There is much more to the restructuring of the countryside than changes in agricultural technology. Refashioning the genetic structure of crops and animals, important as it is, represents only one face of the technological revolution which has marked the appearance of the modern food system. Just as nature has been redesigned from within, through animal genetics and plant biotechnology, it has been transformed from without, leading, in turn, to changes in the physical environment, or countryside. These changes in the "face of the land", themselves stimulated by technological change and accompanying shifts in the labour process have contributed to new social conflicts and political demands, around what has come to be seen as a Green political agenda. As we argue in our book, Refashioning Nature, Food, Ecology, Culture (1991) the development of the food system implies a major change in the "natural" environment, as well as in the genetic composition of the species. The scope of this change can hardly be overestimated, and forms the basis of this chapter.

The environmental effects of modern agriculture point to contradictions within the entire model on which the modern food system is based. Modern agriculture developed out of the partial separation of "farming" activities from the natural resource base, on which these activities were traditionally dependent. This, in turn, led to technological innovation in agriculture and the design of industrially-produced food. Together with the accompanying policy incentives this has presented problems for the planned evolution of the food system. Some sectors, such as the production of chemical fertilizers, plant breeding and pesticides, developed "autonomously", according to a scientific and industrial logic only loosely related to the cycle of agricultural production. The reintroduction of new industrial components into agriculture, and the food system more generally, posed problems in two ways: some processes were taken out of "farm" production (appropriation) and others were substituted, especially in food processing activities (substitution) (Goodman et al 1987).

These transformative technological changes were associated with major shifts in the labour process, not only on the farm but in the household and in the food industry. However, an area of equal concern has emerged during the last decade, which promises to pose even more serious problems for the evolution of the food system. This is the environment. Recent decades have witnessed a series of policy interventions designed to reduce, or reverse, the unforeseen or negative effects of the food system on the environment, especially in the developed countries. No area of concern demonstrates the difficulty of managing the contradictions of the food system as clearly as the environment.

Conflicts over the rural environment, and over food quality, have come to represent the clearest indication yet of the problems which the modern food system poses for sustainable development, and for the model of economic growth based on intensive accumulation which spawned the modern food system itself. This chapter examines the impact of the modern food system on the environment in the developed countries, and the social responses which these environmental changes have evoked in recent years. The wider, global implications of these processes are examined in Chapters Five and Six of Goodman and Redclift (1991).

Our analysis begins by considering the changes within the food system which have undermined long-term sustainability, and which were associated with the transference of economic activities between the farm and other components of the wider system. In the next section the major agricultural policy instruments which have been brought to bear on the rural environment in the industrialised countries are examined, notably the effects of price support policies and economic incentives in the introduction of more capital intensive, "high" technology agriculture. The following section considers the effects on the environment of these policy mechanisms, including the loss of genetic resources, the pollution of water and soils, the threats to sustainable utilization posed by land degradation and the effects of agricultural change on amenity and recreation in rural areas. These environmental effects of the modern food system are considered as first, second and third-order problems, each of which requires major adjustments, at the international as well as the national level. Finally, the chapter examines the role of management interventions and environmental movements in seeking to modify or reverse these processes.

The food system leaves the farm

The description of farming in Hooton Pagnell (Rushton and Whitney, 1934) contains most of the elements of what was still, in the 1930s, looked upon as a "natural" farming system, heavily dependent on the cyclical and seasonal quality of rural life. Animals were left to graze in the fields, or fed on fodder crops produced on the farm, bought inputs such as fertilizers and pesticides played a negligible part in the farm accounts, a sizable part of the food for home consumption was still provided by the farm, marketing was still in its infancy, and the "farm family" (largely the women) processed and prepared food in the home. Each of these elements, it might be noted, has since been removed (partially or fully) from the farm economy and relocated, usually in an industrial form, elsewhere in the food system.

In contrast to this picture modern agriculture is dependent on very high levels of protein and energy transfer, linking the production process on the farm with sectors in which value is added to farm production. These linkages, both upstream and downstream, have broken into the cycle of renewal, failing to return to the resource base what has been removed from it, a principle which marks sustainable agricultural systems. Thus in modern farming animal waste disposal has become a "problem" rather than an essential part of a natural recycling process. In the same way, advanced systems of crop and animal husbandry, using every protective device from pesticides to antibiotics, are made more necessary by the conditions under which animals are kept, and the genetic make-up of delicately engineered plant varieties. Given the commitment to high yields, consistent quality, and the major investments in research and development which underpin these technologies, once they are established there is apparently no cost effective alternative to capital intensive, energy-wasteful production regimes.

Nevertheless in the process of establishing these regimes the "knot" which tied agriculture to the environment has been undone, and the costs of modern agriculture are counted elsewhere. In the United States, for example, it has been estimated that the cost of soil erosion off the farm was $6.1 billion (US) in the mid-1980s (Clark et al, 1985). Similarly, in the United Kingdom, £200 million in capital costs, and an annual expenditure of £10 million will be required, over a twenty year period, to bring all drinking water up the European Community's standard for nitrate concentrations (OECD, 1989). In the developing countries the so-called "externalities" are often higher still (Repetto et al, 1989; Bishop and Allen, 1989).

There are several important respects in which attention has shifted to the problems the modern food system presents to the environment. First, the increased dependence on differently located components of the agricultural production and food processing system, has served to transfer environmental costs from one part of the system to another. For example, as we have argued elsewhere (Goodman and Redclift, 1991), the use of soya and manioc for intensive cattle production in Europe, has served to transfer some of the costs of maintaining feedstock systems to other countries, such as Brazil and Thailand, which can ill afford it. Second, increasingly intensive production has led to problems of waste disposal, pollution and disease control, all of them problems which have accompanied intensification. These problems frequently assume major importance in two directions: for the farm they represent increased costs which need to be incorporated in the farm accounts, and the market viability of the enterprise. For the local environment they represent major threats to the existing ecological systems, species diversity and habitats.

With increasing demands for financial security, but tighter economic margins, per capita investment in what are termed "intermediate goods" now represents nearly half the value of agricultural output of some industrialised countries such as France, as Table 2.1 makes clear.

Table 2.1

Intermediate Consumption in French Agriculture (billion francs)

	1970	1975	1981
Animal feed	6.8	14.9	33.0
Fertilizers	4.2	9.0	19.1
Fuel and repairs	3.2	6.8	15.4
Crop protection	1.2	2.9	9.6
Building maintenance	0.8	1.4	3.2
Veterinary costs	0.9	1.9	4.5
Other goods	2.5	4.8	9.5
Other services	1.4	2.4	5.0
Total intermediate consumption as % of output	30.0%	36.0%	46.0%

Source: European Parliament Working Document A 2-207/85 (1985-6). Report on behalf of the Committee on the Environment, Public Health and consumer protection.

Table 2.1 which expresses the costs of intensification both in current money terms, and as a percentage of total production costs, clearly points to the increasing financial burden of maintaining intensification which is borne by the farmer in the first instance, but indirectly, by the consumer and taxpayer and at another remove by agricultural competitors in less protected markets. As we shall see later in the chapter, the environmental costs of this pattern of financial and resource management on the farm are paid in a number of ways, not all of which are easily "accountable" in monetary terms.

The third aspect of the removal of "natural" processes from the farm, and the relocation of these processes in other sectors of the food system, has been to transform, in some cases fundamentally, the pattern of land use in rural areas. The modern food system has brought unprecedented interference with traditional land uses and the rural landscape especially through activities like drainage, land levelling, and deforestation. There has also been a reduction in soil quality, arising from poor management of soil resources (European parliament 1985/6, p. 13). Current problems, as we shall see, include precipitation of acid rain on land, the discharge of toxic wastes, and the uncontrolled spread of sewage on land. As a result of these, and other factors, the usable agricultural area within the European Community declined by almost eight per cent between 1962 and 1984, from almost 100 million hectares to under 92 million hectares (ibid p.15). The combination of several different processes, whose cumulative effect is to undermine the quantity of undegraded land available for both agricultural and non-agricultural uses (including conservation) has led to a rural resource crisis in Europe of serious dimensions. As the Food and Agricultural Organisation (FAO) of the United Nations has put it, in rather august language:

> "A complex web of economic policies provides, at considerable cost to the environment, many of the incentives and institutional mechanisms needed to support the high level and intensity of agricultural production. This situation is compounded by over-production of some commodities in the agricultural sector and rapidly rising economic costs from policies intended to encourage production and raise income." (FAO 1988, 1)

It is to this "complex web of economic policies" that we need to turn next.

The productivist model: policy instruments and mechanisms

In a document produced by the European Parliament, we are reminded of the lack of attention to long-term sustainability in the development of European Community agricultural policy (European Parliament 1985/6). The document begins by emphasising the five fundamental objectives of the Common Agricultural Policy of the EEC (article 39 of the Treaty of Rome) - to increase agricultural productivity, improve farm living standards, stabilize markets and ensure a secure supply of foodstuffs at a reasonable price - and then continues by stating that "the pursuit of these objectives clearly betokens a productivist and materialist ideology which takes no account of environmental concerns" (p 19). Community preference follows logically from the establishment of a single agricultural market, but it is also clear that establishing this market is expensive in terms of export subsidies "and that it does not necessarily contribute to the rational location of different types of production". (p. 19). Similarly, within the

European Agricultural Guidance and Guarantee Fund (EAGGF) of the European Community, "guidance" to farmers (which might assist the painful process of restructuring for farm households) only amounts to one twentieth of the total. The bulk of expenditure under the fund takes the form of subsidies to agricultural producers.

The scale of agricultural subsidies makes any serious attempt at environmental protection in European agriculture extremely difficult, since farmers who are normally subsidised for doing what is harmful to the environment have also come to expect subsidies for not doing what is environmentally harmful. The cost of the Common Agricultural Policy is, as Simpson (1989) remarks "legendary". The purchase and storage of farm production and the cost of export subsidies alone amounts to a "mere" £18 billion <u>per annum</u>, equivalent to £5.91 a week for a family of four. In addition, the same family has to pay almost twice this amount weekly towards the cost of fixing EEC prices above prevailing world market levels. The total cost is £42 billion <u>per annum</u>. These figures provide an indication of "a policy which <u>sacrifices long-term interests to immediate concerns,</u> and one scarcely needs reminding that most environmental issues arise from a concern for the long-term future" (European Parliament 1985/6, 19).

It is thus worth paying attention to the policy framework for agriculture within the European Community, because in intention, although not always in its choice of mechanisms, it mirrors the approach of other industrialised areas, such as the United States and Japan. The policy framework for European agriculture, as we have seen, was established with a view to protecting rural incomes through production subsidies, and ensuring food sufficiency within member countries. One consequence of these policies is that the benefits and costs of agricultural policy are shared very unequally between both producers and consumers. For example, if we compare France with the United Kingdom, we can appreciate that because of the larger size of the French agricultural sector, the absolute value of protection is higher than in the UK. However, if we take individual farmers the reverse is true; British farmers do rather better under the CAP because they are, on average, larger farmers. In France in 1980 the average farm size was 25.4 hectares compared with 68.7 hectares in the United Kingdom. As Cheshire (1985) makes clear "large farmers, because they produce more, effectively receive more support than poorer, smaller farmers" (Cheshire, 1985, p 11). The aggregate effect of these distributional factors is highly unequal, three-quarters of EC support to farmers goes to the richest "quarter" of farmers (Simpson, 1989, p 15).

The level of expenditure under the CAP far outstrips most other budgetary items within the control of the Community. Taxpayers and consumers effectively supported 40 per cent of the value of farmers' produce during the years 1983-7, when agricultural spending in real terms increased by 4 per cent a year. In the United Kingdom, in 1984, more was spent on farmers and the food industry (£6.9 billion) than was spent on unemployment benefit and supplementary benefit combined (£5 billion). Senior (1989) also points to the fact that only a dozen people work for the European Commission on consumer affairs, while eight hundred work in DG.VI, the directorate responsible for agriculture and making agricultural policy, in consultation with the agricultural producers' group COPA, the Council of Agricultural Ministers and the Agricultural Committee of the European Parliament.

The effect of close collaboration between farming interests, and the virtual exclusion of the consumers' interest from food policy discussions, is that policy not only favours large farmers over smaller ones, it also favours wealthier families over poorer ones. In 1988 in the United Kingdom the poorest 25 per cent of households spent 29 per cent of their disposable income on food. The richest 25 per cent of households spent 14 per cent on food, wile the relatively "poor" Greeks spent 36 per cent. Simpson observes that ".. if poor people were paying to help other poor people and keep them on the land that may be some consolation. But they are not." (Simpson, 1989, p. 15). Very little influence is wielded within the European Community circles by the consumer interest, and environmental considerations still do not enter into the design of agricultural policy, as one might expect. This lack of political influence is in marked contrast with the position of the agricultural lobby. In explaining the ideological dominance of this lobby, we must take account of the level of farm support in the past. The level of farm support has been fundamental to the shift in agricultural practices most of which, as we shall see, are prejudicial to the environment.

It has not been difficult to demonstrate that the mechanisms, and the level, of farm support in the European Community is highly inegalitarian in its effects. Can it now be demonstrated that these policy mechanisms are also ultimately responsible for the environmental problems that afflict the countries of Western Europe?

The cumulative effects of high levels of farm support on the rural environment may be complex and subtle, but they are also increasingly well documented. As we sought to argue in Goodman and Redclift (1991) the agricultural technology/policy model developed in the United States in the 1940s and 1950s encouraged the rapid adoption of new technology. This model was later adopted, in its essential features, by the European Community. The high level of farm support adopted in the model as expressed through high farm prices, has encouraged more investment in research and development, and the acquisition of more capital equipment by farmers. Price support has also stimulated intensification through its effect on land values. For example between the mid 1950s and the late 1970s agricultural land values tripled in real terms in the United Kingdom. After 1979, when the rate of increase of CAP prices began to fall, and particularly after 1984 when milk quotas were introduced, land prices began to decline, for the first time in decades. Before this the intensification of agriculture was given a considerable stimulus by the capitalisation of land as an asset, and the need to maximise on this asset.

It is also clear, from evidence such as that of Traill (1983) that high support prices for farmers induce more capital investment, and the substitution of capital equipment, where possible, for labour. In the early 1980s in what was then west Germany there were 8.5 milking machines for every 100 cows; 2.8 combine harvesters and 12.4 tractors for every 100 hectares of land. This very high level of mechanization is the result of a regime of high support prices, and accompanying subsidised credit and guaranteed markets, which induces even the smallest farmers to mechanize production.

In addition, although the legal and financial inducements to farm amalgamation are few within the EEC, the economic gains from larger units, achieved by "shedding" labour and acquiring ever more capital equipment are considerable. The pressures on the production margins of small farmers, even those with milking machines and tractors, are given a boost by the concentration of farm ownership. One effect of agricultural support, and the technological treadmill is, therefore, greater specialisation. It is an inevitable consequence of inducing investment, and losing employment, in farming. Further consequences of restructuring due to EC policy relate to the environment, and these are now considered.

First order problems with the productivist model: agricultural intensification

The productivist model, which lies at the heart of the modern food system, has both direct (first order) and indirect (second order) environmental effects, and the environmental problems associated with agricultural intensification are, in the first instance experienced as a direct effect of the implementation of the agricultural technology/policy model. For example, the removal of hedgerows (Cheshire, 1985, p.14). Similar accounts could be given of the effects of drainage (Baldock, 1984), or the application of chemicals or intensive livestock production (Long and Rose in Goldsmith and Hildyard, 1986).

Most factors of production are in relatively elastic supply, but land is the exception. The supply of land can normally only be increased through "improvement" or intensification. As agriculture feels the effect of greater capital investment, prices increase and these become capitalised in land. One effect of this process is to increase the opportunity cost of unproductive land, such as hedges and field margins. The farmer will view the conservation of hedgerows as an opportunity foregone - he has forfeited the opportunity to increase his income by producing more food.

This tendency to regard conservation activities as a cost to current income is exaggerated because, under the system of grants to defray capital costs within the European Community, farmers are induced to specialise, substituting capital for labour in many of their operations. As Cheshire argues: "..while labourers could milk cows, tend the sheep and with a simple binder, harvest the corn, milking parlours can only milk cows, and combine harvesters can only harvest cereals" (1985, p.15). By increasing output the farmer was induced to replace organic with chemical fertilisers, and to use chemical sprays for pest control. Both sprays and fertilisers depend on subsidised machinery.

Under specialised production systems hedgerows increasingly became unnecessary, since they served no purpose as livestock barriers, where animals had been brought in from the fields. The use of larger machinery also meant that fields needed to be larger, persuading farmers to recoup their increased capital costs by removing unproductive hedges and ploughing over footpaths, which interfered with the movement of their mechanical equipment. The environmental problems that have accompanied intensification are the "effect of a system which systematically establishes financial inducements to erode the countryside, offers no rewards to offset market failures and increases the penalties imposed ..on farmers who may want to farm in a way which enhances and enriches the rural environment" (Cheshire, 1985, 15). The example of hedgerow removal is just one of many similar examples of foregone production benefits being converted into environmental losses.

Among the most important effects of intensification is the use of nitrogenous and other chemical fertilisers. Within the EEC the use of chemical fertilisers has assumed increasing importance. According to the Food and Agriculture Organisation (FAO) consumption of nitrogenous fertilisers in the Netherlands is 558 kg per ha, Switzerland 436, West Germany 427, and the United Kingdom, 356 kg per ha (FAO, 1988, p.5). There is evidence that these levels of use leave significant residues in the soil. A report on Paris Basin agriculture shows a nitrogen surplus of 240 kg per ha over a seven year period. Eutrophication of lakes, rivers and coastlines caused by excessive nutrient loading from nitrate and phosphate pollution is also widespread. The FAO notes that recent acute deterioration of marine ecosystems in the Kattegat and the Adriatic Sea, for example, has had a significant impact on fisheries and tourism in these areas.

The intensive production of animals in feedlots has had similarly important environmental effects. It is estimated that each year British farmers dispose of 200 million tons of animal manure through the water system. The disposal of slurry is now a major environmental problem A survey by the Water Authorities Association in July 1986 revealed that incidents of silage effluent pollution were almost double those of two years earlier. In 1985 Anglia Water reported that half of all fish deaths leading to prosecutions, and 60 per cent of its pollution prosecutions, were attributable to slurry disposal. The excessive use of animal slurry can lead to concentrations of up to 10 kg of nitrogen per hecatre. The mineralization of the soil from increased large-scale nitrate leaching can pass into both surface and groundwater. Already, in the Netherlands, the nitrate content of shallow sources of fresh water is too high to make it usable (European Community, 1986, p.32). The average nitrate content of aquifers in the Paris Basin has doubled from 20 - 40 mg per litre during the last twenty years, while in some areas of France, such as Beauce and Sologne, the nitrate content of groundwater exceeds 100 mg per litre. Studies of more than six thousand wells in North Rhine-Westphalia showed that two thirds had nitrate contents of 50 mg per litre or above, the maximum permitted under EEC Directive (80/778, 15 July 1980). One third of the wells exceeded the very lenient limit of 90 mg per litre, permitted in West Germany. The cost of reducing nitrate concentration in groundwater, to within acceptable limits in West Germany, has been calculated as 2000 DM per hectare (Vogtmann, 1985, p.5). Facts such as these have led to alarm within European Community policy circles. European Commission guidelines state that: "...indefinite exemption from the principle that the 'polluter pays' can hardly be given to agricultural holdings, least of all those which, in terms of the way they are structured and operated, are to all intents and purposes industrial undertakings" (European Commission 1986, p.20).

The conversion of forests, pastures and wetlands to other uses has led to environmental losses in other directions, notably the loss of wildlife habitats, hydrological changes and increased risk of erosion. Land reclamation practices have brought about radical changes in the environment during the last decades and, although the rate of land conversion is decreasing within the EEC, it is still a contributory factor in further environmental deterioration. In the United Kingdom, for example, a dramatic loss of valuable biotopes and wildlife habitats has occurred since 1945. Almost all unimproved natural grasslands, including herb-rich hay meadows, have disappeared, as have 40 per cent of lowland acidic heaths, 30-50 per cent of lowland woods and 30 per cent of unimproved upland grasslands, heaths and blanket bogs. As the FAO Report to the United Nations Economic Commission for Europe expressed it: "...the combined effects of modification of traditional agricultural landscapes, increased use of pesticides and intensification of agriculture have reduced wild species abundance and diversity in most agricultural areas (in Europe)" (FAO, 1988, p.4).

There are many inter-related reasons for loss of soil productivity which result from agricultural intensification and heavy reliance on external inputs. These effects are not confined to developed countries, like those of Western Europe. The more or less proximate effects of agricultural intensification are also felt in areas of the Third World where modern agriculture has become established, often with fewer controls on adverse environmental effects than exist in the developed countries. These areas, which we can term "enhancement zones", perform a critical role in food production in the South, and particularly the production of food staples such as rice, which are grown under highly intensive irrigated conditions (Redclift, 1990).

Second-order problems with the productivist model: marginal lands

The secondary, or indirect, effects of the food system on the environment in both developed and developing countries, are more difficult to delineate. The processes through which the modern food system becomes established at the farm-level - concentration of holdings, specialisation and intensification of production - carry implications for areas other than those of modern agriculture. The cost of achieving gains in productivity in one locality are often passed on to others; through environmental costs or "externalities". As we have seen intensification needs to be understood not simply in terms of the technology employed, but also in terms of a "package", comprising guaranteed prices, subsidised chemical and mechanical inputs and government procurement after the harvest.

In some developed countries, such as those of the EC, less advantaged regions receive subsidies from central government, precisely because they are adversely affected in social terms, and are less competitive in terms of their economic performance. In developing countries, however, areas where natural resources are poor, especially semi-arid regions, are likely to fall completely outside the ambit of public policy. This neglect serves to accentuate the differences, and the unevenness of the development process. It is more difficult for small farmers, for example, to gain government support for their farming system, and they are left to manage an inadequate technology, even if this technology is environmentally sustainable, and ill-adapted for competition with the technology employed in more favoured regions. Many households, in marginal areas of Europe, Australia and North America, such as the Appalachian Mountains, as well as the Third World, have to supplement the income they obtain from their land by other forms of livelihood. They become part-time farmers, working in the city or in tourism, or migrating on a seasonal basis to other regions of the country. Living in areas that are already poor in terms of productive resources, but frequently rich in terms of natural species or aesthetic quality, they are powerless to do anything in the face of the differentiating effects of modern intensive agriculture.

This chapter has focused upon both the immediate, and the more indirect environmental implications of the modern food system. it needs to be emphasised that a series of "third-order problems" also exist, which we are only beginning to delineate; that is problems such as those arising from the introduction of genetically engineered species into the environment. These "third-order problems" are likely to grow in urgency and include not only the compatibility of "new" life forms and existing ecosystems, but also the relationship between conserving species' diversity in laboratories, and gene banks, as well as in the wild.

Structure and agency in the modern food system: the management response

We have argued in this chapter that agricultural policy instruments have been instrumental in supporting intensification, at the cost of environmental considerations. Given the high visibility of environmental issues and, in the developed countries, the acknowledgment that environmental considerations require changes in agricultural policy, more emphasis has been placed on the various ways in which the rural environment can be more effectively "managed". Beginning with an analysis of environmental management in rural Britain, and extending this to the EEC, this section goes on to assess the kinds of farm-level response which have been induced by recent policy-making. The question posed by this discussion of sectoral, and farm-level decision-making, is whether it carries implications for developing countries, where the penetration of the modern food system is also eliciting environmental management interventions. This means looking very carefully at the assumptions underlying environmental management itself.

As we have seen, policies which encourage agricultural intensification, specialisation and the concentration of farm ownership in fewer hands, have been called into question by the existence of farm surpluses and the heavy financial cost of supporting the agricultural sector. It needs to be emphasised, however, that it is public involvement in conservation, and the lobbying of environmental interest groups in Britain, which has called the model itself into question.

The agriculture and environment debate in the United Kingdom dates back to the early 1960s, although it did not reach the European stage until almost twenty years later (Potter, 1989, p.137). Beginning in the 1960s the public's attention was alerted to the cumulative effects of using pesticides in agriculture. The Nature Conservancy began to reveal that there had been dramatic losses in some wildlife species, such as peregrine falcons, due to the use of organo-chlorines (Hooper 1984). Within a decade this concern, fostered by the growth of the countryside lobby, had extended to the loss of whole habitats, such as moorland, heathland and ancient woodland, losses which were attributed to agricultural intensification and land reclamation.

Groups such as the Council for the Protection of Rural England (CPRE) which had considerable following, especially in the more scenically attractive parts of the British countryside, drew attention to these environmental losses. Other controversies were more long-standing but no less vituperative; the ploughing of moorland in the Exmoor National Park, for example, drew attention to the limited powers exercised over supposedly "protected areas" (MacEwen and

MacEwen, 1982). Land use controversies began to engage public attention as much as environmental pollution or contamination from intensive farming practices. Furthermore, the effect of European Community membership, in accelerating these losses, gave rise to additional concern at the environmental costs of "productivist" agricultural policies.

The loss of the countryside's amenity value was a particularly British concern. As Potter (1989) shows, the agenda was partly set by relatively autonomous bodies, known as "quangos" within the structure of British government, notably the Countryside Commission and the Nature Conservancy Council. In 1974 the Countryside Commission published its "New Agricultural Landscapes" study, which documented the ways in which familiar features of the British countryside, such as hedges, copses and ponds had been removed, as farmers deserted mixed husbandry for more specialised farming operations. By 1977 the Nature Conservancy Council, largely staffed by trained environmental scientists, with no obvious "political axe" to grind, had reported that existing policies, which sought to protect sites of special environmental interest rather than more integrated land use practices, were seriously deficient (Nature Conservancy Council, 1977). By 1984 the Nature Conservancy Council had revealed that only 3 per cent of lowland grassland had remained unaffected by agricultural intensification, since 1945, and that ancient lowland woodlands had been reduced by between 30 and 50 per cent in the same period (Nature Conservancy Council, 1984).

While the environmental lobby was beginning to raise its flag, during the 1960s and 1970s, evidence was emerging that the agricultural lobby was being forced to adapt, slowly and painfully, to the realisation that it could no longer count on the unqualified support of British governments. Two agricultural White Papers in the 1970s (MAFF 1975, 1979) departed, in significant ways, from the conventional wisdom that, as the major land-using industry, agriculture could expect to expand in an exponential direction. Although no revised national policy existed, which integrated the agricultural restructuring being urged on the EEC with more attention to environmental objectives, questions such as the appropriate size of the agricultural industry in terms of food and fibre output, had become matters of policy debate. As a recent research paper makes clear, a subtle shift had occurred, between 1975 and 1979, in which the Ministry of Agriculture conceded that the "national interest" was distinguishable from that of farmers (ESRC, 1989, p.6).

By 1981 the tide of concern over the demise of the British countryside led a Conservative Government to introduce a Wildlife and Countryside Act which provided the legal basis for management agreements between farmers and the Nature Conservancy Council on farmed land of special scientific interest. This Act allowed for payments to be made to farmers, by way of compensation for foregoing modern agricultural practices, in return for agreed conservation practices. Owners and landowners were required to seek permission from the NCC if they intended to change their farming practices. The scheme attracted considerable criticism for being "too little, too late", resting on the farmer's goodwill, and proving very costly to the Exchequer (Lowe et al. 1986, ESRC 1989). Although the shift away from unbridled productivism had occurred, the Government seemed anxious to proceed by agreement and cooperation with farmers, almost whatever the cost. Voluntary and informal structures of land use planning and regulation were very much the method favoured by the Government.

It is this concern with "management agreements" that marks out recent policy interventions in the industrialised countries. According to a recent report from the Organisation for Economic Cooperation and Development (OECD, 1989) there are three desirable aspects of such agreements. First, the environmental benefits have to be realised effectively. For example, if the aim is to prevent cropping, then the cropping rights should be permanently acquired under the agreement. Second, the payment made in compensation for the reduction in expected net farm income, which the adoption of new management practices is likely to produce, should not exceed this "opportunity cost". Third, the agreements should not be in force long enough to enable farmers to bargain about the level of compensation, by refusing to operate under the new conditions until all their demands are met. It will be clear from these "desirable conditions" that it would be impracticable to introduce similar agreements on a large scale in most developing countries.

The mounting debate about agricultural support, however, did begin to alter the policy debate by linking the redirection of agricultural support to rural conservation measures. The structures legislation of the European Community (EC regulation 797/Article 19) and in the United Kingdom, the 1986 Agriculture Act, enabled financial aid to be offered to appropriate farming practices, as well as to farmers who refrained from using inappropriate practices. A number of areas considered "environmentally sensitive" were outlined, under the 1986 Act, and a dozen such areas were designated. Farmers were being paid, for the first time, to "produce" countryside, something which they did without significant agricultural support, in the era before agricultural intensification. The principle that the interests of farmers were distinguishable from those of the British countryside, was conceded in the 1986 Agriculture Act which imposed a statutory duty on Agriculture Ministers to balance the conservation and promotion of the enjoyment of the countryside, the support of stable and efficient agricultural industry and the economic and social interest of rural areas.

Although the agricultural lobby no longer commands undivided support, even from Conservative Governments in Britain, and the environment lobby has increased in size and authority (Lowe et.al., 1986) the mechanisms through which agricultural support can be shifted towards better conservation are still in their infancy. Writing about the United States, where the conflict is more often between agricultural intensification and sustainable agriculture, rather than a "countryside" with amenity and recreational value, Buttel (1982) argues that farmers are most unlikely to change their practices to meet environmental guidelines:

> "State policy-makers have been unable to call upon farmers to collectively and voluntarily reduce their production during phases of overproduction. Given the inability of farmers to control their production, state action to reduce production by rationing land resources has been undertaken because rationing other inputs (i.e. petrochemicals) would be strongly resisted by farmers and by agribusiness firms" (Buttel, 1982, p.21).

Some people, including Agricultural Commissioner McSharry, have argued that the preservation of existing farms is a necessary component of any policy to achieve wider conservation goals in European rural areas, and that the offering of income aids to farmers who agree to make their farming practices more environmentally sensitive, is the most direct and powerful way of advancing future rural environmental policy. However, as Potter observes, there are limitations in the small-farm approach. He writes that:

> "....realistically, though, there are limits to the extent to which a Farm Survival Policy can be orientated towards conservation objectives. With the notable exception of **environmentally sensitive areas** it is unlikely that the disadvantaged and intermediate farms that will be targeted in future will be located in areas of greatest environmental potential or vulnerability. The very transparency of expenditure on income support presents another difficulty: it may not be desirable to seek to achieve long-term environmental goals under expenditure headings that may be vulnerable to political pressure" (Potter 1990,11).

It is not clear, then, that the situation in Europe is as strikingly different from that of North America as first appears. The powerful economic lobbies behind high-input farming have not been seriously affected by the new calls to conservation. Indeed one feature of so-called "Green consumerism" today, is that commercial interests with dubious environmental records are often loudest in their support for more "sustainable" practices. The political climate has changed in recent years, and this is not an unimportant fact in itself, but the model which encouraged agricultural intensification as part of the development of the modern food system, has been dented rather than overturned. In the process, "management" has acquired both greater credibility and a more uncertain future.

This chapter has been principally concerned with the implications of the modern food system for rural land use, and the environmental problems which have accompanied modern agriculture. As long as agriculture remains a land-based activity (which is for the foreseeable future) the effects of changes in production will inevitably conflict with the way in which the countryside is consumed. It is no coincidence that two of the most important areas of political activity in the 1990s are likely to continue to be the environment and food policy, which for most of this century were regarded as complementary policy domains.

References

Baldock, D. (1984), *Wetland Drainage in Europe*, Institute for European Environmental Policy, London

Bishop, J. and Allen, J. (1989), *The On-site Costs of Soil Erosion in Mali: a Natural Resource Accounting Approach*, World Bank, Washington

Buttel, F. (1982), *Environmental Quality in Agriculture: some observations on political-economic constraints on sustainable resource management*, Bulletin No. 128, Cornell University Department of Rural Sociology. Ithaca, New York State.

Cheshire, P. (1985), 'The environmental implications of European agricultural support policies', in D. Baldock and D. Conder (eds) *Does the CAP Fit the Environment?* Institute for European Environmental Policy, London.

Clark, E.H., Haverkamp, J.A. and Chapman, W. (1985), *Eroding Soils: the off-farm impacts*, Conservation Foundation, Washington DC.

ESRC (Economic and Social Research council) 1989, *The Countryside in Question: a research strategy*, ESRC Countryside Change Initiative, Working Paper No. 1, ESRC, Swindon.

European Commission (1986), *A Future for Community Agriculture: Commission Guidelines*, Brussels, The Commission.

European Community (1986), *Report on behalf of the Committee on the Environment, Public Health and Consumer Protection*, European Parliament Working Document (A-2-207/85), Brussels.

European Parliament (1985/6), *Working Document A2-207/85 Report on behalf of the Committee on the Environment, Public Health and Consumer Protection*, The Parliament, Brussels.

FAO (Food and Agriculture Organisation) (1988), *Integration of environmental aspects in agricultural, forestry and fishery policies in Europe*, XVI Regional Conference for Europe, Cracow, Poland, 23-26 August.

Goldsmith, E. and Hildyard, N. (1986), *Green Britain or Industrial Wasteland?* Polity Press, London.

Goodman, D.E. and Redclift, M.R. (1991), *Refashioning Nature: Food, Ecology, Culture* Routledge, London.

Hooper, M. (1984), 'What are the main impacts of agriculture on wildlife?' in D. Jenkins (ed) *Agriculture and the Environment*, Cambridge: Institute of Terrestrial Ecology.

Lowe, P., Cox, G., MacEwan, M., O'Riordan, T. and Winter, M. (1986), *Countryside Conflicts: the politics of farming, forestry and conservation*, Aldershot: Gower.

MacEwan, A. and MacEwan, M. (1982) *National Parks: conservation or cosmetics?* London: Allen and Unwin.

MAFF (1975), *Food from our own resources*, Cmnd.6620, HMSO, London.

MAFF (1979), *Farming and the nation*, Cmnd.7458, HMSO, London.

Nature Conservancy Council (1977), *Nature Conservation and Agriculture*, London: Nature Conservancy Council.

Nature Conservancy Council (1984), *Nature Conservation in Great Britain*, London: Nature Conservancy Council.

OECD (Organisation for Economic Cooperation and Development) (1989), *Agricultural and environmental policies; opportunities for integration,* OECD, Paris.

Potter, C. (1989), 'Approaching limits: farming contraction and environmental conservation in the UK', in Goodman,D. and Redclift, M. (eds) *The International Farm Crisis,* Macmillan, London, pp 135-155.

Potter, C. (1990) "Conservation under a European farm survival policy", Wye College (University of London) unpublished ms.

Redclift, M. (1990), 'Developing sustainably: designating agro-ecological zones', *Land Use Policy* 7(3).

Repetto, R., Magrath, W., Wells, M., Beer, C. and Rossini, F. (1989), *Wasting Assets: natural resources in the national accounts,* World Resources Institute, Washington.

Rushton, A. and Whitney, D. (1934), *Hoston Pagnell,* Edward Arnold, London.

Senior, S. (1989), 'European interest groups and the CA',*Food Policy,* 14(2) pp 101-106.

Simpson, R. (1989), "Feeding Poverty", *New Statesman and Society,* December 8.

Traill, B. (1983), 'Simulating changes in investment grants, interest and tax rates and inflationary pressures on input prices in UK agriculture', *Journal of Agricultural Economics* XXXIV, pp 473-492.

Vogtmann, H. (1985), 'Environmental and Socio-Economic Aspects of Different Farming Practices', *The Other Economic Summit,* London, unpublished .

3 Rural restructuring: Mechanisation and the agricultural workforce

NIGEL WALFORD

Introduction

In the current debate about the restructuring of the countryside considerable emphasis has been placed on how the economic basis of so-called rural areas has become increasingly linked into a larger system operating at national and even international scales (Hodge and Monk, 1991). In this system agriculture is rightly seen as itself having such links in both the political and economic dimensions. However, it is also now generally accepted that the economic importance of agriculture to rural areas in terms of income and employment generation has diminished. Agriculture may be the predominant land user nationally as well as in the countryside, but as an industry it is by no means a major employer. This has of course not always been the case and even less than a half a century ago fairly substantial numbers were working on the land. The decline in the farm workforce, although perhaps not very large in absolute terms, has been important because of the diminished relative position of the agricultural worker in the countryside.

The technological and organisational changes that have taken place in agriculture over this period of rising agricultural productivity have had profound effects on the social and economic life of the countryside in many advanced industrial societies. The major changes in agriculture with regard to inputs relate to the combination of land, labour and machinery. These inputs are usually regarded as part of the fixed resource base of a farm, however, the historical viewpoint reveals that they have undergone considerable change and are far from fixed. Two of the main changes in agriculture since the Second World War have been the decline in the employment of labour and the counterbalancing process of mechanisation. Although these trends have been well established for a number of years and academics have been familiar with the patterns of change during a period of rising productivity in the industry, rather less is known about the situation under the pressures that the industry is currently experiencing both to control surplus production and to undertake environmentally friendly farming. Errington (1988) is perhaps one exception to this, since he has looked at certain aspects of the agricultural workforce and asserted that there is evidence of "disguised unemployment".

This chapter examines empirical information from both primary and secondary sources with three objectives in mind. The first is to review historical trends in the agricultural workforce and mechanisation; the second is to examine the extent to which any trends emerging from this historical analysis have continued during the restructuring of the last 5 to 10 years, taking the early 1980s as a watershed in the agricultural industry; and the third is to assess the future prospects for the agricultural workforce in the light of current political and secular changes. The underlying aim of the chapter is to examine how the restructuring of the countryside and of agriculture are affecting the farm workforce. However before looking at these specific issues, it is useful to examine in more general terms the nature and process of agricultural change.

Nature of Agricultural Change

There is a persistent and popular belief that agriculture is distinguished by continuity and the endurance of past traditions. This belief is linked to four factors. The first is agriculture's relationship to the natural environment, making it more closely allied to and affected by the pace of the biological, chemical and physical processes than many other industries. Second, the periodicity of production cycles gives a feeling of relative changelessness. Third, the long history of agriculture as a socially organised system of food production supports a belief in its continuity and slow evolution. A fourth factor is the extent to which agriculture is now far removed from the ordinary lives of the majority of individuals and inaccurate impressions, based on romantic notions of what happens in the countryside and of the character of rural life, are more easily sustained than destroyed. Juxtaposed to, and seemingly in conflict with, this belief in the continuity of farming, is an acknowledgement that agriculture is not the same now as it was 100 or even 50 years ago. In an attempt to resolve this paradox, the changes in agricultural organisation and practice that have occurred are often characterised as an 'agricultural revolution', creating the image of an activity that experiences long periods of consolidation and continuity interspersed with concentrated and relatively sudden upheavals.

One of the features of agriculture is that producers have to keep pace with changes in technology in order to survive or to grow. Dexter (1977) has suggested the concept of the technological treadmill, in which the economic system does not allow technology to stand still, but demands continual development and change. In the context of agriculture, this treadmill leads to farmers continually capitalising their production in order to maintain a 'competitive edge', as old machinery and systems become outdated (Marsden *et al*, 1986). This process of capitalization has led to the progressive loss of labour in the industry, since one of the attractions of new technology is its ability to enable work to be done both faster and at lower cost by reducing the labour requirement per unit of output.

However, farmers are not a uniform group, and those operating smaller units do not necessarily have the assets against which to borrow money for the purchase of the most up-to-date, and inevitably expensive, technology. Large farms often have the necessary reserves and are therefore able to maintain their competitive advantage. This process of the 'rich getting richer and the poor getting poorer' is of course not unique to agriculture, but is a symptom of capitalist economic systems. Thus there is unequal growth in the industry. Smaller farms can acquire yesterday's technology at a secondhand price after it has been discarded by their larger counterparts, but they inevitably remain a few steps behind on the treadmill and the smallest approach ever closer to the margin of economic production.

The technological treadmill is kept in motion not only by the forces of competition in agriculture, but also by similar forces in those industries that supply agriculture. The technical advances that are made by the agro-chemical and machinery manufacturers have a limited life, or, as Dexter (1977) has maintained, scientific knowledge is perishable. Thus established manufacturers have the incentive to search for new developments in order to maintain their market share and newcomers to the market are driven on by the desire to improve on the technology that is already on offer. This process of technological change is one of the main reasons why agriculture has developed greater links with other sectors of the economy over recent years. These links are not simply represented by new machinery or new chemicals, but by the sources of capital and finance that have taken an investment interest in agriculture. Thus although a far smaller proportion of the populace are now directly involved in agriculture, a substantial number of people do have an indirect interest through the investment policies of pension funds, insurance companies and other financial institutions such as banks and building societies.

Agricultural change involves the reorganisation of working practices and a restructuring of social and economic relationships. From an analytical point of view, a distinction is often made between agriculture as a productive economic activity and farming as a way of life, in which the activity "extends far beyond the merely economic into the wider social aspects and organization of life" (Buchanan, 1959). Under the first heading, the focus is on agriculture as the economic process that societies carry out in order to produce food and other plant and animal products, either for home consumption or for export. Under the second heading, the concern tends to be with the social relationships that develop in the context of this productive process between the owners of capital and the owners of labour, and between these groups and society at large, both in the countryside and beyond. This separation mirrors Newby's (1982) division between the interests of agricultural economists and rural sociologists.

Newby (1979) has suggested that agricultural communities had very largely disappeared by the mid 20th century and that the social life of villages is now more diffuse and therefore perhaps more uncertain. Many 'modern' villagers have thus less sense of place in both a geographical and social context. This situation engenders latent and overt conflict, instability and insecurity. The changes in British agriculture since the Second World War, which have been acclaimed the 'New Agricultural Revolution', have extended the process of social and economic change in the countryside. The new revolution, as distinct from its historical counterpart, has encompassed a change in the technology of agriculture defined in both the narrow, physical sense of new machinery and in the broader sense of "techniques and processes for bringing about desired actions and for controlling and managing systems" (Elliot and Elliot, 1976). An important feature of the new revolution is the application of scientific techniques to agricultural production, both in the field and in the laboratory. Furthermore, the need for farm management to become an active process for producing change and monitoring production has arisen partly in response to these technical changes and partly as an important development in its own right. At the same time recent changes in the agricultural landscape have reversed some of the effects of the enclosure movement, with the removal of hedgerows increasing field size in order to take full advantage of mechanisation. It is nearly 20 years since a Countryside Commission report suggested that the contemporary changes in the rural landscape were as extensive as the "ruthless" changes of the 18th Century which "gave the landscape a consistent quality, ... thought of by many as the traditional English landscape" (Countryside Commission, 1974).

Trends in Labour and Machinery

Developments in the relationships between and levels of labour and machinery inputs used in agriculture during the productionist phase of the post Second World War era have attracted considerable academic comment and investigation (Britton, 1968; and Culpin, 1969). In this historical analysis two basic and to a large extent inseparable trends have been identified: the increased use and size of machinery; and a reduction in the workforce. These two trends are closely related because many farmers have reorganised their businesses so that higher levels of capital inputs are required while labour usage is reduced. This process of capitalization has been observed both on this side of the Atlantic (Sturrock, 1966; Nix, 1968; and Sturrock *et al*, 1977) as well as in North America and other developed countries (Inhen and Heady, 1964; Donaldson, 1970; and Fulton *et al*, 1978). Before investigating developments in the 1980s, a review of the important changes in the period after the Second World War and some detail of the key trends is appropriate. This is undertaken on a national scale by reference to official statistical sources and, in relation to large arable farms, by means of sample survey results.

Labour

The decline in the size of the agricultural labour force has taken place over many decades, with agricultural workers becoming a residual group in the national workforce. In Great Britain at the start of the 1980s, they constituted about 2 per cent of the total compared to 10 per cent in 1881 and 35 per cent in 1811 (Gasson, 1974; MAFF, 1982; and Burrell *et al*, 1984). Farming is an industry dominated by family businesses and a higher proportion of the owners of farm capital do manual work than in many other industries. Agriculture also has a far larger number of individual production units (ie farm businesses) than many other industries. Within these scattered production units the typical division of labour into owners, managers and workers is more difficult to apply, because individuals may have overlapping functions. Many small, and even medium to large, farms have a workforce that is composed entirely of members of the farm family, who share or divide the owning, managing and labouring functions. At the other extreme some of the large agribusinesses mimic the structure of companies in other industries by having directors, managers, office staff, foremen and workers. This variability has important practical and theoretical implications. The person on a small full-time family farm, who is classified as 'farmer, partner or director' for statistical purposes in the Agricultural Census, is functionally different from the farmer or director of an agribusiness, who is unlikely to do any manual work at all. This definitional problem is a further consequence of the Agricultural Census being essentially a head counting exercise (Errington, 1988). It is therefore difficult to derive an accurate measure of the human input into agriculture from this statistical source, let alone to differentiate between management and manual labour.

Nevertheless, the difficulties of measurin the size of the agricultural labour force cannot disguise the decline in numbers. Using data for England and Wales from the Agricultural Census, it is possible to calculate annual percentage change for various groups in the workforce as shown in Table 3.1. In the period between 1960 and 1979 an overall reduction in the workforce is clear, despite a definitional discontinuity in the time series in 1969/70. In the 1960s the annual rate of loss was 3.8 per cent for regular full-time hired workers, while in the 1970s the figure was 2.9 per cent. Phillips and Williams (1984) record full-time family employees as having "fallen by half during the 1970s", and part-time family workers almost as quickly. The number of full-time farmers, partners and directors had also declined, although there is some indication that the number of part-time farmers was starting to increase.

Another important change has been in the number of seasonal and casual workers, which rose by about a third between 1971 and 1981 (Walford, 1981a). This is a heterogeneous group that at one time included gangs of city dwellers who migrated seasonally to work on farms. Two notable examples of this are the Londoners who joined the hop harvest in Kent and people from the Midlands who worked on horticultural farms in the Vale of Evesham. Although this colourful component in the agricultural workforce may now be a part of history, seasonal and casual labour is very important. There are still gangs of gypsies who move between farms in the potato growing parts of the country - Lincolnshire, Cambridgeshire and on a smaller scale the Romney Marsh in Kent - supplying labour at harvest time on a piecework basis. Many farms employ casual workers in smaller numbers at some stage in the production cycle and the increase in this element in the total labour force during the 1970s suggests that farmers have been using this type of labour in place of having a large regular workforce. In some areas of the country the growth of 'pick your own' enterprises has also contributed to the decline in the size of the regular labour force.

<u>Machinery</u>

There are also difficulties with trying to measure level of machinery input and mechanisation in agriculture. Most items of agricultural machinery are designed to carry out specific tasks and hence they are difficult to compare and measure against one another. It is obviously difficult to assess the relative contribution of different types of machinery, for example a plough and a chemical sprayer, but it is also problematic to evaluate between functionally the same machine produced by different manufacturers. Furthermore, since machinery manufacturers are competing with each other, the equipment that they develop is promoted as being more useful and efficient than that of their rivals. Some manufacturers in the 1970s, for example, introduced multiple cultivating equipment that cultivated, harrowed, drilled and rolled in one operation. The measurement of mechanisation is further complicated by the fact that the official statistics tend to be collected intermittently and the size groups into which the different machinery items are classified vary considerably over the years.

Table 3.1
Agricultural Labour in England and Wales 1960-1979

	Regular Hired Family Wkrs		Farmers, Ptrs Directors		Seasonal Casual		Total
	WT	PT	WT	PT	M	F	
1970 '000	217	63	159	42	36	35	553
Change %							
1970/71	-1.4	+4.8	+11.9	+2.7	+0.8	-4.3	-4.0
1971/72	-3.7	+1.5	+0.5	+1.6	-5.6	-1.5	-0.7
1972/73	-1.5	+3.0	+3.0	-8.8	+8.1	+14.8	-0.2
1973/74	-4.9	-1.4	-2.8	+4.4	-2.9	-6.6	-3.8
1974/75	-4.7	-1.5	-4.0	+0.7	-0.8	-11.4	-2.4
1975/76	-3.3	-3.0	-0.6	+3.2	+2.2	+7.6	+0.9
1976/77	-4.5	-13.8	+4.2	+1.3	+17.0	+13.5	-1.1
1977/78	-4.7	-1.8	+0.6	+1.8	+6.9	+1.8	-0.4
1978/79	-4.3	-5.5	0.0	+3.5	-4.8	-4.6	-2.6
1979 '000	155	52	167	61	46	37	526
Change %							
1960/69	-38.4	-19.2	NA	NA	-34.7	-20.0	NA
Change %							
1970/79	-28.5	-17.4	+5.0	+45.2	+27.8	+5.7	-4.9

Notes:
NA: Not Available.
Wkrs: Workers, Ptrs: Partners, WT: Whole Time, PT: Part Time,
M: Male, F: Female.

Source: MAFF Statistics (MAFF annual).

A partial solution to these problems is reached by using the tractor as a basis for estimating the level of mechanisation on a farm. As a general rule, large equipment requires large tractors and therefore the power rating of the tractor's engine is an indirect indicator of overall mechanisation. Total numbers of tractors on farms in England and Wales increased from 295,000 in 1950 to of tractors on farms in England and Wales increased from 295,000 in 1950 to about 408,000 in 1980 (a rise of 38 per cent). As far as the statistics allow there is evidence of a general trend towards larger tractors as shown in Table 3.2. During the 1970s the number of tractors on farms in England and Wales rated at over 37.3 kW more than doubled. Smaller tractors, although fluctuating from year to year, declined overall by 12.6 per cent.

Combine harvesters are another important and expensive item of farm machinery which have increased dramatically in numbers since the Second World War. The increase is clearly related to the expansion of cereals and other combinable crops that has occurred. In 1950, 10,000 combine harvesters were in use on farms in England and Wales, and over the next 30 years this rose to 51,000 in 1976 (an increase of 410 per cent). As with tractors, there have been major developments in the range and sizes of combine harvesters that are available. The tractor drawn combine was dropped as a separately identified type in the agricultural machinery census in 1968 when they had fallen to only 11 per cent of the total, from 41 per cent 10 years before. During the 1970s there was an overall decrease in the total number of combine harvesters (-6.1 per cent), although there appears to have been a shift towards investing in larger models. Self-propelled combines with a cutterbar width of 4.6 metres or more rose from 300 to 800 between 1968 and 1976, an increase of 166.6 per cent, and those under 3 metres decreased by 27.3 per cent.

Labour and Machinery on Large Arable Farms

The published agricultural statistics cannot be used to chart or to help understand changes in the size of the labour force or machinery complement on individual farms. In order to examine such issues more detailed survey information is needed. A sample of arable holdings over 300 ha were surveyed for this purpose in 1978 within the counties of Kent, Surrey, East and West Sussex. The sample was representative of the distribution of this type of holding across the four counties (see Walford, 1981b for further details). In 1982 a follow-up postal questionnaire was administered to the same sample of farms in order to investigate changes over the 1978-82 period. Some 66 per cent of the farms in the first survey responded to the postal questionnaire. This subset of the farms appears to be broadly representative of the whole sample, with a similar range of sizes and spatial distribution across the survey area.

The timing of these two surveys corresponds with the heyday of productionist agriculture. Agricultural policy was mainly concerned with growth and efficiency. The information gained from these two surveys therefore provides a very useful insight into the activities and motivations of large scale farmers at this important time. The surveys also constitute an important starting point for examining developments in labour and machinery usage during the 1980s.

The farms' production systems were dominated by cropping enterprises, especially cereals, which were grown on all farms and accounted for 50 per cent of the average farm area. A further 26 per cent of this 'average 540 ha farm' was devoted to herbage seeds, temporary grasses and other fodder. Just over half of the farms had dairying and in some cases this enterprise was large enough to support two or even three separate herds or units. According to the Standard Man Day (SMD) classification of the survey farms in 1978, 21 per cent, 8 per cent and 43 per cent were respectively 'cropping mostly cereals', 'general cropping' and 'mixed farming'.

Table 3.2
Tractors and Combine Harvesters on Agricultural Holdings in England and Wales 1950-1976

	Tractors (wheeled)		
	Up to 37 kW	Over 37.3 kW	Total
1970	246,000	92,000	338,000
Change %			
1970/71	+0.8	+6.5	+2.4
1971/72	-12.1	+9.2	-6.1
1972/73	-4.6	+3.7	-1.8
1973/74	+3.8	+39.6	+20.3
1974/75	-2.3	+6.5	-6.8
1975/76	-3.3	+4.2	+5.0
1976/77	+2.5	+4.7	+3.5
1977/78	+4.8	+4.4	+4.6
1978/79	-1.8	+2.7	+0.2
1979	215,000	193,000	408,000
Change % 1950/59	NA	NA	+42.1
Change % 1960/69	NA	NA	-3.7
Change % 1970/7	-12.6	+109.8	+17.1

	Combine Harvesters (self-propelled)			
	Cutterbar width			
	Up to 3 m	3 to 4.6 m	Over 4.6 m	Total
1968	22,000	31,000	300	53,300
Change %				
1968/72	-13.6	0.0	+200.0	-4.5
1972/74	0.0	+6.5	-22.2	+3.5
1974/75	-15.8	+6.1	+14.3	-1.7
1975/76	0.0	-2.8	0.0	-1.9
1976	16,000	34,000	800	51,000
Change % 1950/59	NA	NA	NA	+314.3
Change % 1960/6	NA	NA	NA	+48.3
Change % 1968/76	-27.3	+9.7	+166.7	-6.1

Notes:
NA: Not Available because sizes not separately recorded.
kW: Kilowatts (1 kW = 0.746 horsepower)
Source: MAFF Statistics (MAFF annual).

The average area of the 41 farms providing data in the two surveys was 558 ha (1978) and 550 ha (1981). The average for this group of farms in 1978 was sufficiently close to the full sample in that year (540 ha) to enable the subset of farms to be regarded as reasonably comparable to the whole survey. Looking closer at the figures, it appears that 10 per cent of the 41 farms had decreased in size by over 25 per cent of their 1978 land area, and 5 per cent had increased by the same order of magnitude. These changes in size ranged from a decrease of 429 ha to an increase of 139 ha. This evidence suggests that even over this relatively short time period, when the overall size structure of agriculture remained fairly constant, there was a considerable amount of land changing hands at the individual farm level. Furthermore, the changes were not all in the direction of small farms being amalgamated to form larger units, since some farm fragmentation had also occurred.

The national statistics confirm that it is larger farms, measured in terms of their area or business size, that are the main employers of hired labour in agriculture. In 1978 all of the survey farms employed regular, full-time male workers and up to 9 such employees were present on 68 per cent of the survey farms, which compares with 69 per cent of all holdings of the same size in England in the same year. Other groups of workers, such as part-timers, farm managers and casual workers, were also present on the survey farms. As would be expected, the number of farms with salaried managers and secretaries was considerably higher than the national average. The importance of casual workers revealed by the national figures is confirmed by the survey, since 82 per cent employed casual labour at least once a year.

The impression is sometimes given that the regular, full-time workforce on farms is a fairly homogeneous group of people and that there is little differentiation in working practices, wage rates or qualifications. In the survey regular, full-time workers were classified according to the nature of their work. Four groups were identified: tractor drivers; specialist dairy and livestock workers; general farm workers; and maintenance workers (mechanics, estate workers and carpenters). Some specialisation was apparent with only a very small proportion of the workers classified as General Farm Workers and 39 per cent of the original survey farms employing between 5 and 9 tractor drivers.

Nearly a quarter of the 41 farms that supplied data for 1978 and 1981 had not changed the overall size of their regular full-time labour forces. The remaining 31 farms were divided almost equally into those with an increase (16) and those with a decrease (15). The size of the changes ranged from a loss of 13 full-time workers to a gain of 8. However these were the extremes and the majority of farms experienced much smaller fluctuations, between a loss of 3 and a gain of 2 people. In general, an increase or decrease in labour was associated with a similar change in land area, however there were a few cases where a modest reduction in area was accompanied by a small increase in the workforce.

The overall decline in the number of regular full-time workers overlays changes in the composition of the workforces on the farms. Significantly most groups, apart from managers, declined. However this may be due to the fact that the figures for 1981 are based on farmers' allocation of workers to the different categories, whereas the original classification was carried out on a more rigorous basis. In 1981 there were fewer farms employing people in certain groups, notably maintenance workers, although general farm workers were found on a larger number of farms. The composition of the workforce does appear to have changed, with the disappearance of one group, for example of dairy specialist workers, on a particular farm signifying the removal or diminution of an enterprise from the farm's production system. Other changes are perhaps more subtle and, in the case of the decline in maintenance workers, possibly indicate efforts at cost-cutting.

An analysis of the age of the machinery on the full sample of farms in 1978 reveals that some 36 per cent of the items were less than 4 years old and 26 per cent were over 10 years old. This suggests a broad division into new and old equipment with a relatively small proportion (14 per cent) between 7 and 9 years in age. There were contrasts between the age profiles for different types of machine. Four-wheel drive tractors, for example, showed a marked skewness towards younger, newer machines, with 73 per cent of these tractors under 4 years of age. In contrast, cultivation machinery tended to be older than some other groups, with 26 per cent under 4 years old. Size of machinery is a more difficult attribute to measure, but there is some evidence that the machinery on the survey farms tended to be larger than on holdings in England and Wales as a whole. For example, 21 per cent of combine harvesters in the survey had cutter-bar widths over 4.6 m compared with only 2 per cent nationally. There is also some support for the notion that farmers were replacing old machinery with larger and more sophisticated equipment. The analysis of the age and size of tractors on the farms showed that the majority of more powerful tractors were also relatively new.

The changes in machinery on the survey farms between 1978 and 1981 can only be examined on a comparatively limited basis as it was impractical to collect many details in a postal questionnaire. Between 1978 and 1981, 40 per cent of the farms did not change the number of tractors, and of those that did the majority increased or decreased by only one tractor. As in the case of workers on the farms, there was a negative correlation between the number of tractors and hectares per tractor. However, unlike the labour force changes, it does not appear that a decrease in area was necessarily associated with a decrease in the number of tractors. This feature may be associated with the retention of the machinery on a farm until the end of its useful life.

These figures are simply aggregate counts and do not take any account of changes in the characteristics of the tractor complements. The two surveys provide an opportunity to look at the detailed changes in the size and age of tractors on large farms at two specific points in time. Table 3.3 summarizes these changes and confirms that the size of tractors has been rising steadily, since there were 11 per cent more large tractors in 1981 than in 1978. Average tractor size increased on 87 per cent of the farms. Furthermore, the proportion of farms with an average tractor size of more than 57.7 kW had doubled to 40 per cent by 1981. These changes, which suggest continuing mechanisation, must be counterbalanced by evidence of a general ageing of the tractors on the farms. In 1981, the farms had 8 per cent fewer tractors under 4 years of age (47 and 39 per cent in 1978 and 1981 respectively). The percentage of farms with the average age of their tractors under 4 years old also fell by a similar amount. An examination of the age and size profiles of the tractors bought and sold between these years reveals that it was the younger, relatively larger machines in 1978 that had been disposed of and replaced by even larger models in 1981. This empirical evidence must be placed in an historical context and related to changes in other aspects of agriculture. The period 1980 to 1981 represents the start of a squeeze on farm incomes and a resultant lack of investment in agriculture. Thus labour and machinery use during the 1980s needs to be examined in order to determine whether the trends established in the productionist era continued into a period of adjustment.

Table 3.3
Age and Size of Tractors on Large, Arable Farms 1978-1981

	7.5-37.3	37.3-57.7	>57.7 (kW)
Size of Tractors			
1978	21	51	28
1981	17	44	39
Mean size of Tractors			
1978	0	81	19
1981	0	60	40

	0.1-5	5.1-10	10.1-15	Over 15 (kW)
Change in mean size 1978/81				
Increase	56	38	6	0
Decrease	50	0	0	0
Difference in mean size of tractors bought or sold				
Increase	26	22	26	26
Decrease	67	0	0	33

	0-3	4-7	8-11	12+ (Years)
Age of Tractors				
1978	47	32	15	6
1981	39	33	16	12
Mean age of tractor per farm				
1978	34	61	5	0
1981	26	54	20	0

Notes:
All figures are row percentages.
kW: Kilowatts (1 kW = 0.746 horsepower)
Source: Survey data.

Restructuring Labour and Machinery in the 1980s

The last decade, and more particularly the last 5 years, has been a period in which agriculture and farmers have come under increasing pressure from a number of directions. Swinbank (1985) has suggested that price-support policies, taken with other pressures such as investment subsidies, tax incentives and high inflation, have resulted in a "formidable squeeze on the need for a hired labour force" and help to explain the relative stability in the number of farmers. During the 1980s it has become widely accepted that the CAP has contributed to the build up of structural surpluses in a number of products. As a consequence there has been pressure on farmers to reduce levels of production. Quotas for dairying were introduced in 1984 and threats and murmuring about input or output quotas for arable cropping continue to feature in the farming press. Other pressure on farmers has arisen from the general public in two main directions. The public have become more concerned about the quality of the food they eat rather than just its price. This important change of emphasis has increased the demand for organically produced food and lead to demands for better quality. The second point is that the message in official reports and the academic literature about the effects of modern farming on the environment has now filtered down to the general public. People have started to become more concerned and informed about cnservation and environmental issues, including the effects of farmers' activites.

The emphasis in the mid to late 1980s shifted from production to diversification and survival as income levels from agriculture fell. Agricultural policy still emphasises efficient production, but in the presentation of policy more stress is now being placed on what the consumer wants from agriculture in respect of methods of production, food quality and the impact of agriculture on the countryside. Indeed restructuring of the agricultural industry through the Common Agricultural Policy has become a priority on the political agenda. Policy measures, which are intended to take land out of agriculture have been introduced in the late 1980s, such as set aside and incentives for forestry in lowland arable areas, but have tended to receive relatively modest levels of support from the industry. In 1991 it is anticipated that development control restrictions under the Town and Country Planning Legislation will be extended to farms under 5.1 hectares (12.5 acres), which represents a significant departure from the privileged position that agriculture has enjoyed previously. Pressure to raise the limit to 10.1 hectares (25 acres) was unsuccessful with the Planning Minister (Sir George Young) telling Parliament that such a limit would "double the number of farm units under planning control" (Planning 1991). The purpose of this section is to see if there is any evidence that these pressures are affecting the patterns of labour and machinery usage in agriculture.

It inevitably takes some time for these pressures to take effect and still longer for the implications to be revealed in official statistical sources. Nevertheless some features can already be detected. The decline in the agricultural labour force, which had been intimately connected with increasing productivity, gained momentum in the 1980s as shown in Table 3.4. Overall the agricultural workforce in England fell by 10.7 per cent between 1980 and 1989, compared with a decrease of 4.9 per cent between 1970 and 1979. The trend for using seasonal and casual labour in place of regular labour identified earlier did not continue into the 1980s. The number of male and female seasonal and casual workers in England fell by 6.1 and 24.4 per cent respectively between 1980 and 1989. It is significant that the number of women employed in this fashion on farms fell by nearly a quarter. The reduction in the number of regular full-time family and hired workers in the 1970s (-28.5 per cent) continued into the next decade (-26.6 per cent).

Table 3.4
Agricultural Labour in England and Wales 1980-1989

	Regular Hired Family Wkrs		Farmers, Ptrs Directors		Seasonal Casual		Total
	WT	PT	WT	PT	M	F	
1980 '000	150	53	162	69	49	41	590
Change %							
1980/81	-3.0	-3.2	-1.9	+2.9	-0.0	-7.3	-1.3
1981/82	-2.0	-0.2	-1.1	+1.8	-1.0	+4.2	-0.4
1982/83	-1.3	-1.2	-0.1	-8.9	-1.0	-1.3	-1.6
1983/84	-4.0	+0.6	-0.1	+5.8	+0.2	-5.4	-0.8
1984/85	-2.2	+1.8	-1.9	+2.9	+2.7	+1.1	+0.1
1985/86	4.4	+1.0	1.0	+1.8	-0.8	-1.6	1.1
1986/87	-4.8	-1.5	-1.9	-0.3	-1.6	-0.5	-2.0
1987/88	-5.0	+0.2	-2.2	+1.6	+1.2	-4.1	-1.3
1988/89	-3.8	-4.5	-2.2	+4.0	-5.7	-11.7	-2.7
1989 '000	110	48	143	77	46	31	527
Change %							
1980/89	-26.6	-9.4	-11.7	+11.6	-6.1	-24.4	-10.7

Notes:
Wkrs: Workers, Ptrs: Partners, WT: Whole Time, PT: Part Time, M: Male, F: Female.

Source: MAFF Statistics (MAFF annual).

It is perhaps even more significant that there has also been a change in the number of farmers, partners and directors doing farm work. In the 1970s in England and Wales there was a 13.4 per cent increase in this group, but during the next decade there was a decrease of 4.8 per cent. Furthermore, these figures conceal the fact that full-time farmers, partners and directors decreased by 11.7 per cent in the 1980s, while those working part-time increased by 11.6 per cent. The increase in part-time farmers continues a trend established in the previous decade. It is probably too early to say whether the increase in part-time farmers is only a temporary development, but given the interest in farm diversification it is very significant.

The pressures on agriculture do therefore appear to have produced a response from the farmers in terms of the use of labour in the industry. In the case of machinery the number of wheeled tractors in England and Wales increased by 17.1 per cent between 1970 and 1979 as shown in Table 3.5. Although there was a lower increase between 1981 and 1987 (+2.2 per cent), the trend for larger tractors was clearly apparent. The number of tractors with engine sizes of 60 kW and over increased by 98.2 per cent between 1981 and 1987. Very small tractors (under 25 kW) show a marked decrease in numbers, falling by 26.4 per cent between 1981 and 1987. Similar trends have occurred in the case of combine harvesters. The number of combine harvesters in England and Wales with engine sizes over 100 kW increased by 125.0 per cent

England and Wales with engine sizes over 100 kW increased by 125.0 per cent between 1981 and 1986, while those below 60 kW decreased by 33.8. The overall number fell by 4.3 per cent over the same period. The implication of these statistics is that, irrespective of pressures for change and for cutting production, farmers have been continuing to purchase larger machinery.

Table 3.5
Tractors and Combine Harvesters on Agricultural Holdings in England and Wales 1981-1987

	Tractors (wheeled)				
	Up to 37	25 to <60	60 to <100	Over 100 (kW)	Total
1981	53,000	301,000	56,000*		407,000
Change %					
1981/82	-9.6	-1.4	+20.9*		+2.6
1982/84	-10.4	-4.5	+25.1	+55.0	+0.1
1984/85	-10.3	-0.1	+8.8	+6.5	+0.6
1985/86	+0.3	+3.6	+5.3	+4.5	-1.1
1986/87	+1.3	-2.7	+6.1	+10.1	-0.1
1987	39,000	266,000	103,000	8,000	416,000
Change %					
1981/87	-26.4	-35.0	+98.2		+2.2

	Combine Harvesters (self-propelled)				
	Engine size				
	Up to < 60	60 to < 80	80 to <100	Over 100 (kW)	Total
1981	5,000	18,000	10,000	4,000	47,000
Change %					
1981/82	-4.9	-2.3	-1.9	+18.2	-4.7
1982/84	-21.3	-13.9	+7.8	+74.4	-3.6
1984/86	-13.1	-2.0	-4.5	+29.4	+0.9
1986	10,000	15,000	1,000	9,000	45,000
Change %					
1981/86	-33.8	-16.6	+10.0	+125.0	-4.3

Notes:
* Combined figure for tractors over 60 Kw.
kW: Kilowatts (1 kW = 0.746 horsepower)

Source: MAFF Statistics (MAFF annual).

<u>Future Prospects for Labour and Machinery</u>

Agricultural change does not occur in isolation, it is part of wider social and economic developments. The changes in the use of labour and machinery both during the productionist and the restructuring phases have been part of a broader change in the organisation of agriculture and in the development of society. Questions are raised about the place of a primary economic activity such as farming in a post-industrial society. Agriculturalists appear to have adjusted their use of labour and machinery to the new economic and political circumstances. The flexibility in the use of labour and machinery has a number of dimensions. On the one hand it relates to differences between farms in the extent to which these inputs are combined at a given point in time. Another dimension concerns change in the use of these resources over time. The analysis has confirmed that there is still scope for some considerable measure of change and that labour and machinery complements are not static with regard to both total numbers and composition.

However, there are other ways in which the process of restructuring has been manifested. In the past when the rural economy was dominated by agriculture and a substantial proportion of country dwellers depended directly or indirectly on this industry for their employment and livelihood, the social system was part and parcel of the agricultural system. However, when most rural residents are in the country but not of the country and are employed in towns and cities, then the social cohesion of villages may be weakened and conflicts can arise.

The changes occurring in agriculture and the countryside are an emotionally charged issue. Farmers claim rights to stewardship of the countryside but also that change must be accommodated to maintain profitable production and food supplies. The counter arguments revolve around the ecological issues of protecting endangered species and valued environments, and the assertions that modern agriculture is associated with over-production and the creation of surpluses. It is difficult to see how the counter arguments can be reconciled, since they start from opposing premises. For the farmers, the land is a factor in the agricultural production process, whereas for the general populace the countryside is part of the consumption sphere, a place for recreation and relaxation. This division is not entirely watertight, since farmers often claim that working in an attractive environment is one of the reasons for continuing in farming. Nevertheless the division is a useful one and points to certain underlying conflicts. It would therefore seem that political action is necessary if the continuing process of change in land, labour and machinery is to be managed in a way that reduces the unwanted consequences for both the environment and for rural society.

The empirical evidence from a sample of large arable farms in the South-East of England has indicated that rural employment problems will not be solved by vain hopes that farmers will voluntarily increase the numbers of workers that they employ. The statistical evidence of the last 10 years supports the same conclusion. Indeed there are clear signs that the established trends will continue and that agriculture still has a surplus of labour, both in terms of workers and farmers. Experience suggests that this will mean further mechanisation and the enlargement of holdings. Farmers want to retain the right to make the economic decisions that bring about such changes, yet as the countryside moves increasingly into the consumption sphere of a wider public we see the potential for deep-seated conflict developing and the need for a comprehensive strategy for rural areas becoming increasingly more vital.

In many respects the fact that the Common Agricultural Policy has been at the heart of the European Community and its institutions reflects the need to accommodate the transition to an economic and social system in which farming is not a major employer of the national workforce. The restructuring of agricultural policy is involving a broader perspective on rural issues. Agricultural policy is slowly being converted into a rural policy and funding from agricultural budgets is now being used to help alleviate problems in the countryside. Whether such a change in policy can intervene to control the ongoing reduction in the farm labour force or to limit remains to be seen.

References

Britton, D. K. (1968) 'Agricultural manpower: the current situation', in Agricultural Manpower, National Economic Development Office, London.

Buchanan, R. O. (1959) 'Some reflections on agricultural geography', Geography, 44, pp. 1-13.

Burrell, A., Hill, B. and Medland, J. (1984) Statistical handbook of UK agriculture, MacMillan, London.

Countryside Commission (1974) New agricultural landscapes, Countryside Commission, Cheltenham.

Culpin, C. (1969) 'Mechanisation', Journal of the Royal Agricultural Society of England, 130, pp. 93-111.

Dexter, K. (1977) 'The impact of technology on the political economy of agriculture', Journal of Agricultural Economics, 28, pp. 211-19.

Donaldson, G. F. (1970) Farm machinery capacity, Royal Commission on Farm Machinery, Canada.

Elliot, D. and Elliot, R. (1976) The control of technology, Wykeham, London.

Errington, A. (1988) 'Disguised unemployment in British agriculture', Journal of Rural Studies, 4 (1), pp. 1-7.

Fulton, C. V., Heady, E. O. and Ayres, G. E. (1978) Farm machinery costs in relation to machinery and farm size, Centre for Agricultural and Rural Development Bulletin No. 80, Iowa State University.

Gasson, R. (1974) Mobility of farm workers, Department of Land Economy, University of Cambridge.

Hodge, I. and Monk, S. (1991) In search of a rural economy, Department of Land Economy, University of Cambridge.

Inhen, L. and Heady, E. O. (1964) Cost functions in relation to farm size and machinery technology in southern Iowa, Department of Economics and Sociology Research Bulletin No. 527, Iowa State University.

MAFF (annual) Agricultural statistics - England and Wales, HMSO, London.

MAFF (annual) Agricultural labour in England and Wales: earnings, hours and number of persons, HMSO, London.

MAFF (1982) Annual review of agriculture 1982, HMSO, London.

Marsden, T., Munton, R., Whatmore, S. and Little, J. (1986) 'Towards a political economy of capitalist agriculture: a British perspective', International Journal of Urban and Regional Research, 10, pp. 498-521.

Newby, H. (1979) Green and pleasant land, Hutchinson, London.

Newby, H. (1982) 'Rural sociology and its relevance to the agricultural economist', Journal of Agricultural Economics, 33, pp. 125-65.

Nix, J. S. (1968) 'Labour organisation on the farm', Agriculture, 75, pp. 59-63.

Phillips, D. and Williams, A. (1984) Rural Britain: a social geography, Blackwell, Oxford.

Planning (1991) 'Department delivers farm controls and fees', Planning, No.

922, 14 June.
Sturrock, F. G. (1966) 'Economic aspects of mechanisation in advanced countries', Advancement of Science, 23, pp. 171-77.
Sturrock, F. G., Cathie, J. and Payne, T. A. (1977) Economies of scale in farm mechanisation: a study of costs on large and small farms, Agricultural Enterprise Studies Economic Report No. 56, University of Cambridge.
Swinbank, A. (1985) 'A note on price support policy and hired farm labour', Journal of Agricultural Economics, 36, pp. 259-61.
Walford, N. S. (1981a) The development and significance of alternative strategies in agricultural labour and machinery use, Geography Research Paper No. 8, University of Sussex.
Walford, N. S. (1981b) Present and future labour and machinery usage on the larger, mainly arable farm, PhD Thesis, University of London.

4 Elderly farmers as countryside managers

CLIVE POTTER AND MATT LOBLEY

Introduction

Family farms are arguably still the most important units of decision making in the countryside. Over 90 % of agricultural land in the UK is under their ownership or management control; decisions made daily on thousands of full time agricultural holdings have a profound impact on the appearance of the rural landscape and the quality of its wildspace. Indeed, in a formal sense family farms are structures for the accumulation and management of a very large stock of natural capital (hedges, trees, woodland, rough grazing, hay meadows). They are also vehicles for its transmission to future generations. This was recognised by European policymakers when they affirmed that

> 'sufficient numbers of farmers must be kept on the land. There is other way to preserve the natural environment, traditional landscapes and a model of agriculture based on the family farm as favoured by society generally. This requires an active rural development policy and this will not be created without farmers' (Commission of European Communities, 1988, p. 3).

The paper goes on to reject a European agriculture modelled on the USA 'with large reserves of land and few farmers'. In following this strategy however, policymakers are to a large degree working against the grain of economics. The secular trend, disguised in the past by the CAP, is towards a much slimmer farming industry composed of many fewer farmers each capable of earning a reasonable living by claiming a relatively larger share of a shrinking cake (Britton, 1990). By agreeing to limit the price guarantees offered to farmers under a reformed CAP, policymakers might appear to be reinforcing this restructuring process, though in practice widespread liquidation of holdings is less likely under the 'decoupled' CAP which farm ministers seem to favour. Under decoupling, price guarantees will be substantially reduced but with farmers' income being supported selectively and transparently through direct income aid schemes. Decoupling thus refers to the separation of the market regulation role of price from its income support function.

In fact, recent years have seen the emergence of a 'farm survival policy' (Potter, 1990) in the guise of an invigorated and extended set of socio-structural measures which offer farmers payments to set aside land, extensify production or diversify their businesses. An important feature of these schemes is the linking of payments to environmental management or improvement on the farms in question, reflecting the revised social contract between farmers and the state, with farmers in receipt of income aids agreeing to desist from certain environmentally damaging operations or even gearing their farming practices to countryside management. A new environmental protection scheme launched by the Commission in 1991 for example, aims to promote less intensive forms of production throughout the countryside (Commission of European Communities, 1991). In some cases, specific farmers are being targeted for these direct payments precisely because they own land which must be farmed traditionally if it is to retain its conservation value. This is the principle behind the EC's Environmentally Sensitive Areas (ESA) programme which protects characteristic landscapes and habitat mosaics in places like the Somerset Levels and South Downs in the UK by supporting the traditional, extensive systems of farming that lie behind them (MAFF, 1989). This policy signals for the first time a recognition that farm support monies should be used to preserve the 'particular character' of farming in an area for environmental reasons. Other socio-structural measures such as the pilot farm extensification scheme (MAFF, 1990) indicate that agriculture departments are now willing to purchase part of a farmer's right to property in the interests of environmental protection and landscape conservation. This represents a significant shift in conservation behaviour, away from the traditional, more investment orientated approach often appealing to more progressive innovative farmers who could afford the 'luxury' of conservation. Now, following the lead of the ESA programme, conservation is becoming ever more managerial and positive in approach, utilizing principles from the traditional agricultural practices that created and maintained our present landscapes.

A consequence of all this could be that farmers previously not interested in conservation could find themselves involved for the first time. It has already been suggested that conservation contracts such as those on offer to farmers in ESAs are likely to appeal most to agricultural 'laggards' (Potter, 1990). The recruitment of 'laggards' into conservation schemes means that conservation can be seen as another 'crop' which farmers produce as a means of earning a living. Taken a little further, it is not unrealistic to expect entire sections of the farming community to be retrained and recast as managers of countryside instead of solely producers of food. But which farmers are best equipped for this role and how should incentive schemes be designed to attract them? There is a need for applied research which can begin to identify these target farmers and the parts of the conservation resource that are under their management or ownership control. Policymakers need information which can be used to 'fit' new schemes and programmes to those farms and farming situations that can make most use of them and deliver the greatest environmental benefit.

Serious contenders must be the large number of farmers who are now near or past retirement age. Of the European Community's 6.3 million farm operators in 1985, 1.7 million were aged between 45 and 55 but there were 1.8 million between 55 and 65 and 1.3 million over 65 (Eurostat, 1989). In member states like France and Italy, elderly farmers make up a large share of the total farming population, 15% and 25% being over 65 in these two countries respectively. In the UK in 1985 27% of farmers were aged between 55 and 65 and 21% were over 65. There are long-standing proposals from commentators such as Franklin (1971), Green (1985) and Statham (1986) which envisage elderly farmers becoming countryside managers. It is assumed that many such farmers may actually be 'running down' their holdings as they approach the end of their working life, especially those without successors, and doing so in ways which increase their value to nature conservationists. For Franklin (1971) however, the 'park-keeper formula' is simply an expedient way of dealing with what are often marginal holdings, anachronisms in a modern industry. Certainly the attitude of policy-makers towards elderly farmers has tended this way, the many small scale holdings run by elderly farmers being of interest only as sources of land for the amalgamation and restructuring of farms (Revell, 1986). Franklin envisages elderly farmers becoming 'wards of the welfare state .... (maintaining) an agro-cultural environment for the enjoyment of urban dwellers' (Franklin, 1971, p. 23). More recently, Hodge (1988) has canvassed the idea of conservation trusts buying up land released by (amongst others), elderly farmers without heirs or successors.

While intriguing, such proposals raise more questions than they answer concerning the amount of land held by elderly farmers and its value to conservationists and about the willingness and ability of elderly farmers to take on the radically different role that is being cast for them. Do elderly farmers own or manage land that is likely to be of interest to conservationists ? Or to put this another way, is there any evidence to suggest that farms run by elderly farmers are managed any more extensively than those at other stages in the life cycle? And do elderly farmers possess the necessary skills, interest and motivation to become heritage farmers? If so, how easily can they be recruited into conservation schemes?

The land holding of elderly and pre-retirement farmers

The amount of land presently owned or managed by elderly farmers or pre-retires (aged between 55 and 65) is difficult to estimate, though we know that farmers aged 55 and over occupied some 4.7m ha or 41% of the total agricultural area in 1983 (Eurostat, 1989, see table 4.1).

It is often assumed that much of this land is concentrated in hill and upland areas, elderly farmers clustering in the national parks for instance. The Uplands Landscape Study (Sinclair, 1983) in the UK discovered a pronounced skew towards farmers aged 50 or more in their study areas (54% compared to 47.6% for the UK as a whole). Table 4.2, based on an analysis of MAFF census returns, suggests however that in terms of numbers elderly farmers are widely scattered, with no significant differences in the age structure of LFAs compared to non-LFAs.

An interesting question is what proportion of the undoubtedly considerable amount of land held by farmers over 55 will actually be 'shaken out' on retirement or death. A determining factor is whether successors exist and are willing and able to take over the farm [1]. From a review of the available evidence, which is by no means comprehensive, Fennell (1981) points to the alarmingly low number of farms in the EC with a successor working alongside the farmer (between one quarter and one third of holdings where the farmer is middle aged). However, given that many successors need to work away from the farm until they inherit (due to small farm size and limited income potential) the true level of succession is likely to be higher. Evidence on total successors suggests that at least half of EC farmers have no obvious family successor. In a survey of UK farmers Harrison (1975) indicates higher levels of

Table 4.1
Land farmed by elderly and pre-retirement farmers

Farmers aged 55 and over

	Farms No (10³)	Member State % of all farms	% of EC 10	Area Farmed Total 10³ Ha	Average Per Farm (Ha)
Germany	219	29	7	2581	11.8
France	501	47	16	8583	17.1
Italy	1488	54	49	6889	4.6
Netherlands	51	38	2	697	4.6
Belgium	41	41	1	423	10.3
Luxembourg	1.8	43	0	35	19.4
UK	100	54	0	4782	47.8
Ireland	105	49	3	2182	20.8
Denmark	40	41	1	913	22.8
Greece	511	53	17	1862	3.6
EC-10	3060	48	100	28948	9.5

Source: Commission of European Communities, various dates.

Table 4.2

Distribution of farmers aged >55 in LFAs and non LFAs

	England			Wales			Northern Ireland			Scotland			United Kingdom		
	LFA	Non LFA	Total	LFA	Non LFA	Total	LFA	Non LFA	Total	LFA	Non LFA	Total	LFA	Non LFA	Total
No.	8634	56723	65357	8567	5866	14433	17549	6998	24547	9261	2930	12191	68946	72517	116528
%	41.8	46.9	46.2	48.7	50.3	49.4	58.1	54.3	56.9	46.1	44.2	45.6	49.7	47.7	48.4

Source: MAFF census data.

succession, with 24% of business principals having no identified successor compared to 76% who wished for a successor (64.3% of all principals had a successor identified). Although there are no data on the spatial distribution of farmers with successors, an Agricultural Economic Development Commission survey found that 'the highest proportion of bachelor farms were in Wales and North of England' (Agriculture Economic Development Commission, 1972 p 83). Considering the amount of land likely to fall vacant, Fennell (1981) observes that, regardless of location, this is likely to be a smaller proportion of the total area of land held by elderly farmers than these figures would suggest; farms at the greatest risk tending to be smaller than average for obvious reasons. So far as the UK is concerned, assuming a succession rate of 60%, simple arithmetic suggests that some 47,000 farmers over 55 could presently be without a successor. The rate of succession itself is affected by both farm and farmer factors. In cases where the farmer has children, parents' attitudes towards the farmer's retirement and their children will be significant, as will childrens' own interests, skills, ability and the availability of alternative employment. These factors can result in higher levels of succession in poorer farming regions because of limited alternative employment opportunities for successors. Farmers themselves would say (with good reason) that the transformation of rural communities in social and economic terms has had a significant impact on succession. These days farmers children are likely to mix with more 'non-farm' children and faced with wider job opportunities may settle for regular employment in preference to years of self exploitation.

The use and management of land held by elderly farmers

The case for focusing on elderly farmers as conservation targets rests on two assumptions: first, that such individuals are more likely than their younger counterparts to be managing land in ways which somehow increase or maintain conservation value and interest, and secondly, that farmers approaching retirement and old age might be more willing than those earlier in their careers to enrol in government conservation schemes.

On the first point, there is some evidence to show that the ageing of a business principal may be the signal for important changes in the way a business is managed and organised, leading to shifts in both the pattern and intensity of land use (Commins and Kelleher, 1973). In particular, farmers may choose to 'run down' their holdings and extensify production in a manner which adds to its conservation value. Previous research suggests that farmers adopt various coping strategies as they near the end of their working lives, a time when the transfer of accumulated wealth and farm property to a successor becomes a preoccupying concern. As Marsden, et al (1989) point out, successfully passing on a business to the next generation to ensure family continuity is one of the basic imperatives which drives the decision making of family farmers. Unfortunately, although researchers have assiduously studied the linked processes of succession and inheritance (Commins and Kelleher, 1973; Fennell, 1981; Hastings 1983, 1984; Hutson, 1987; Rogers and Salamon, 1983) and the mechanics of passing on business assets and management control, there are
surprisingly few analyses of the way approaching retirement and death affects the way a farm is actually managed, let alone how ageing affects the stock of natural capital on a farm.

What emerges from studies like those by Commins and Kelleher (1973) however, is that decisions made in old age are often prefigured much earlier in the life-cycle as farmers take precautions against old age and plan for eventual succession and the transfer of wealth and assets. The way capital is accumulated and maintained over the family life-cycle is intimately bound up with the likelihood of its being passed on or transmitted to a successor. Decisions which affect the accumulation, maintenance and transmission of natural capital are inextricably linked.

An important finding is that farmers with successors may follow a different development trajectory compared to those where successors do not exist or cannot be persuaded or are unable to take over the farm. The running down of a farm business in old age is more likely to take place where the elderly farmer is working alone on the farm and lacks the incentive to maintain capital assets and lay the grounds for future expansion which a younger successor or heir is likely to provide. And indeed, there is some anecdotal evidence to suggest that farmers without successors may be farmed more extensively as old age approaches, though this is disputed by others. Harrison (1967; 1975) observes that the existence of a successor plays a determining role in investment decision making, with farmers without successors having a lower level of investment than those with a positively identified successor. In the latter stages of the family life cycle elderly farmers will begin to make changes in the business which release funds for consumption or investment elsewhere or which simply reduce their workload and indebtedness. Symes (1973) found that land on farms without successors was less intensively farmed than those with successors. He suggests that on such farms the production system 'declines closer to subsistence mode than at any point in the normal cycle' as the farmer enters old age (p.101). According to Crow (1986), on farms without a successor 'the enterprise will be characterised by a period of gradual decline as the farmer ages and approaches retirement' (p.3). Harsche (1987) also found that an ageing farm population lacking sufficient number of successors has created a situation where there is 'a pronounced lack of will and ability to maintain adequate levels of agricultural investment' (p.30). Similarly Jones and Green (1987) in a study of rough grazings in Wales found that on the third of farms with no plans for future improvement, an important explanatory variable was the age of the farmer and the non-availability of a successor. An elderly farmer with a successor, by contrast, may be handing over the reins of the business to a younger, more vigorous successor.

It would appear that while successor and non-successor farmers share certain common motives in developing a viable farm business (such as increasing net worth and maximising returns) the two groups are separated in old age by rather different concerns and objectives. Those without successors or heirs for instance, could be characterised as 'life-cyclers' in the sense that they take decisions to build up the business and accumulate capital as a precaution against a childless old age but do not plan to pass on accumulated wealth to the next generation. Many farmers without successors though cannot be characterised as pure 'life cyclers' as they might have heirs who will one day inherit the farm or benefit from the proceeds of its sale, thus providing a check against the farmer running down the holding to such an extent that it seriously erodes its market value. Farmers with successors, on the other hand, might have significant bequest motives which shape decisions about accumulation throughout the life-cycle, especially in the middle and later stages. In Figure 4.1 we propose a model which can be used to analyse how this bifurcation could lead to distinct management changes and environmental opportunities on farms run by elderly farmers.

To repeat, running down a farm and 'consuming' capital seems much less likely to take place on farms where a successor is already taking over the reins of control or is being positioned to do so. According to Hutson (1987, p.223) 'the existence of children is a significant incentive for a policy of (continued) improvement and development'. Far from ushering in a quieter period of extensification and 'decumulation', approaching old age could be associated with abrupt changes in the way the land is used and managed. The farmer himself will withdraw from the business, passing on management responsibilities to his successor over what is typically a long period of time. Past studies of this process (Hastings, 1983) suggest that the inter-generational dynamics of the retirement and transfer process are complex and often highly idiosyncratic. The business will become 'segmented' as the farmer withdraws first from management and then from investment and financial decision-making, shifting the burden onto the shoulders of his successor. This segmentation may well have environmental consequences as younger and more vigorous successors embark on new rounds of investment and land use intensification. But it is the making of bequests that particularly marks out farmers with successors from those without.

There is an extensive literature dealing with the bequest motive (Bernheim et al, 1985; Kessler and Masson 1988; 1989; Kotlikoff, 1988; Kotlikoff and Summers, 1988; Modigliani, 1988). A mixture of utilitarian and altruistic concerns appear to be involved. According to Hochman and Rodgers' (1969) utilitarian model, parents agree to transfer assets to their children in return for support (financial or otherwise) in their twilight years. Reduced to essentials, parents and children in this model enter into an implicit risk-sharing agreement, the risk shared being the length of time parents actually survive in old age! Altruistic bequests are made because parents are concerned to make provision for the future welfare of their children. In Becker and Tommes' (1979) model of 'compensated bequests', parents are concerned with their childrens' lifetime income and will make bequests which discriminate between high and low earning offspring.

As an occupational group farmers can reasonably be expected to have very strong bequest motives, given the high net worth of most owner occupied farms. Peters (1980) claims that many owner-occupiers are among the richest members of society in terms of wealth and material assets, 'large cropping and livestock farms easily being in the top half percent' (Peters, 1980, p. 390). According to Lifran (no date), the transfer of accumulated wealth and farm property to successors is one of the basic imperatives driving the decision making of family farmers. Boehlje (1973) explains how farm assets 'particularly land, become an integral part of the family structure, an heirloom in many cases' (p. 25). In addition, a farmer will be concerned with transferring to a successor the skills and values he associates with good farming alongside the material resources required to practice them (see Hastings, 1984; Rogers and Salamon, 1983). This has been characterised by Rogers and Salamon as a transfer of farm property and farming as an occupation. Indeed, Symes (1990) argues that today 'the concept of succession and inheritance apply more to ensuring the continuity of occupation in farming than to the specific transfer of property rights to land' (p. 284). Keating and Munrow (1987) quoted in Maroz-Baden (1988) have developed the idea of a 'generational stake' in which a successor provides an older generation the opportunity to pass on, not only the physical assets of an enterprise - which ensure family continuity - but also site-specific skills which increase the value of the transferred assets. The size of the farmer's 'generational stake' in his successor will be small at the beginning of the transfer process but obviously much greater by the time the successor is effectively managing the business. According to Rogers and Salamon, the existence of multiple or single heirs will be an important determinant of estate division and the planning of bequests.

One might ask whether the bequeathing of environmental assets is something which family farmers presently consider in old age. In most cases natural capital is probably unintentionally bequeathed to the next generation along with the farm and its tenant's capital. It is increasingly possible, however, that should farmers begin to compete for places on conservation income aid schemes, bequeathing a stock of natural capital in good repair which could improve a farmer's

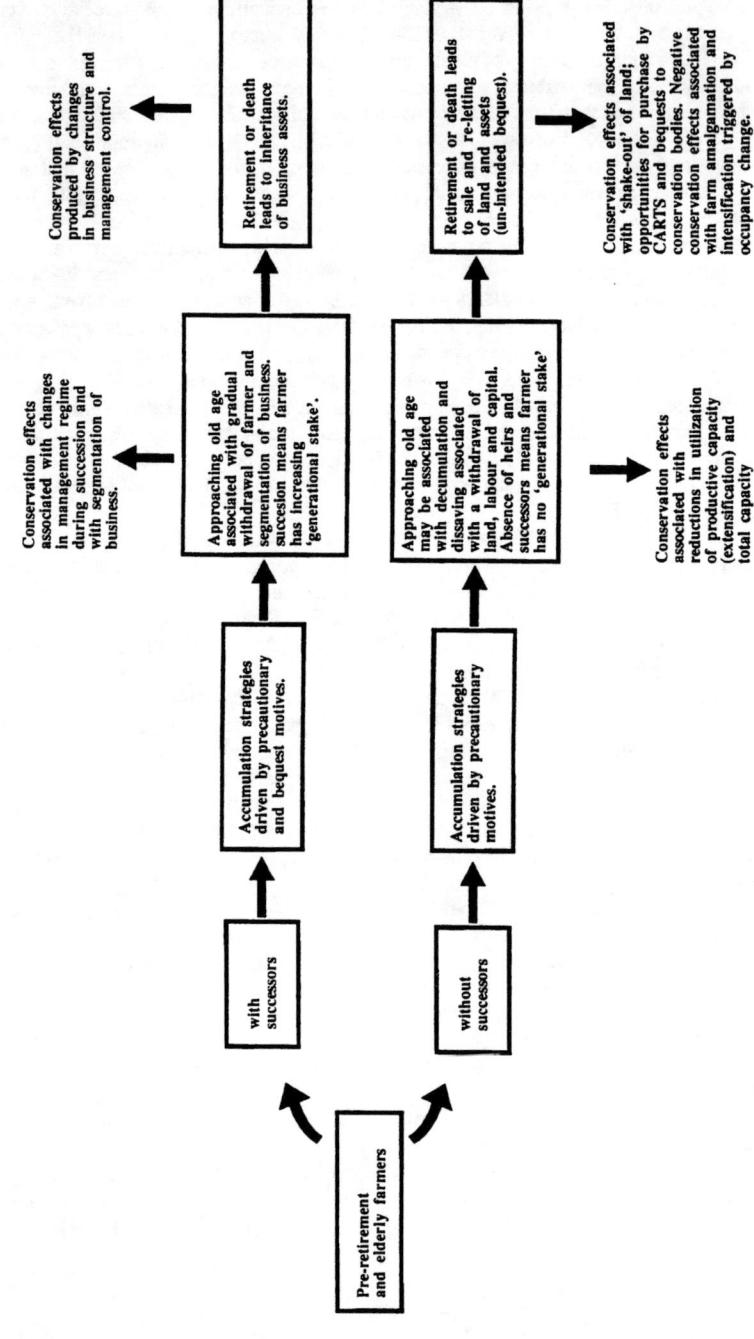

Figure 4.1 The Conservation Effects of Ageing on Family Farms

qualification for joining, may become a more conscious part of the transfer process. Some forms of natural capital are already consciously passed on through succession and inheritance. Take for example a farmer who has always laid his hedges; he will pass this skill on to his son and will expect (hope) that he will continue the practice. If laid hedges had a value in terms of entitlement to income aid it would encourage the expansion and intergenerational transfer of this form of natural capital.

It is on farms without successors that the much vaunted 'running down' process of such interest to conservationists will probably occur. There are many reasons why succession may not take place: first, the farmer has never married. Whilst this does not preclude inheritance by a relative it certainly limits the chances of succession; second, the farmer is married but has no children or the children are unable or unwilling to take over the business. Symes (1972, 1973) makes a useful distinction between what he terms 'residual households', resulting from a childless marriage or an inability to retain children on the farm and 'relic households' where the farmer has not married. In both cases 'family failure' could produce environmental benefits, if only because such farmers will be disinclined or unable to pursue the expansionary strategies adopted on farms where succession is assured (see discussion above). In the case of residual households there is a problem of causality in that succession may not take place precisely because the farm is too small or under-capitalised to be viable in future. Gasson, et. al. (1988) observe that farms near the margin of viability are less likely to be held by the same family for more than a generation for this very reason. Denied the option of putting the burdens of running a farm onto younger shoulders, farmers without successors may actually proceed to run down or 'consume' their material assets and tenant's capital as old age approaches, effectively extensifying production in an effort to reduce working time and managerial effort. The resulting process of 'decumulation' may create holdings that are important strongholds of conservation value in the countryside (though a lack of systematic applied ecological research in this area means that this cannot yet be substantiated). Figure 4.1 again shows some of the relationships involved.

In these circumstances shedding assets and running down the business may be more than the absence of accumulation; it can be an active and positive process (in the sense that it can be planned). Although in most cases this process seems likely to be confined to the latter stages of the life cycle, the first moves towards 'run down' may occur when it becomes clear that a successor is not available. The reaction at this point is likely to be limited to a recognition that there is no need to invest so furiously in the business although eventually this must translate into decisions not to invest at all and to gradually run the business down. The paucity of information concerning this process on farms makes it very difficult to do anything but speculate and hypothesise about the form that it might take.

Survey evidence suggests that old age will be characterised by the diminishing physical capacity of the farmer and more conservative decision making ie the farmer becomes more risk averse, has a shortened planning horizon and is reluctant to expand (Tauer, 1984). In the absence of a successor (who can act as a check against some of these processes), one hypothesis derived from Weinschenck and Kemper (1981) is that initial changes associated with decumulation may involve a reduction in the utilization of capacity and the burden of work (reduced hours, lower level of use of buildings, machinery, land and a move towards extensification). This may also involve a switch in enterprises for example, from dairy to less intensive beef production. Such changes could have a positive environmental impact if they resulted in the stocking density coming closer to the ecological grazing requirements or a reduction in fertilizer and chemical applications. In addition it may be possible that elderly farmers seek to avoid certain tasks. The 1972 Agriculture Economic Development Commission survey found that farmers over 55 were less likely to be involved in driving certain mobile equipment (other than tractors) than young farmers. (It is unclear whether this is due to reduced vigour associated with old age or because elderly farmers are less familiar with modern mobile equipment). More radical reductions in capacity itself (sale or leasing of land, reduction in utilised agricultural area) will probably occur only after such adjustments have been made to the intensity of the farming system. The sale or leasing of land is perhaps more likely than abandonment given the farmer's desire for financial security and reluctance to see the land 'go to waste'.

Such farmers are less likely than successor farmers to be planning to leave bequests, at least to individuals (though conservation bodies like The National Trust and the RSPB are occasional beneficiaries of bequests from farmers in such circumstances). However, because elderly farmers without successors do not usually know when they will finally leave farming (through death or retirement) they cannot plan to run down the farm completely (nor would this be desirable in most cases). It seems reasonable to assume that elderly farmers who remain in farming until they die will leave a stock of capital and environmental assets as 'unintended bequests'. While environmental assets could have built up during the farmer's more active years, perhaps more importantly they could result from decisions taken as the farmers career draws to a close. This raises some intriguing policy issues; what happens to any 'unintended bequests' depends on the fate of the farm; it is arguably the role of policy-makers and those involved in conservation to 'capture' such bequests for public benefit. In certain cases these 'bequests' could indeed be captured and transmitted to future generations by bringing the farm into the 'conservation estate' via direct purchase (Colman and O'Carroll, 1990).

Recruiting elderly farmers into conservation schemes

The existence of precautionary and bequest motives and the important differences between farmers with and without successors are significant factors which policy-makers would do well to consider should they decide to target elderly farmers for conservation contract schemes. The possible existence of 'unintended bequests' also raises interesting policy questions. For farmers with successors the later stages of the life cycle will be dominated, as we have seen, by the precautionary motive, concerned with security and the wish not to take chances that might endanger this, and the bequest motive, based on the desire to maintain the family farm, and pass it on to a successor. A conservation contract could provide guaranteed income (security) and could perhaps provide an added degree of stability during what could be a difficult period of adjustment. However, the views of the successor would be critical here, particularly if he had 'other plans' for the farm; extensification may be viewed as a constraint to the further expansion of the business.

By contrast, elderly farmers without successors face no such constraints. Indeed, with falling asset values and a tightening cost-price squeeze, but lacking the incentive to adjust and diversify, there may be many such farmers who, in Harvey's (1987) words, 'cannot afford not to' join such schemes. And indeed Warnock and Bell (1987) in a study of participation in hypothetical extensification schemes, found that elderly farmers without successors were much more interested in the idea of extensification than their younger counterparts. Potter and Gasson (1988) similarly found that farmers aged 55 and over and without successors were prepared to accept below average payments to enter land into hypothetical land diversion schemes. It appeared entirely feasible for such individuals to enrol their entire holdings into land diversion schemes, continuing to live in the farmhouse but engaging in simple farming operations to keep the land in good heart. Research in Greece into attitudes towards such schemes there (Fanariotu and Skuras 1989), also found elderly farmers interested in the notion of being paid to extensify production, though it was notable that their willingness to make marginal adjustments to fertilizer use and return to old fertilization practices was greater than their interest in more thorough-going changes to the system of farming. But do elderly farmers possess the necessary skills, interest and motivation to become heritage farmers? In pointing out that 'the pool of knowledge and experience available from the generation of farmers whose farming methods sustained valued grasslands is diminishing', Way (1989, p. 109) appears to be suggesting that elderly farmers, especially in the uplands, may well possess latent skills and knowledge that are valuable to conservationists. Here, as elsewhere, there is a need for research which can fully assess the conservation potential and importance of this section of the farming community.

Conclusions

At a time when policy-makers are beginning to think more seriously about targeting conservation policies at farms as well as conservation sites and heritage landscapes, the existence of a sizeable proportion of farmers nearing or past retirement age cannot be ignored. With their lower consumption needs and distinctive goals and values, older farmers, especially those without successors, are arguably already in a good position to respond to the new generation of environmental schemes now on offer. In the countryside of the future they may have an important role as managers of countryside, especially in more remote, upland areas. A lack of relevant research means however that their precise conservation status is still in doubt, with only anecdotal evidence concerning the way ageing affects the way land is used and managed and sketchy data from which to predict the willingness of elderly farmers to enter conservation schemes.

This chapter has posed some of the questions which policymakers and researchers will need to address if the full potential of elderly farmers is to be understood. The process of succession and inheritance, or indeed its absence, on farms held by elderly farmers appears to have very powerful consequences though we still lack research which probes some of the motives which lie behind the behaviour and decisions of farmers in old age; a clearer understanding of these motives is essential if conservation schemes are to be properly designed and targeted. The need to plan the transfer of assets to a successor, driven as it is by a bequest motive, can lead to the segmentation of farm businesses as a successor gradually takes over a greater share of management functions and the 'generational stake' increases. An intensification of land use and new programmes of capital investment may be the result. Farmers without successors, on the other hand, may begin to run down their holdings and extensify production as retirement and death approaches, conceivably in ways which enhance their conservation value and lead to the accumulation of valuable 'natural capital'. Finally, the eventual future shake-out of land from such farms when the farmer retires or dies in harness creates opportunities for conservation trusts and conservative agencies to purchase land in an effort to capture these 'unintended bequests' for public benefit.

Note

1. At this point a distinction needs to be made between succession and inheritance in order to avoid confusion later. Succession is the lengthy process of handing over managerial control of the farm, typically starting when the successor is in his 20's and extending in to his 30's or even 40's. (In the majority of cases the successor would be a son/s, occasionally son-in-law or a more distant relative, rarely a daughter.) Inheritance on the other hand is the transfer of the ownership of property usually occuring on death, although as Symes (1990) points out, the division of patrimony can occur under other circumstances, for example, financing continuing education (often of non-succeeding heirs).

Acknowledgements

The research for this paper was funded by the Nature Conservancy Council and the Economic and Social Research Council under their joint research programme 'People, Economies and Nature Conservation'.

References

Agriculture Economic Development Commission (1972), *Agricultural manpower in England and Wales*, National Economic Development Organisation and HMSO, London

Becker, G. and Tomes, N. (1974), 'An equilibrium theory of the distribution of income and intergenerational mobility', *Journal of Political Economy*, vol. 85, no. 6, pp. 1153-89.

Bernheim, B., Shleifer, A. and Summers, L. (1985), 'The strategic bequest motive', *Journal of Political Economy*, vol. 93, no. 6, pp. 1045-76.

Boehlje, M. (1973), 'The entry-growth-exit process in agriculture', *Southern Journal of Agricultural Economics*, no. 5, pp. 23-36.

Britton, D, (ed) (1990), *Agriculture in Britain: Changing pressures and policies*, C.A.B International, Wallingford.

Commission of European Communities (1988), *The future of rural society*, COM (88) 501 final, Brussels.

Commission of European Communities (1990), *Proposal for a Council Resolution on the introduction and maintenance of agricultural methods compatible with the requirements of the protection of the environment and the maintenance of the countryside*, COM (90) 366 final, Brusses.

Colman, D. and O'Carroll, L. (1990), *Public policy and the conservation estate: setting up a research agenda*, paper presented to the Countryside Change Conference, University of York, April 1990.

Commins, P and Kelleher, C. (1973), *Farm inheritance and succession*. Irish Farm Centre, Dublin.

Crow, G. (1986), *"One day all of this will be yours": Continuity and change in patterns of transmitting property within family farms*. Paper presented to the 1986 British Sociological Association Conference, Loughborough.

Eurostat (1989), *Structures survey, 1985 report*. Eurostat, Brussels.

Fanariotu, I. and D. Skuras, (1989), 'Environmental protection under the EEC's Socio-Structural policy for agriculture'. *Journal of Environmental Management*, vol. 28, no. 3 pp. 269-75.

Fennell, R. (1981), 'Farm succession in the European Community', *Sociologia Ruralis*, vol. 21, no. 1, pp. 19-42.

Franklin, S. (1971), *Rural Societies*, Macmillan, London.

Gasson, R., Crow, G., Errington, A., Hutson, J., Marsden, T. and Winter, M. (1988), 'The farm as a family business: a review', *Journal of Agricultural Economics*, vol. 39, no. 1, pp. 1-42.

Green, B. (1985), *Countryside Conservation*, Second edition, Allen and Unwin, London.

Harrison, A (1967), *Farming change in Buckinghamshire: some features revealed in a study of farm business structures 1961-1963*, University of Reading Department of Agricultural Economics Miscellaneous Study No. 43.

Harrison, A. (1975), *Farmers and farm businesses in England*. University of Reading Department of Agricultural Economics, Miscellaneous Study No. 62.

Harvey, D. (1987), 'Extensification schemes and agricultural economics: Who will take them up ?' In *Farm Extensification: implications of EC Regulation 1760/87*, Jenkins, D and Bell, (eds). Merlewood Research Paper 112, Institute of Terrestrial Ecology (ITE), Merlewood.

Harsche, E. (1987), 'Regional economic potentials, the age structure and the social security of aged farming populations: the structural transformation of agriculture and the reduction of farm surpluses in an industrial Europe', *Land Agrawirtschaft und Gesellschaft*, September 1987, pp. 29-41.

Hastings, M. (1983), *Succession on farms; a study of the transfer of management on owner occupied, family farms in Warwickshire*, Unpublished Msc Thesis, Cranfield Institute of Technology.

Hastings, M. (1984), 'Succession on farms', *Agricultural Manpower*, vol, 8, no. 2, pp. 4-8.

Hochman, H. and Rodgers, J. (1969), 'Pareto optimum redistribution', *American Economic Review*, no. 2, pp. 524-57.

Hodge, I. (1988), 'Property institutions and environmental improvement', *Journal of Agricultural Economics*, vol. 39, no. 3, pp. 369-75.

Hutson, J. (1987), 'Fathers and sons: family farms, family businesses and the farming industry', *Sociology*, vol 21, no. 2, pp. 215-29.

Jones, W.D. and Green, D.A. (1987), *Rough grazings in the hills and uplands of Wales: productivity and potential*, Department of Agricultural Economics and Marketing, University College Wales, Aberystwyth.

Kessler, D and Masson, A. (1988), *Modelling the accumulation and distribution of wealth*, Clarendon Press, Oxford.

Kessler, D. and Masson A. (1989), 'Bequest and wealth accumulation: are some pieces of the puzzle missing?' *Journal of Economic Perspectives*, vol. 3, no. 3, pp. 141-52.

Kotlikoff, L. (1988), 'Intergenerational transfers and savings', *Journal of Economic Perspectives*, vol. 2, no. 2, pp. 41-58.

Kotlikoff, L. and Summers, L. (1988), 'The contribution of intergenerational transfers to total wealth: a reply', In Kessler and Masson, 1988, op cit.

Lifran, R. (no date), *Land ownership structures of farms and the wealth of farmers*, Station d'Economie et Sociologie Rurales, Montpellier, unpublished.

MAFF. (1989), *Environmentally Sensitive Areas*, First Report, HMSO, London.

MAFF. (1990), *Beef and Sheep pilot extensification schemes*, The Ministry, London.

Maroz-Baden, R. (1988), *Transferring the family farm: survival in an uncertain world*, Research Briefing Paper, Montana State University.

Marsden, T., Whatmore, S. and Little, C. (1989), 'Strategies for coping in capitalist agriculture: an examination of the response of farm families in British agriculture', *Geoforum*, vol. 20, no. 1, pp. 1-14.

Modigiliani, F. (1988), 'The role of intergenerational transfers and Life cycle saving in the accumulation of wealth'. *Journal of Economic Perspectives*. vol. 2, no. 2, pp. 15-20.

Peters, G. (1980), 'Some thoughts on capital taxation', *Journal of Agricultural Economics*, vol. 31, no. 3, pp. 381-97.

Potter, C. and Gasson, R. (1988), 'Farm participation in voluntary land diversion schemes', *Journal of Rural Studies*, vol. 4, no. 4. pp. 365-75.

Potter, C. (1990), 'Conservation under a European Farm Survival Policy', *Journal of Rural Studies*, vol. 6, no. 1. pp. 1-7.

Revell, B. (1985), *EC Structures Policy and UK Agriculture*, Centre for Agricultural Strategy Study 2, Centre for Agricultural Strategy, Reading.

Rogers, S. and Salamon, S. (1983), 'Inheritance and social organisation among family farmers', *American Ethnologist*, vol. 10 pp. 529-50.

Sinclair, G. (1983), *The Uplands Landscape Study*, Environmental Information Services, Dyfed.

Statham, D. (1986), 'Upland land uses', *The Planner*, February 1986, pp. 19-21.

Symes, D.(1973), 'Stability and change among farming communities in South West Ireland'. *Acta Ethnographica Academiae Scientiarum Hungaricae*, vol. 11, pp. 89-105.

Symes, D (1990), 'Bridging the generations: Succession and inheritance in a changing world', *Sociologia Ruralis*, vol. 30, 280-91.

Tauer, L. (1984), 'Productivity of farmers at various ages', *Central Journal of Agricultural Economics*, vol. 6, no. 1, pp.81-7.

Warnock, S. and Bell, M. (1987), 'Likely farmer response in the hill and uplands: results of a survey based on the ITE sample framework', in Jenkins, N. and Bell, M. *Farm Extensification: Implications of EC Regulation 1760/87*, Merlewood Research Paper 112, Institute of Terrestrial Ecology (ITE), Merlewood.

Way, J.M. (1989), 'Reconstruction of habitats on farmland', in Buckley G.P. (ed.) *Biological Habitat Reconstruction*, Belhaven Press, London, pp. 102-114.

Weinschenck, G. and Kemper, J. (1981), 'Agricultural policies and their regional impact in Western Europe', *European Review of Agricultural Economics*, vol. 8, pp. 251-81.

5 'All winds and weathers': Uncertainty, debt and the subsumption of the family farm

STEVE PILE

Introduction

In this chapter, I will take a close look at farmers' experience of the restructuring of their economic relations. This experience suggests that our theories of the subsumption of the family farm do not take account of the ways in which farmers create, respond and reproduce the family farm. Our understanding of the intersection of internal and external relations within the family farm is still underdeveloped. Perhaps the best examination of internal relations is Whatmore's (1991) analysis of domestic political economy; while the most developed account of external pressures is outlined by Goodman and Redclift (1985), who located the transformation of the family farm in an understanding of capitalist processes in general. Even so, Whatmore does not tell us how farmers actively re-produce their changing economic circumstances; while Goodman and Redclift do not allow a theoretical space where farmers are active in the restructuring of their economic relations, and so subsumption takes on an air of inevitability.

Farmers however are actively engaging and disengaging with various capitalist relations; they are continually thinking about what is going on, and they try to predict the future in order to decide which economic options to choose. Moreover, farmers have a strong desire to continue to farm; as Whatmore's (1991) analysis suggests, this is because farmers' aspirations lie at the intersection between farm-based (class) and family-centred (gender) relations. These are the issues which I will raise here, through the voices of Somerset dairy farmers; but first I will deal with the theory of subsumption.

The Subsumption of the Family Farm

I would like to begin with a coincidence.

[Reg rents a 400 acre mixed dairy and arable farm. Reg is in his late 60s.][1]

Reg   The numbers of employees on the land have gone down drastically in the last 40 years.

SP   Hhmm.

Reg   [Unclear] There used to be employed 12, 14 men on this place.

SP   Hhmm.

Reg   Two teams of three horses plus one other horse, what they used to call a half-way horse, used to do odd jobs, to do the more day-to-day jobs like taking milk to the [railway] station. But you couldn't possibly do that now. This has been going on, the change in agricultural practices has been going on now for 40 years. Its become less an' - less and less - well, the reason was the labour force left. It wasn't a question of the labour force being told to go. The labour force decided that - well, a lot of the labour force - decided it was gonna go to the town because it was - things were much more easy to do and you weren't left with having to work in all winds and weathers.

SP   Hhmm.

Reg   You took a job in the town, all the men in this parish went off working in the urban areas.

SP   So did your father sack people, did they retire?

Reg   No! No. They left. They just left "I've got a better job, more money, less hassle in the town". So, this was happening throughout the whole of agriculture and what agriculture did, it geared itself up to do its own job with less and less people.

SP   So was there a shortage of labour then?

Reg   There wasn't a shortage of labour the labour just decided that it was going to go elsewhere.

SP   Hhmm.

Reg   Course when the [Second World] War came a lot of them were taken away anyway. But even when they came back they didn't want to come back to the farms. Go to British Leyland, you see (...) But it was patently obvious that the labour wasn't going to be forthcoming and the type of labour you wanted was not forthcoming so you had to gear yourself to do the job with less and less people. Hence the technology advances within the agricultural profession over the last 40 years far outstrips the advances in any other industry. Its had to.

Marx's description of the continual progress of capitalist transformation in modern industry echoes Reg's description of the situation in agriculture over the last 40 years.

> "By means of machinery, chemical processes and other methods, [modern industry] is continually transforming not only the technical basis of production but also the functions of the worker and the social combinations of the labour process. At the same time, it thereby also revolutionizes the division of labour within society, and incessantly throws masses of capital and of workers from one branch of production to another" (Marx, 1867, p. 617).

This coincidence worries me; it raises a series of questions about the supposed insightfulness of theory. Perhaps our theoretical discussions of the modernization of the family farm are no more than farmers already know. Recent debate on the restructuring of the family farm has been framed in terms of Marx's analysis of the emergence of capitalist enterprises, and relies on an analytical division between "formal" and "real" subsumption of labour (Marx, 1867, pp. 1019-1038). In the *formal* subsumption of the labour process the worker is still able to undertake the labour process as an independent producer and surplus value is extracted as absolute surplus value. The transition to a specifically capitalist labour process occurs when capital transforms the *real* nature of the labour process as a whole and extracts surplus value as relative surplus value. This transition involves the *real* subsumption of labour because the new labour process is beyond the capacity of workers operating as self-employed producers. For Marx, capitalist production can be based on both *formal* and/or *real* subsumption. It is argued that subsumption of the family labour farm is usually *formal*, because the direct producer in agriculture usually retains control of the labour process and the technical basis of production (Goodman and Redclift, 1985, p. 240).

In agriculture, wage labour relations and the persistence of family farm businesses do not represent the *real* subsumption of agriculture. Instead, *real* subsumption is represented by the tendency of capital towards the elimination of the labour process as a land-based activity (Goodman and Redclift, 1985, p. 241). Meanwhile, the family farm has been subsumed by capital largely through the *formal* expropriation of surplus value from the labour process, without directly transforming the *real* labour process (Marsden et al., 1986, p. 512). Industrial and finance capitals have progressively appropriated activities related to production and processing, and these activities have undergone subsumption, thus removing barriers to accumulation and expanded reproduction. Thus, many family producers have retained considerable control over their businesses as well as establishing close links with industrial and finance capitals (Marsden, 1984).

Family producers have been able to retain *formal* control of the labour process, both through technological innovations and through the reduction of the labour inputs. Even so, they have become increasingly dependent upon external technical and economic factors, which are beyond their control (Marsden et al., 1986, p. 512). Financial and industrial capitals continually attempt to penetrate all productive activities and to exploit technological innovations, in order to extract surplus value from the labour process. However, the land-based nature of agriculture obstructs the full valorization of agricultural production and its associated labour process. Once again, family farmers have been able to retain considerable control over the labour process.

Against this, the State has facilitated the subsumption of the agricultural labour process; it has attempted to guarantee minimum returns, creating financial confidence in the industry, and this has stimulated investment by industrial and financial capitals. State actions have encouraged capital investment and accumulation in agriculture despite the obstacles presented by land being an 'awkward' means of production and a monopolised use value under exclusive property rights (Whatmore, 1986; and, Marsden, 1986). It is argued that the increase in owner-occupation, indebtedness and institutional land ownership within agriculture, together with the general inflation of land prices, are all facets of the increasingly complex operation of capitalist relations (Stinchcombe, 1961, p. 16). These are especially important for agriculture, as they affect the uneven spatial pattern of accumulation and the *formal* subsumption of the labour process (Marsden et al., 1987).

The analytical priority of all this approach is to describe the nature of capitalist relations and the internal and external relations of farm businesses. Since Marx's dictum 'people make history, but not in circumstances of their own choosing' has been ignored (see Mooney, 1987, p. 290), marxist political economy has failed to account for the reproduction of structures through people's actions; failing to understand both what the reproduction of the family farm means to farmers and why they adopt the accumulation strategies they adopt. Even where farmers' beliefs and motivations are considered (e.g. Newby et al., 1978; Buttel, 1983; Goodman and Redclift, 1985; and, Friedmann, 1986), these are treated as a feature of the ideological superstructure rather than as a means to understand the way in which farmers farm. By treating people as the bearers of the logic of capital, they fail to appreciate that it is *people* who do things, not *capital*.

"People Worry Too Much . . . It'll all be the Same in 100 Years Time": farmers, farming and change

Exciting Times: uncertainty and complexity

Fundamental to the restructuring of family farms is the way farmers read their historical circumstances; that is, the way they understand and experience threats to the reproduction of the *family farm*. Farmers' accumulation strategies are fundamentally linked to the transformation of the family farm both in terms of 'the family' and 'the farm'. Therefore, the concept 'accumulation strategy' is concerned with the relationship between changing forms of production and the domestic structure through which the immediate material needs of the household are met (Redclift, 1986, p. 218; Whatmore, 1991). The problem for farmers, in deciding which accumulation strategy to adopt, is to understand the present situation. In complex and uncertain times, farmers confidence in their capacity to cope with crises depends on the predictability of the outcomes of the various decisions which they take.

Amongst the Somerset dairy farmers, there was a growing feeling that agriculture, economically and politically, is becoming more uncertain and complex; for example, Sam described the situation as being "all upside-down". Uncertainty undermines the faith that farmers have in their knowledge and skill and, therefore, their ability to cope with this situation. Crises appeared to farmers to be essentially economic; nevertheless, they threatened not only the reproduction of the family farm, but also farmers' independent yeoman self-image and their authority. In this sense, economic crises can lead to a crisis in what it means to be a farmer (see Habermas, 1976, pp. 46-48). That is, threats to the continuity of the farming family undermine the (potential) fulfilment of farmers' farm-based and family-centred aspirations; yet, these aspirations mean that farmers are unwilling to admit defeat, or that things will not be alright in the future.

```
SP      Does it worry you - the decline of the small family
        farm?
Reg     Umm, it's unfortunate, umm, but if I let things like
        that worry me I'd be in my grave, wouldn't I?
SP      [Laughs]
Reg     If you start worrying about everything that might
        happen or might not happen, umm, you'll never do your
        job. I think this is - I think this is one of the
        malaises of this country today that people worry too
        much about things. My philosophy is this: as far as
        I'm concerned it'll all be the same in a 100 years
        time.
SP      Hhmm.
Reg     It won't make any difference in that sense. And I
        think people's performances have been drastically set
        back by the fact that they worry too much (...) Not
        so much to worry about as to go out and do something
        about it. Scramble into a hole and worry, it's a sure
        sign that you're on the way out, I think.
```

Only where farmers feel confident in their predictions about the future can accumulation strategies be safely deployed, but these farmers saw a situation in which the state was no longer acting with "common sense". This lack of faith in the state manifested itself as a crisis of authority. The problem, then, was that there was no apparent lead: no-one seemed to be able to predict what was going to happen. Nevertheless, even without a lead, farmers could make themselves feel better about their decisions by being optimist about the future; the source of optimism was their understanding of the way history works. If history is seen to be cyclical, with good and bad times; then, when there are bad times, you need to work and wait for the good times to return.

[Sam is a dairy farmer in his early 50s, who rents a 150 acre farm.]

Sam	So I don't think they [computers] will come in, miself. The big farmer might, but they're cutting down, you see. Like Nichols and that now they've got their own milk tankers but it's costing them so much to get them out they'm getting Wincanton Transport to haul it now, you see.
SP	Oh really!
Sam	And Seldens. So you see we'm going back, it's gradually slowly going back, aren't we?
SP	Yeah, that's right, going back to...
Sam	Yeah! And I said it would! I said years ago, when all this, I said it'd go back, go back to stage one again.
SP	Because things seem to go in cycles...
Sam	Yeah, they do, I think we're gonna have three or four years and it'll be on the climb again.

Not all farmers believe this; particularly in the mid 1980s, the complexity of conditions under a regime of quotas enhanced farmers' uncertainty, sapping any optimism that the future would be better. While uncertainty threatened to undermine farmers' faith in themselves as farmers, this is not the whole story: uncertainty is also a reason to keep farming. The "challenge" difficulties represent, together with the incorporation of business-like attitudes, can enhance the satisfaction of being a farmer. More often, though, increasing uncertainty is understood negatively; that is, as increasing risk to the reproduction of the family farm. And European Community (EC) agricultural policy has made the market seem more risky; so farmers may make decisions designed to reduce risk by 'selectively disengaging' from uncertain market-based enterprises, until risk seems reduced.

[Sam talking about stopping doing calves.]

Sam	Well, you see, I might go out and ... now calves are very very expensive, dearest they've ever been. I could go out there now and buy a lot of calves and the price in the spring could...
SP	Yeah could drop.
Sam	You've lost a lot of money (...) This is why really I said "Well, we'll pack it in".
SP	Yes, very dodgy at the moment.
Sam	Yeah. This beef is in the gloom. With the beef at the moment - mountains and that. So I thought if we do all our own calves, we'm bound to make money out of it.

'Selective disengagement' is mirrored by 'selective engagement' with other less risky sectors of the economy, where possible. The running of the farm has to be continually adapted to changing circumstances for it to survive.

[Dave is in his late 20s, he now owns half of a 300 acre farm and rents the rest.]

Dave   We've diversified, yeah.
SP   Going back to sheep, corn...
Dave   Umm, I started to get diversified, or had plans to get diversified before there was this reversal in trend. I think the more noticeable diversification has come because people, for example, with dairy quotas said we've got to do something, we'll either keep on a few of the calves and fatten them and sell them as beef, or grow a little bit of corn (...) A lot of dairy farmers I think survived before - depending on their level of borrowing and that - some well, some surviving, some struggling but still surviving. They haven't had to go out and do anything extra. And so this nice bit of job or task or enterprise has been there but not used.

Uncertainty and complexity inform farmers' assessments of the risk of the farm going under, and they modify their farming behaviour as a result (see Gasson et al., 1988, p. 16). Assessments are made, not only in terms of the economy but *also* polity and the family; that is, farmers' accumulation strategies are set by the interaction between their aspirations and their external relations. For these farmers, the world is historical, so reactions to uncertainty are bound up with their reading of the process of subsumption; which sets the economic limits on the future reproduction of the family farm.

Exciting Times: the future of family farming

Farmers read the future in terms of what they believe has happened in the past. There is no simple reading or making of history. It is read in different ways and that reading is linked to the interrelationships between the economy, polity and the family. Thus, for Gerry, the phrase "dog and stick" not only refers to a traditional, disappeared world, but it is also a prediction of the direction of change; what is lost to the past becomes the inverse-image of what the future will be like.

[Gerry is in his early 60s, he owns a 250 acre farm.]

Gerry   We shall have to go back to the old days of dog and stick farming, you know, produce most of it off grass, and go dry in the winter, or something [Laughter] Kill the cows and salt them [Laughter] Oh! Dear. I'm in the wrong business I think, but still a lot of people think they're in the wrong business, come to that (...)
SP   It seems, generally, that things are becoming more and more aggressive, but you have to be.
Gerry   Yeah, that's right, to survive you can't go on being little family firms or...

SP	It's the same for dairy farmers as well, isn't it? (...)
Gerry	It will be a part of big business or increasingly big business.
SP	The dairy farmers will be different people, won't they?
Gerry	Oh yes, they will become more sort of managerial or managers or something, you know (...) I don't know, the whole world is in a state of flux - the economy...
SP	Yeah.
Gerry	There, I suppose it always was, but things move - these days - so fast, in business like everything else.

Uncertainty and complexity mean that one way farmers read the future is using evidence culled from other areas of life, since predictions based in their own direct experience are increasingly untrustworthy. At that time, farmers felt that farming was depressed, but their experience of history is longer term, stretching across generations. They had a long term view of future development based on a partial and interested reading of the trends; farmers saw the ups-and-downs of history. Since the thirties, farming has moved from unfavourable to favourable circumstances; they are now unfavourable again. And farmers were widely anticipating the cycle's upturn (see Sam's comments above).

In fact, it was common knowledge for farmers that other farmers were already selling up and getting out. However, farmers want there to be continuity in family farming. They were there to farm and they were *going* to grin and bear the tightened belts. But the future is not simply a question of home economics. Agriculture is becoming increasingly administered; and this made farmers uneasy, because they could not trust the EC. At that time, farmers felt they could make enough money out of milk production to fulfil their farm-based and family-centred aspirations, but they knew the future was not secure; either economically or politically.

These farmers were all concerned to secure their future, but their accumulation strategies were conditioned by their personal readings of the general circumstances which they all face. The effect was that while each farmer picked an individual route through the crisis, the routes paralleled those chosen by others, producing similar outcomes (see Pile, 1991). Accumulation strategies, in practice, are selective engagements and disengagements with capitalist relations. Farmer's (contingent) choice of strategy is based on the their partial and interested reading of history, and social relations; and this can be illustrated by Dave's and Sam's different attitudes towards debt.

Accumulation and Debt: the loss of control over money

Farmers are aware that the reproduction of the family farm is becoming "harder and harder" and they are beginning to wonder where this trend will take their farms.

[Sam talking about being unable to pay himself for all the hours he works]

Sam	You don't know where to go today. That's - honestly you just don't know what to do, really.
SP	You'd still like to farm, though?
Sam	Well, yeah, yeah. But there ain't the interest out there like there used to be, really.
SP	What, you're not...?
Sam	Because you're working, because we're just working harder. All the time - t'in't very much now, really. Working for - you can't get all your hours you'd put in now you'd be at a dead loss.

The amount of land required to provide a decent living for an individual family member has increased progressively over the years; this is partly financial, but it is also related to changing attitudes towards what is a decent living. Small-farm farmers felt an unremitting pressure to keep expanding; for them, it was demonstrably true that large-farm farmers had the economic edge, witnessed in their seeming ability to keep expanding. Many farmers have borrowed to expand, but expansion is both fuelled and undermined by indebtedness. Small-farm farmers have become embroiled in a cycle of increasing debts requiring expansion and/or increasing work and/or the greater use of technology. At the same time, increasing debt constrains the amount of expansion that can take place.

Debt is also one of the key means of the penetration of external capital leading to the extraction of surplus value and the *formal* subsumption of the labour process (Goodman and Redclift, 1985). Farmers are aware of this, but their continued control over the labour process disguises the extent, not only of the penetration of external capital but also of the limits set by wider economic forces; such as interest rates and inflation.

Most farmers do not have enough money to finance their investments, so the availability of credit is crucial at some point in their lives. Although paying off the debt is a constraint, the money it provides can be an enabler. At the least, farmers need to use a working overdraft because of the wide gaps in cashflow and circulation. This costs them money: first, in overdraft charges; second, in opportunity costs; and, third, in terms of undercapitalised money in times of surplus.

SP	Do you use a working overdraft to run your business?
Sam	It d'fluctuate up and down.
SP	Depending on...?
Sam	Depending on what we want, you see.
SP	Is the bank manager quite happy about that?
Sam	Yeah yeah.
SP	Have you ever ... didn't you use the AMC for a mortgage?
Sam	No, no. You can't, you can only do it with land, see. Cos that's fairly cheap money, innit? Really.
SP	You were on FHDS, weren't you?
Sam	Yeah, I done all that?
SP	Did you get a loan from the bank for that?

Sam	You can't, you can't, you've got to do it all out of your own pocket.
SP	So have you ever had a proper loan from the bank?
Sam	Only in the short term, really.
(...)	
SP	It's unusual not to take out big loans and get everything. Is it...?
Sam	Well, wouldn't want that wrapped round your bloomin' neck, can't do very much can you?
Adrian	You'm working all the time for the bank really.
Sam	Really, yeah.

While he has a working overdraft, Sam sees loans as a millstone around the "bloomin'" neck. The idea of working for the bank is an anathema. Sam's attitude makes him particularly resistant to restructuring in the form of debt relations. For others, like Dave, it has become an unavoidable fact of life. Many dairy farmers are caught in a financial trap set by decreasing assets against increasing liabilities (Reid, 1981; Poole, 1985). Dave's situation over the year illustrates this trap.

Dave	We haven't made perhaps the money in the last five years that we'd like to.
SP	Umm.
Dave	We've stayed static. We owe a great deal of money, purely because, Okay we own 91 acres of land, 25 years ago we owned no land, that's all been borrowed, and some of it at times when land was not cheap (...) If we were to sell up we would ... the land would basically pay off the debts. The cattle and machinery would be left for [Walter] to buy a home and retire. Basically, for the amount of money invested the return is not very great (...) So, you wonder if it is worth continuing with, same as we wonder about when you talk about starting up again somewhere else (...) There's endless possibilities. There always is. Umm, I like to think I'm gonna be here quite - for quite a few number of years, but you can't tell, farming can easily change things.

In June, Dave was fairly contented; although he realised that things were not all they could be, they were going along to his satisfaction. By January, a "bad" bank statement put paid to this feeling, and the announcement of a further cut in quota, without the reassurance of official information, compounded his pessimism. Dave and his father were once again talking about cutting their losses by selling up.

In fact, far from selling up, Dave decided to increase his indebtedness in order to purchase a neighbouring farm, belonging to Mr Steedman; taking on a debt of £100,000. In the course of our conversation, Dave refused to talk about why Mr Steedman had sold up. In many ways, Mr Steedman is typical of the first casualties of milk quotas; as a small-farm farmer, who is approaching retiring age. Dave, of course, would prefer not to consider who is next.

For Dave, one of the most important aspects of buying the new farm is the ownership of land; not because of an 'ideology' of ownership, but because he hoped it would ensure his succession to farming, assuming the farm survives. It meant that he could stay on: in the village (his pride of place); in farming (his farm-based ambition); as is his birthright (his family-centred desire). Taking on the farm was intended to secure his future; but the debt he had to take on endangered that future, the central problem was how to pay off the increased debt. For Dave, this meant diversification of the farm business (see above); he also had to give the bank manager a series of assurances about the future profitability of the enlarged farm.

While Dave was pleasing the bank manager with dubious assurances, Sam was trying not to break the (presumed) trust between himself and his bank manager by keeping out of financial difficulties. Different attitudes towards the banks (a part of their personal history) meant that Dave and Sam choose different accumulation strategies. Dave's bank is an institution to be exploited, much as he is himself. While Sam's bank is full of people that can be hurt and let down, much as he can himself. For Sam, debt is also a matter of pride and of traditional values; getting into debt almost took on an air of dishonesty, for him.

The way in which capitalist interests (such as the bank) are seen by farmers mediates the kind of capitalist penetration that takes place. While Dave's and Sam's interlocking with capitalist relations may both result in the *formal* subsumption of the labour process; a monolithic theory of subsumption cannot conceptualize the differences in the experience, context and consequences of farmers' actions; nor does it understand their different interpretations and responses to those relations. In short, the concept of subsumption remains descriptive because it cannot account for the multiply-layered reasons behind peoples' actions.

To sum up, while Dave is locked into greater and greater debt (to increase outputs), Sam is locked into higher and higher technological inputs (to decrease costs). Both are ensuring the survival of the family farm by tolerating a degree of *formal* subsumption of the family farm. The criteria for judging survival are central to the farmers response and these criteria are grounded in their farm-based and family-centred aspirations.

Conclusion

How the restructuring of the family farm takes place is the result of the intersection of the farm's structural location and wider capitalist forces, and the family's feelings and wider social aspirations. The intersection of countryside, family, polity and work brings with it a commitment to farming which farm families find it hard to desert. Farmers' partial resistance to, and corresponding acceptance of, capitalist relations is grounded in the duality of family feelings and job satisfaction. And this is why farmers' desire to continue farming is so strong. So, the accumulation strategies of the farmers and their farm-based and family-centred aspirations are fundamentally interwoven. Accumulation strategies involve a selective engagement and disengagement with capitalist relations; farmers have a partial reading of these relations, avoiding those which threaten, while embracing those relations which they feel will secure the family farm's survival.

While these farmers' farms are all partially resistant to *formal* subsumption, this does not mean that they are totally resistant and that traditional family farming will inevitably persist. Indeed, the partial success of accumulation strategies adopted by farmers, given their different structural (dis)advantages, means that farm businesses are becoming increasingly differentiated. The *real* subsumption of the labour process may be restricted by the availability of land, diminishing returns on investment in land, site specificity, and the immobility of capital in land and property relations (Whatmore et al., 1986; and, Marsden et al., 1986); but farmers are partially complicit in the restructuring of both farm and family relations, they have welcomed some of the possibilities that capitalism brings, while rejecting others.

Previous work has suggested that capital penetrates farming but it is prevented, permanently or temporarily, by obstacles (Mann and Dickinson, 1978). And, in the exploration of contemporary agricultural relations, a number of acronyms have been generated: PE, DPE, PCP, SCP and so on. Each (political economy, domestic political economy, petty commodity production, simple commodity production, and so on) explains specific relations, but each also defines a limit; they deal only with the processes they have already conceptualized. Instead, I have described the 'situated practices of everyday life'. This formulation acknowledges structure (situatedness) and agency (actions), but resolves this dichotomy at the level of people (everyday life). I have shown that the process of subsumption is disorganised by the intersection of each farmer's situation and their actions, and this is further disrupted by the way farmers' live, understand and (re)produce their everyday life.

In practice, all the farmers are embracing certain capitalist relations, which may endanger the survival of family farming. Increasingly, this threat is being brought into sharp relief by the modernization of agriculture. There is a tension between family and farm aspirations that is not just about decision-making on farms or the ownership of property, but about the mutation of its internal/external economic, political and social relations. Moreover, the *formal* subsumption of the family farm involves the transformation not only of farmers' economic relations, but also of the everyday lives of farm families. Each dimension sets limits on the extent of restructuring. At that time, at least, farmers were prepared to continue to work in all winds and weathers.

Acknowledgements

I would like to acknowledge the financial support of the Economic and Social Research Council and the Central Research Fund of the University of London. This research would not have been possible without the enthusiasm of the participating farmers, I owe them a very great deal. Many thanks are due to Richard Munton, Terry Marsden and Roger Lee.

Notes

[1] The evidence presented here is based on a case study of dairy farming in Somerset (for a full analysis, see Pile, 1990). The major part of the field work was a series of monthly interviews with six farmers conducted over one year. These sessions were informal and tape-recorded. The farmers' names and certain locations have been changed to protect their identity. The farmers' names are Dave, Toby, Reg, Ted, Harry, Sam and Gerry. Further details are given in the text.

References

Buttel, F. H. (1983), Beyond the Family Farm. In G. F. Summers (ed.) Technology and Social Change in Rural Areas: a Festschrift for Eugene A. Wilkening, Boulder, Co., Westview Press, pp. 87-107.

Friedmann, H. (1986), Family Enterprises in Agriculture: Structural Limits and Political Possibilities. In G. Cox, P. Lowe and M. Winter (eds.), Agriculture: People and Policies, London, Allen and Unwin, pp. 41-60.

Gasson, R. et al. (1988), The Farm as a Family Business, Journal of Agricultural Economics, 39, pp. 1-41.

Goodman, D. and Redclift, M. (1985), Capitalism, Petty Commodity Production and the Farm Enterprise, Sociologia Ruralis, 25(3/4), pp. 231-247.

Habermas, J. (1976), Legitimation Crisis, London, Heinemann.

Mann, S. A. and Dickinson, J. M. (1978), Obstacles to the Development of a Capitalist Agriculture, Journal of Peasant Studies, 5(4), pp. 466-481.

Marsden, T. (1984), Landownership and Farm Organisation in Capitalist Agriculture. In T. Bradley and P. Lowe (eds.), Locality and Rurality: economy and society in rural regions, Norwich, Geo Books, pp. 129-46.

Marsden, T. (1986), Property-State Relations in the 1980s: an examination of landlord-tenant legislation in British agriculture. In G. Cox, P. Lowe and M. Winter (eds.), Agriculture: People and Policies, London, Allen and Unwin, pp. 126-145.

Marsden, T., Munton, R. J. C., Whatmore, S. and Little, J. K. (1986), Towards a Political Economy of Capitalist Agriculture: a British perspective, International Journal of Urban and Regional Research, 10(4), pp. 498-521.

Marsden, T., Whatmore, S. and Munton, R. J. C. (1987), Uneven Development and the Restructuring Process in British Agriculture: a preliminary exploration, Journal of Rural Studies, 3(4), pp. 297-308.

Marx, K. (1867), Capital: Volume 1, 1976, Penguin, Harmondsworth.

Mooney, P. H. (1987), Desperately Seeking: one-dimensional Mann and Dickinson, Rural Sociology, 52(2), pp. 286-295.

Newby, H., Bell, C., Rose, D. and Saunders, P. (1978), Property, Paternalism and Power: Class and Control in Rural England, London, Hutchinson.

Pile, S. (1990), The Private Farmer: Transformation and Legitimation in Advanced Capitalist Agriculture, Aldershot, Dartmouth Press.

Pile, S. (1991), Securing the Future: 'survival strategies' amongst Somerset dairy farmers, Sociology, 25(2), pp. 255-274.

Poole, A. H. (1985), The Effect of Liabilities on the Farm Business, Farm Management Service Information Unit, Report 46, Thames Ditton, Milk Marketing Board.

Redclift, M. (1986), Survival Strategies in Rural Europe: continuity and change. An Introduction, Sociologia Ruralis, 26(3/4), pp. 218-227.

Reid, I. G. (1981), Farm Finance and Farm Indebtedness in the EEC, Journal of Agricultural Economics, 32, pp. 265-74.

Stinchcombe, A. (1961), Agricultural Enterprise and Rural Class Relations, American Journal of Sociology, 67(2), pp. 165-76.

Whatmore, S. (1986), Landownership Relations and the Development of Modern British Agriculture. In G. Cox, P. Lowe and M. Winter (eds.), Agriculture: People and Policies, London, Allen and Unwin, pp. 105-125.

Whatmore, S. (1991), Farming Women: Gender, Work and Family Enterprise, Basingstoke, Macmillan.

Whatmore, S., Munton, R. J. C., Marsden, T. and Little, J. K. (1986), Internal and External Relations in the Transformation of the Family Farm, Sociologia Ruralis, 26(3), pp. 396-398.

SECTION 2
CASE STUDIES

6 Patterns and implications of policy-induced agricultural adjustments in the European Community

DAVID J. BRIGGS AND ELAINE KERRELL

Introduction

The Common Agricultural Policy clearly represents one of the most far-reaching influences on the rural environment in the European Community. In its early decades, this policy was aimed explicitly at increasing agricultural production and maintaining agricultural incomes through processes of price support and intensification. Since the mid 1980s, however, these motives have changed. Faced with continued overproduction, rising costs of the CAP, and growing concerns about the environmental impacts of intensive agriculture, the Community has started to make attempts to control output and reverse the process of intensification. With this aim, various new policy instruments have been introduced, amongst them the Regulations on Extensification and Land Conversion (1094/88, 1273/88), and Set-Aside (1094/88, 1272/88). In addition, a Directive on nitrates has recently been adopted, aimed at reducing levels of fertiliser usage in so-called vulnerable zones (Anon, 1991). Recently, the need to restructure the CAP has also been given both force and urgency by, firstly, the revival (and subsequent abandonment) of the Uruguayan round of the GATT talks, and by the proposals for reductions in output put forward by Mr. McSharry, the Commissioner for Agriculture.

These changes to the CAP are likely to be prolonged and wideranging. It is therefore important that new policy developments are both appropriate and effective. The costs, otherwise, are likely to be considerable - not only in financial terms (e.g. the direct costs of policy formulation and implementation), but also to the rural communities and environments they affect. Given the sensitivity of some of these communities and environments, and the precarious foothold they retain in modern rural areas, many of these effects may also be irreversible. Traditional farming systems, cultural landscapes, rare ecosystems, whole societies may be damaged or lost.

The importance of careful evaluation of policy proposals before their adoption, and the monitoring and assessment of policy measures thereafter, is consequently paramount. As with other EC policies, however, the opportunity for evaluation and assessment is limited. In particular, problems arise due to:

- the scale of analysis;
- the limitations of data;
- the regional diversity of the European Community;
- the complexity and specificity of the land use; decisions involved; and
- the lack of clear criteria on which to base such an analysis.

This paper presents preliminary results from a broader study aimed at assessing the environmental and cultural implications of policy-induced agricultural adjustment in the European Community. Specifically, it examines early experience with the set-aside scheme as a basis for:

i. developing and testing policy appraisal methods;
ii. interpreting responses to the first year of the set-aside scheme; and
iii. drawing preliminary lessons for future policy development.

The set-aside scheme

Policy mechanisms

Regulation No. 1094/88 of the European Community, establishing the set-aside scheme, was adopted on April 25th 1988. Its primary objective was explicit: to help reduce the production of cereals in the EC, as a step towards restoring market equilibrium in the cereal sector, and thus reducing the cost of the CAP. At the same time, the Regulation recognised the importance of agriculture in maintaining the quality of the environment, and stressed that action was needed to diversify farming.

To this end, the Regulation provides a framework for set-aside of cereal land in the member states. Set-aside is permitted according to specific conditions, including:

  i. that the set-aside area is at least 20% of the arable area of the holding, and that each set-aside plot is at least 1.0 ha in area (0.5 ha in Greece);
  ii. that land set aside has been in cereal production for at least one marketing year prior to set aside;
  iii. that the land set aside is used only for (defined) environmentally acceptable uses;
  iv. that land set aside to fallow is maintained in good condition, is not irrigated or manured, is not treated with agricultural chemicals (except in defined circumstances) and that grazing and cutting are kept within specificied limits; and
  v. that the land is held in set-aside for at least five successive years (for set-aside to fallow the actual area set aside can be rotated provided that the same proportion of the farm remains in set-aside).

The Regulation gives guidelines for the level of aid to be paid for set-aside land (100-600 ECUs/ha), although member states are free to set lower levels of aid, or vary the aid regionally, according to national need. Member states may also apply for exemptions for regions on the basis of possible adverse effects on soil conditions, social conditions or employment. All member states, however, were obliged to introduce and implement acceptable schemes by the 1989 production season, and to report to the European Commission by June 1989.

In the event, there were a number of delays in introducing national schemes. The UK was the first to implement a scheme, in July 1988, but Italy and Luxembourg did not establish schemes until well into 1989, and Denmark had still not complied by the reporting deadline, as shown in Table 6.1. Portugal was exempt from introducing a scheme until December 1994. Exemptions from the scheme were also agreed for the Comunidades Autonomas of Castilla-La Mancha, Castilla-Leon, Aragon, Extremadura and Andalucia in Spain (for socio-economic reasons); for ca. 2% of the arable area in France (considered to have a high fire risk); and for the province of Trento in Italy (because of the risk of depopulation) (Commission of the European Communities 1989a). In addition, as Table 6.1 indicates, member states adopted highly variable levels of aid, both in absolute terms and in proportion to the regional or national farm net value added (FNVA). As will be seen, these circumstances have significantly influenced uptake of set aside during the first year.

Table 6.1
National set-aside schemes, 1989-90.

Member state	Date of establishment	Compensation rate ECU/ha	Aid/FNVA[1]
Belgium	18/10/88	170-420	0.58
Denmark	-	-	-
France	19/11/88	280-335	0.48-0.83
FRG	12/08/88	450-600	1.02-1.26
Greece	13/12/88	100-250	0.56-0.69
Ireland	09/12/88	220	0.80
Italy	06/02/89	380-550	1.15-1.16
Luxembourg	12/04/89	220	1.02
Netherlands	16/08/88	600	1.51
Portugal	-	-	-
Spain	12/12/88	100-300	1.01
UK	29/07/88	270-300	0.82

Notes: 1. Ratio of compensation rate to regional farm net value added.

Source of data: Commission of the European Communities (1989a)

Set-aside targets and performance criteria

In order to assess the effectiveness of any policy, it is clearly necessary to have explicit criteria or targets against which its performance may be judged. The set-aside Regulation does not specify quantitative criteria or explixit targets - for example, the area of land to be set-aside or the total saving in output to be achieved.

Broad, quantitative targets may nevertheless be imputed from these wider policy objectives. In 1988, when the set-aside scheme was adopted, cereal output was ca. 163 million tonnes/year, compared to a maximum guaranteed quantity of 160 million tonnes. In the case of wheat and barley, production was averaging 10-20% above an internal market demand of around 130-135 million tonnes. Moreover, annual production of cereals had been rising during the late 1980s by ca. 2-3 million tonnes/year, whilst internal market capacity had declined by 1.5 - 2.0 million tonnes/year. To control overproduction, therefore, a short-term reduction of at least 3 million tonnes was required. In order to maintain output thereafter at 160 million tonnes/year (a level which can itself be absorbed only under the protection of external import controls) will require that production of an additional 3.5 - 5.0 million tonnes (as implied by current trends in productivity and falling demand) is deferred each year.

Clearly set-aside is not the only means by which this saving can be made. Nevertheless, currently it is the only policy measure directed specifically towards this end, and as such must bear much of the burden of output control. As a realistic target, it may thus be suggested that the scheme will need to result in the withdrawal of 2-3 million tonnes of new cereal production annually, over the foreseeable future. To be effective, much of this saving will need to come from wheat and barley production.

Environmental protection

In the case of its environmental objectives, the set-aside Regulation is also not explicit. It merely states the general intent to help create rural wildlife habitats and to reduce pressures on the environment, by the conversion of set-aside land to less intensive, and environmentally more compatible, land uses. Nevertheless, broad criteria may be specified, against which to judge policy performance.

The provisions for environmental protection and improvement provided by the set-aside policy are clearly relatively weak. It requires merely that set-aside land be converted to a specified range of uses, and spared from certain management practices, for a minimum of five years. There is thus no permanence to the habitats created, nor, in most instances, will the alternative land uses necessarily provide habitats of significant ecological value. As such, the scheme is unlikely to make any great contribution to habitat protection in areas of existing ecological diversity and wildlife importance. Instead, its main environmental benefits are likely to occur in areas of intensive cereal production, where wildlife habitats are inherently scarce and where pressures on surviving species are high. Here, for example, many of the more common bird species are already in decline because of the loss of even low-grade habitats, and the changes in farming practice (e.g. conversion from spring- to winter-sown cereals) which have occurred in recent years (see for example Shrubb and O'Connor, 1986). Within these regions, set-aside may help to maintain a mosaic of habitats for these more common species, and establish at least temporary corridors along which species may disperse.

Policy constraints

In assessing the performance of the set-aside scheme, the need to reduce cereal production and improve environmental protection must clearly be paramount. The attainment of these objectives, however, cannot ignore other policy constraints. In particular, the scheme involves significant economic costs, most especially through the provision of compensation to farmers adopting set-aside. No budget is attached to the scheme, nor is there a limit on the total permissible expenditure, but as has been seen maximum levels of compensation are defined. More generally, the pressure to reduce the costs of the CAP mean that these costs must be kept as low as possible. This is likely to have significant implications for both policy implementation and evaluation. At the same time, an intrinsic aim of the CAP is to protect the incomes of farmers throughout the European Community, and to maintain agriculture as a part of the rural economy in marginal areas. Indeed, in pursuit of this objective, various policy measures, such as the establishment of Less Favoured Areas (268/75), have already been adopted. The same responsibility must also apply to the set-aside scheme.

The need to minimise social impacts has, again, significant implications for the way in which the policy is implemented and assessed. In general, it may be suggested that the areas most susceptible to policy-induced social impacts are the more marginal agricultural regions (e.g. the Less Favoured Areas), where incomes are low, profitability poor, environmental constraints on farming severe and the population ageing. Opportunities for incremental adjustments in land use practice are thus limited because the disincentives to farmers to remain in farming, instead of being offset by measures to sustain farming but, are now reinforced by attractiveincentives to remove land from production (such as set-aside). As a result, farming is entering a state of narrowly confined metastable equilibrium, in which relatively small changes in either the physical or the policy environment may result in fundamental disruptions to existing land use systems. The establishment of set-aside in these areas may therefore have far-reaching, and adverse, social effects.

Optimal uptake models

The policy targets and performance criteria outlined above provide a basis for defining optimal responses to set-aside. As has been noted, the scheme should ideally:

- generate a saving of ca. 3 million tonnes of cereal output per year;
- help create at least low-grade wildlife habitats in areas of existing low ecological value;
- avoid significant social impacts (especially in marginal agricultural regions); and
- involve the minimal possible implementation costs.

These requirements are broadly compatible. They all point to the need for set-aside to be concentrated in the core cereal-

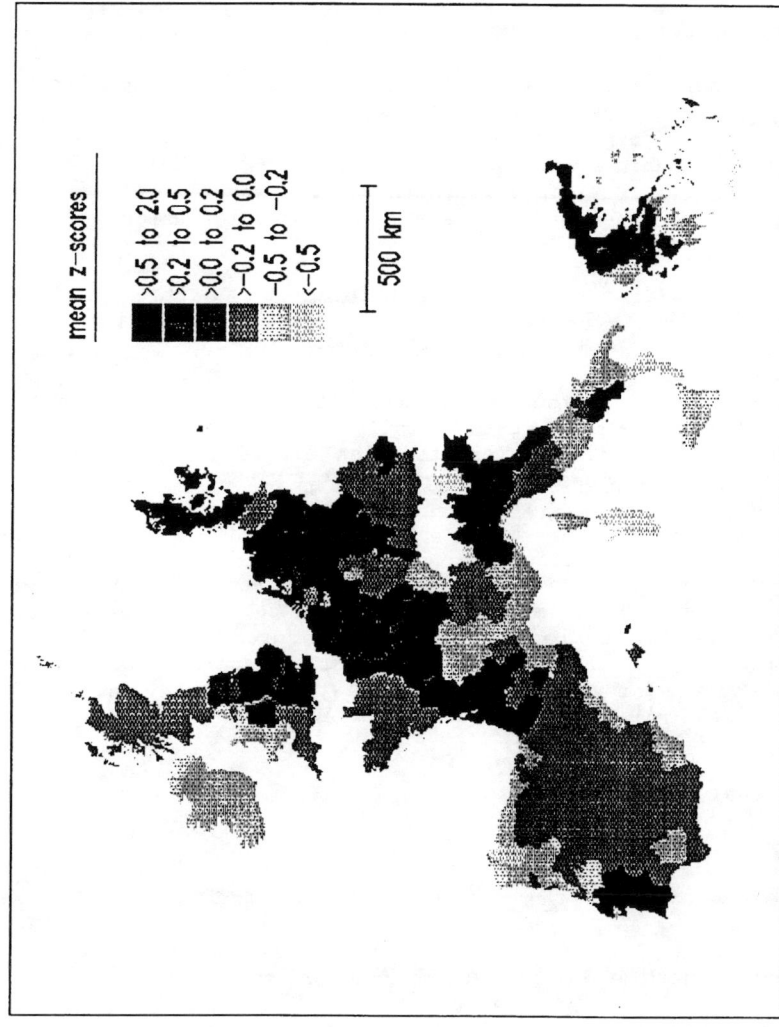

Figure 6.1. Suitability for set-aside in the European Community
Note: for explanation of mean z scores see text.

producing areas of the European Community, where yields and profit margins are high, farms relatively large, agricultural pressures on the environment strong and wildlife habitats scarce.

Figure 6.1 represents a regional classification of the European Community according to these criteria. Analysis was carried out using six regional indicators, as follows:

- percentage of agricultural land under cereals
- average cereal yield (t/ha);
- mean farm size (ha);
- standard gross margin for cereals (ECUs/ha);
- fertiliser application (ECUs/ha); and
- percentage of total area designated for nature protection.

Data on the first five of these indicators were obtained from Eurostat sources (Commission of the European Community 1989b and 1989c) and relate to the period 1985-87. Data on designated areas was obtained from the CORINE database (Whimbrel Consultants/Huddersfield Polytechnic 1989 and Briggs 1990). All data have been compiled for the standard NUTS (Nomenclature des Unites Territoriales Statistiques) level II and III regions used by Eurostat. Each indicator was standardised as a z-score, then overlayed and combined using the SPANS GIS system. Results are expressed as the average (i.e. unweighted) z-score for each region.

The results thus show the broad suitability of each region for set-aside on the basis of the criteria outlined above. The optimal area for uptake focuses on the core cereal-producing area of the EC, in northern and south western France, the north-German plain, southern and eastern England, northern Italy, northern Denmark and part of Greece.

Policy evaluation: 1988-89

Patterns of uptake

The extent to which the set-aside scheme has met its policy objectives can, as yet, be only provisionally assessed. Whilst the Regulation specifies that member states must supply information to the European Commission on the progress of the scheme by July 1st each year, at the time of writing (June 1991) regional data from the Commission are available only for 1988-89, and even for that year they are incomplete. No regional data is yet available for later years, except for the UK (where data have been obtained frim MAFF). Moreover, the available data relate only to initial applications; they do not include the (often substantial) cases which are subsequently

Table 6.2
Set-aside 1988-89: applications and actual area.

Member state	Applications[1]				Actual area set-aside[2]	
	Holdings		Area			
	No.	% total	Total (ha)	% cereal area	ha	% applied
FRG	25289	3.57	169729	3.6	165125	97.3
France	1002	0.10	15707	0.1	15707	100.0
Italy	9301	0.33	155606	3.1	91617	58.9
Netherlands	195	0.15	2621	1.3	2582	98.5
Belgium	32	0.01	329	<0.1	339	103.0
Luxembourg	-	-	-	-	6	-
UK	1750	0.66	54779	1.3	51991[3]	94.9
Ireland	77	0.04	1310	0.3	1141	87.1
Denmark	-	-	-	-	-	-
Greece	-	-	-	-	-	-
Spain	518	0.03	34229	0.4	34229	100.0
Portugal	-	-	-	-	-	-
EC	38164	0.44	434310	1.3	362737	83.5

Notes: 1. data from Commission of the European Communities (1989a)
2. data from Commission of the European Communities (pers. comm.)
3. data from MAFF (pers. comm.)

considered to be ineligible, and are thus not supported. National statistics are, however, available, for actual uptake for 1988-89, and for preliminary applications for 1990-91.

Table 6.2 summarises the extent of set-aside applications for 1988-89, while Table 6.3 shows the uses to which set-aside land was to be put. As can be seen, applications were made for 434,000 ha of land to be set aside, amounting to about 1.3% of the cereal area. Highest rates of uptake were seen in the Federal Republic of Germany, the UK and Italy (despite being one of the last countries to establish a national scheme). No applications had been reported for Luxembourg or Greece, whilst schemes were not in operation in either Portugal or Denmark. Most of the set aside applications were for conversion to either rotational or permanent fallow, less than 10% being assigned to grazing and only 2% to forestry.

As has been noted, however, these initial data for 1988, reflect the number of applicants who <u>desired</u> to take part in the scheme and not the actual number who did so. Subsequently, many applicants were found to be ineligible and were excluded. As can be seen from Table 6.2, considerable adjustment took place, particularly in Italy, where initial applications covering an area of 155,606 ha were reduced to a total area set aside of 91,617 ha. On the other hand, Luxembourg entered the scheme belatedly, setting aside 6 ha of land. Overall, therefore, ca. 363,000 ha were set-aside in 1988-89, ca. 84% of the original area for which applications were made.

The regional distribution of set-aside applications in 1988-89 is shown in more detail in Figures 6.2 and 6.3. Figure 6.2 indicates the percentage of agricultural land covered by applications for set aside in each NUTS level II or III region, for which data were available. Set-aside tends to be concentrated in western and southern Italy, throughout the Federal Republic of Germany, in northern Spain, southern and western England. When expressed as a percentage of holdings a broadly similar pattern is seen, as shown in Figure 6.3.

Table 6.3
Intended uses of set-aside land, 1988-89 (%)

	Rotat. fallow	Perm. fallow	Forestry	Extens. grazing	Non-agric.	Chick-peas
FRG	46.3	52.8	0.5	1.1	0.3	0.0
France	28.8	62.6	4.9	0.0	3.6	0.0
Italy	25.4	44.4	3.4	23.7	0.7	2.2
Netherlands	63.5	31.7	4.0	0.0	0.4	0.0
Belgium	18.1	42.5	10.1	7.4	21.6	0.0
Luxembourg	-	-	-	-	-	-
UK	11.0	79.6	1.4	0.0	0.7	0.0
Ireland	2.5	23.5	3.1	64.5	6.2	0.0
Denmark	-	-	-	-	-	-
Greece	-	-	-	-	-	-
Spain	29.0	41.3	4.1	5.1	0.9	19.8
Portugal	-	-	-	-	-	-
EC	32.4	52.0	2.1	9.4	1.6	2.3

Source of data: Commission of the European Communities (1989a)

Neither of these distributions follows closely the optimal pattern indicated by Figure 6.1. Instead, it is apparent that applications tended to concentrate in the more marginal cereal-growing areas, where yields are lower and cereals are a smaller component of the agricultural system. The implication is that set-aside has not generally been sufficiently attractive to more intensive growers, but has perhaps been seen as an economically viable alternative for cereals on more marginal land.

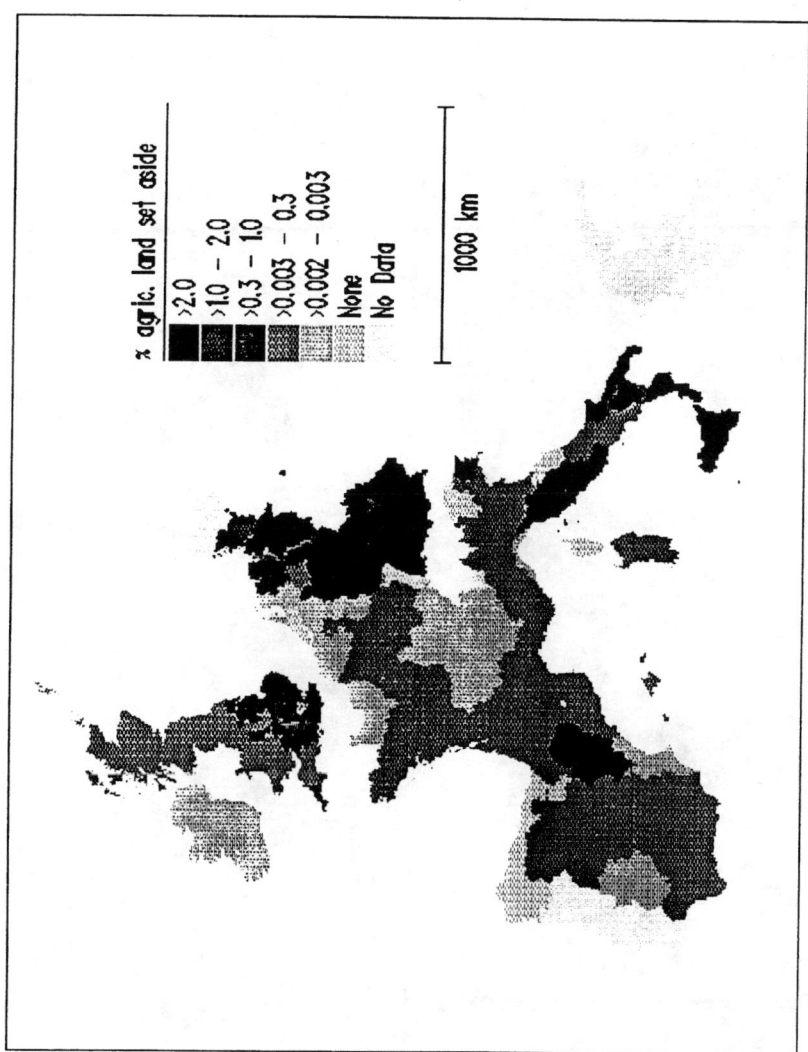

Figure 6.2 Distribution of set-aside, 1988-89: area of agricultural land set aside

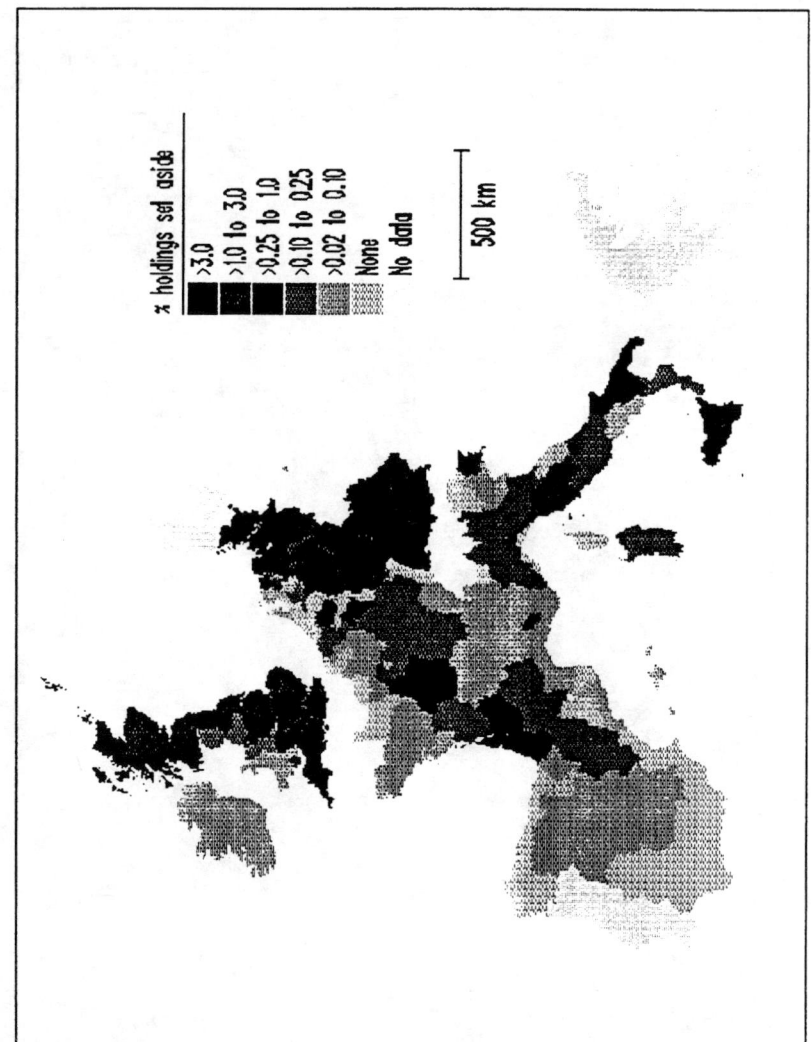

Figure 6.3 Distribution of set-aside, 1988-89: percentage of holdings taking up set-aside

In order to evaluate this interpretation, data on set-aside applications for 1988-89 were analysed using multiple regression techniques. Levels of uptake, expressed both as the percentage of agricultural land set aside in each region, and as the percentage of holdings applying for set-aside, were regressed against the following regional indicators, using SPSSPC+:

- cereal yield (t/ha);
- standard gross margin for cereals (ECU/ha; ECU/holding);
- mean farm size (ha);
- farms <20 ha (%);
- farms 20-50 ha (%);
- farms =>20 ha (%);
- farms >50 ha (%);
- farmers <35 yrs age (%);
- farmers 35-55 yrs age (%);
- farmers =>35 yrs age (%);
- farmers >55 yrs age (%);
- agricultural work units (no/ha; no/holding);
- fertiliser usage (ECU/100ha; ECU/holding);
- guidance funds (ECU/100 ha; ECU/holding);
- less favoured area (%);
- hill, mountain and less favoured area (%);
- population density (no/ha); and
- set-aside compensation rate (ECU/ha).

Data on the area of agricultural land set aside, the number of holdings set aside and the compensation rate paid were obtained from the first annual report on set-aside (Commission of the European Communities, 1989a). To derive regional estimates of the different compensation rates, a degree of interpretation was necessary, taking account of the various extraneous factors used by member states, such as less favoured area and mountain and hill-land status (UK, Spain, Greece, Belgium, Italy), topography (Italy), soil type (Belgium), standard gross margin (France) and irrigation (Greece, Spain). Data on the remaining variables were obtained from Eurostat sources (Commission of the European Communities, 1989b and 1989c).

The original data set obtained in this way contained a number of data gaps. As previously explained, the revised data for 1988-89 were only available at national level (except for the UK), and some countries had not taken up the scheme by the reporting date; no regional data on set-aside uptake were therefore available for Luxembourg, Portugal, Denmark, and Greece, so these were excluded from the analysis. Other gaps, for individual data points, were filled by computing predictive regression equations from the available data. In this way, a complete data set for 85 NUTS level II and III regions was constructed.

Initial analysis produced highly unstable correlations, due to the presence of six outliers in the data set. These six regions (Toscana, Hamburg, Sicilia, Hainaut, Brussels, Berlin) were all areas for which several missing data points had been computed on the basis of surrogate variables, or were small regions with little agricultural land. They were therefore removed from the data set and the analysis rerun. The results are shown in Table 6.4.

As these results show, the area of set-aside is seen to increase with an increasing area under cereals and higher compensation rates, but is negatively correlated with standard gross margin and cereal yield. Adoption of set-aside is greatest in areas with a high proportion of land under cereals and relatively young farmers, but lower yields and population densities. Compensation rates are also important, with both the rate of adoption and the area of set-aside increasing as levels of compensation rise.

Table 6.4
Set-aside response models, 1988-89

Model 1: Area of land set aside

Variable	Weight	Change in r^2	Significance
Area under cereals (%)	0.211	0.175	0.0000
Compensation rate (ECU/ha)	0.020	0.141	0.0000
Standard gross margin (ECU)	-0.018	0.175	0.0001
Cereal yield (t/ha)	-0.116	0.073	0.0006
Constant	-0.627		0.7310

Model 2: Holdings adopting set-aside

Variable	Weight	Change in r^2	Significance
Compensation rate (ECU/ha)	0.029	0.151	0.0000
Area under cereals (%)	0.306	0.152	0.0000
Age >55 yrs (%)	-0.499	0.071	0.0000
Population density (no/ha)	-1.262	0.065	0.0040
Cereal yield (t/ha)	-0.217	0.054	0.0056
Constant	8.356		0.0022

Without more detailed data, on individual holdings, it is difficult to interpret these results. The importance of compensation rates, however, is clear. Differences in the compensation rates offered in different member states (and from one region to another) undoubtedly affect responses to the scheme. Yet it also seems that set-aside is proving attractive not on the most intensively-farmed cereal land, but in more marginal areas, where yields are lower. Similar patterns of response were also found in England (Ilbery, 1990) and in Germany (Jones, 1991). In both cases, this response may be considered entirely logical and predictable, since, at any level of compensation, farmers will inevitably tend to withdraw only the less productive land. Nevertheless, it also demonstrates the power of compensation rates in determining policy response. Clearly, by manipulating the level of compensation, member states (or the European Commission, centrally) can control the rates and pattern of uptake.

Insofar as it is legitimate to translate these regional responses into farm-specific interpretations, the results also indicate the importance of local factors in determining uptake. Rates of adoption, for example, would seem to be greatest for younger farmers. This possibly reflects the greater willingness of younger farmers to adopt innovations, or their greater awareness of what is on offer. At the same time, remoteness also seems to favour set-aside, holdings in areas of low population density tending to be offered more readily.

Saving in cereal production

The amount of cereal production saved by set-aside in 1988-89 is not known. Estimates may, however, be made by making assumptions about potential yields on the land involved. If, for example, the average yield for the European Community (4.6 t/ha) is applied, a total saving of almost 2 million tonnes is implied. Had set-aside been concentrated in the highest-yielding land, a reduction in output of ca. 3 million tonnes, close to the imputed annual target, would have been achieved.

In practice, however, it is clear that the saving in production was considerably less than either of these estimates. As has been shown, set-aside applications were not concentrated in the areas of highest production. A more realistic estimate can be made, by assuming that the land set aside within each region had a yield equivalent to that of the regional average. In this case, set-aside may have led to a saving of ca. 1.8 million tonnes. Yet even this is likely to be an overestimate of the actual situation, for three reasons. Firstly, it seems clear that the areas selected for set aside within each region are often those which are more marginal for cereal production, and thus have lower yields. Secondly, it seems clear that considerable 'slippage' in uptake occurs, as farmers compensate for loss of output on set-aside land by intensifying production elsewhere. No accurate measures of slippage have been made, but estimates suggest that it may negate as much as 50% of the saving in output (Commission of the European Communities 1989a and Lambert 1990). Finally, as has been noted, total set-aside in 1988-89 was only 84% of the initial extent of applications due to the refusal of some applications.

Taking account of these factors, the actual level of saving in production in 1988-89 may thus have been as little as 0.75-0.9 million tonnes - less than 30% of the imputed target.

Due to lack of regional data, similar estimates cannot yet be made for 1989-90. Provisional data, showing applications for that year, are however shown in Table 6.5. As can be seen, Greece made applications in 1989, so that by that date the scheme was operating in all but two countries - Portugal (which was exempt until 1994) and Denmark. The total area of new applications, however, was only 434,000 ha, comparable to that in the previous year. The implication is thus that, again, savings in output will be well below the amount necessary to stabilise cereal production.

Table 6.5
Area of set-aside applications: 1989-90

Member state	Area set-aside (ha)
FRG	57259
France	39702
Italy	265192[1]
Netherlands	6155
Belgium	151
Luxembourg	31
UK	48818[2]
Ireland	1627
Denmark	-
Greece	250
Spain	12074
Portugal	-
EC	431259

Notes: 1. Provisional only, the final figure is expected to be ca. 160,000ha
2. UK data from MAFF (pers. comm); other data from Commission of the European Communities (pers. comm.)

Conclusions

As has been noted, the set-aside scheme is still in its infancy, and the regional data available for this analysis relate only to its first year. It would therefore be inappropriate to draw definitive conclusions from the results presented here. On the other hand, a number of indicative interpretations can be made. In particular, it is clear that the response to set-aside in its first year was relatively limited. The total saving in cereal production was probably no more than 0.9 million tonnes, insufficient to negate the anticipated increase in output due to technological development. The distribution of applications also indicates that the scheme is, as yet, not sufficiently targetted on the key cereal-growing areas. Instead, adoption tends to be most extensive in the 'secondary' cereal-growing areas, where yields are lower. As a result, relatively large areas will need to be set aside to meet the imputed target of 3 million tonnes of cereal production per year On current response patterns, ca. 1.4 million ha. of land would have to be set-aside, representing uptake by ca. 126,000 holdings. At the same time, it would appear that the costs of implementation are relatively high. The direct costs of compensation in 1988-89 probably amount to ca. 185 million ECUs; to achieve a target saving of 3 million tonnes of cereal output would, on this basis, cost ca. 610 million ECUs (ca. 5% of the annual cost of the CAP).

Because of this pattern of uptake, it is also likely that the environmental benefits presently being provided by set-aside are small. Little habitat generation is occurring as a result of the scheme in the areas of greatest ecological need (i.e. the intensive cereal-producing regions). The relatively low-grade habitats which are being created by conversion to fallow and extensive grazing in the main areas of uptake can probably add little to the ecology of the landscapes concerned. On the other hand, neither is set-aside proving popular in the most marginal agricultural regions, where the potential social effects are greatest. To date, therefore, the scheme poses no significant social threats.

For the future, the scheme clearly needs to be developed and improved. The scenario set out here provides an indication of the outcome which should perhaps be sought. The results of the analysis of uptake during the first year imply that this can perhaps best be achieved through greater discrimination in the levels of compensation offered. Clearly, higher levels of compensation are necessary in the core cereal-production regions of the EC (as defined in Figure 6.1). Yet, at the same time, other measures are also needed. Extended areas of exemption, or less favourable compensation rates, may be required to limit uptake elsewhere. Levels of slippage need to be reduced, perhaps by controls on overall levels of production on holdings claiming compensation for set-aside. If the scheme is to have serious environmental benefits, encouragement is necessary to take set-aside land permanently out of production. In addition, methods for monitoring and reporting on the scheme need to be greatly speeded up and improved. Together with policies such as extensification, set-aside can clearly provide a useful means of both agricultural and environmental control. To achieve its potential, however, the scheme must be kept under close and critical review.

References

Anon (1991) 'EC Ministers approve nitrate and exhaust cuts', Environment Business 19 June 1991 pp.1-2.

Briggs, D.J. (1990) 'Establishing an environmental information system for the European Community: the experience of the CORINE Programme', Information Services and Use 10, pp.63-75.

Commission of the European Communities (1989a) Report on the application of the Community scheme for the set-aside of arable land and proposal for a Council Regulation (EEC) amending Regulation (EEC) No 797/85 as regards the rates of reimbursement for the set-aside of arable land. COM(89) 353 Final. Brussels, 12 September 1989.

Commission of the European Communities (1989b) Regions statistical yearbook. Theme 1: General statistics, Series A, Eurostat, Luxembourg.

Commission of the European Communities 1989c Agricultural statistical yearbook Theme 5: Agriculture, forestry and fisheries, Series A, Eurostat, Luxembourg

Ilbery, B.W. (1990) 'Adoption of the arable set-aside scheme in England', Geography 75, pp.69-73.

Jones, A. (1991) 'The impact of the EC's set-aside programme. The response of farm businesses in Rendburg-Eckernfoerde, Germany', Land Use Policy 8, pp. 108-24.

Lambert, A.J. (1990) 'Scaling the surplus down to size', Geographical Magazine 62, pp.32-6.

Shrubb, M. and O'Connor, R.J (1986) Farming and Birds Cambridge, Cambridge University Press

Whimbrel Consultants Ltd/Huddersfield Polytechnic (1989) Corine Data Base Manual. Version 2.1. Whimbrel Consultants Ltd/ Huddersfield Polytechnic, Huddersfield.

7 The success of set-aside and similar schemes

IAN BROTHERTON

Introduction

As agricultural policy in Europe turns from a productive to a more protective phase, the number of schemes encouraging farmers into conservation oriented husbandry proliferates. This is evidenced in the UK in various ways, not least through the advice and grants offered by central government's agriculture departments. Thus, the essential purpose of the grant schemes that ran until 1988 was the encouragement of increased production. But with the closure of the Agriculture Improvement Scheme (AIS) and its replacement in early 1989 by the current Farm and Conservation Grant Scheme (FCGS), grant aid for agricultural operations seen as particularly damaging by conservation interests is no longer available; grant aid for agricultural operations in general is now offered at low rates, and is designed to encourage the maintenance of farmland in good heart without increasing production; while grant aid for pollution control and environmentally beneficial operations is available at a relatively high rate.

This change in emphasis is also indicated by the designation in 1986 and 1987 of eighteen Environmentally Sensitive Areas (ESAs). Within the ESAs, annual area payments are made to farmers who manage eligible land in defined, environmentally acceptable ways (MAFF, 1989a). Similarly, under the cereal set-aside scheme implemented in the summer of 1988, farmers also receive annual area payments if they agree to divert at least 20% of their eligible land into fallow or trees or other approved use (MAFF, 1988a). The planting of trees on agricultural land is being encouraged inter alia under a farm woodland grant scheme (FWGS) which came into effect on 1st October 1988 and this provides payments for participating farmers over periods ranging from 10 to 40 years (MAFF, 1988b).

The key features of these recent schemes, including eligibility are shown in Tables 7.1 and 7.3. Importantly, all the schemes are entirely voluntary. All too send signals to farmers quite

Table 7.1
Environmentally Sensitive Areas (ESAs)

Designations	First round 1986/87: second round 1987/88
Main purpose	Environmental
Eligibility	Farmers with eligible land in defined areas (Breckland, Broads, North Peak, Pennine Dales, Shropshire Borders, Somerset Levels, South Downs, Suffolk River Valleys, Test Valley, West Penwith; Cambrian Mountains, Lleyn Peninsula; Mourne and Slieve Croobe; Breadalbane, Loch Lomond, Stewartry, Machair Lands of West Uists and Benbecula, Whitlaw/Eildon).
	Areas selected because of national importance for conservation which depends on farming type but is threatened by changes in farm practice.
Requirements	Prescriptions specific to each ESA but require farmers to follow traditional methods of agriculture and to avoid intensive farming techniques, for 5 years, on all or part of their land in the ESA.
Payment	Depends on particular ESA, ranges from £10/ha/annum for maintenance of in-bye moorland in North Peak up to £300/ha/annum for reversion of arable to grass in Breckland
Source	MAFF (1989a)

Table 7.2
UK Set-Aside

Introduced	Summer 1988
Main purpose	Reduction of surplus arable crops
Eligibility	Arable land in UK in blocks of at least 1 ha
Requirements	20% or more of eligible area per holding to be entered for 5-year period and put to fallow, woodland or other approved non-agricultural use.
Payment	Depends on land quality and use (maximum £200/ha/annum for permanent fallowing of non-LFA land)
Source	MAFF (1988a)

Table 7.3
Farm Woodland Grant Scheme (FWGS)

Introduced	October 1988
Main purpose	Reduction of surpluses/environmental
Eligibility	All agricultural land in UK except unimproved grassland in lowlands, with a maximum of 40ha/holding and subject to overall limit of 36,000 ha over 3 years
Requirements	Acceptance by Forestry Commission (FC) for receipt of planting grant
Payment	FC payments towards establishment costs, depend on area and species composition (£240/ha for conifer plantings > 10 ha up to £1,375/ha for broadleaved plantings < 3 ha
	MAFF payments as compensation/income support: amount depends on land quality, duration on species composition (maximum for beech and oak on arable or improved grassland in lowlands is £190/ha/annum for 40 years)
Source	MAFF (1988b)

different from those they are accustomed to receiving. The recent schemes are designed to reduce surplus production, maintain farmland in good heart and secure environmental benefits, as well as provide income support. Yet throughout almost the whole of the post-war period and until the mid-1980s at least, the expansion of productivity and production have been goals of government policy. Given this history of contrary thinking, the encouragement of farmers into conservation oriented schemes might be expected to meet with not a little resistance, at least initially. But in practise entry has varied enormously.

This chapter reviews the initial entry into the ESA schemes, set-aside and the FWGS. It does so in terms of the entry sought since, in none of the schemes, is the intention to encourage the participation of all of the eligible holdings but a target number or area. It is shown that, in general terms, overall participation in ESAs has met the target entry set by the agriculture departments whereas participation in set-aside and FWGS has not. On the face of it, this is perhaps surprising. Thus, ESAs typically involve farmers in conservation oriented husbandry which is expected to be less appealing than fallowing, the option that most farmers take under set-aside and which involves an agricultural practice of long pedigree. An attempt is made therefore to explain why the agriculture departments have attracted farmers into ESA schemes, but not into set-aside and farm woodlands, in the numbers intended.

The participation sought and achieved

Environmentally Sensitive Areas

In some of the ESAs (for example in the Breckland and the South Downs), payments are available inter alia for reverting arable to grassland. The aim in these schemes is to secure the participation of a relatively small proportion of the eligible holdings. However most ESA schemes are designed, in landscape terms at least, to maintain the status quo and the entry of 75% of the eligible area is sought in these. There are difficulties in gauging the extent to which this target has been met. This is not because the area that has been entered is not known (it is, see House of Commons, 1989) but because not all ESA land is eligible for entry and the area that is eligible has not been accurately measured. However estimates have been made (see Brotherton, 1990), at least for the twelve ESAs in England and Wales. This suggests that the 75% target has been approximated, if not exceeded, in overall terms although participation (as a percentage of the eligible) shows marked variation from ESA to ESA, being particularly low in the Lleyn Peninsula and Test Valley and particularly high in

West Penwith and the North Peak (see also Brotherton, 1991).

Set-aside

The eligible area for UK set-aside is readily calculated (for example, from MAFF et al, 1988) while the number of holdings participating and the area entered is given in MAFF (1990a). This indicates some 2-3% of eligible land in the scheme after three years. The difficulty comes in relating this to the area sought since a target entry for set-aside has not been publicly declared. But the 3% achieved is a negligible almost token area in relation to the over-production both in the UK and European Community and is viewed within MAFF, in private if not in public, as disappointing. This is evidenced perhaps in the headings that MAFF gives its press notes which invariably, as may be expected, proclaim success. If the success is genuine, as in the case of the ESAs, the press note can say so, witness <u>Environmentally Sensitive Farming a Huge Success, says John MacGregor</u> (MAFF, 1989b). But MAFF cannot claim success in its absence. It can however imply success and this is typically done by playing the big numbers game. MAFF's portrayal of set-aside indicates this well. Thus, its press notes have not claimed that set-aside is a huge success nor indeed any kind of success. Rather they have resorted to implying success, with headings such as <u>26,000 Farmers Respond to Land 'Set-Aside' Scheme</u> (MAFF, 1988c). This is itself an inflation since the number responding, that is registering an interest, was well over ten times the number entering the scheme.

Farm Woodland Grant Scheme

As with set-aside, MAFF has not claimed the FWGS to be a success but has again played the big numbers game. Thus, <u>Ten Million Trees will Grow from Scheme, says Minister</u> (MAFF, 1989c). On this basis, the expectation is that the FWGS has failed to meet its target and this is in fact the case. MAFF's target was to secure the planting of 36,000 hectares in three years (MAFF, 1988b). In the first year, 7,000 hectares were entered to the scheme and in the second year 4,000 hectares (MAFF, 1989d and 1990b). The strong likelihood is that well under 40% of the target will have been met by the end of the three-year period.

Explaining participation

In general terms therefore, ESA schemes seem to have been successful in securing their target entries whereas set-aside and FWGS seem not to have been. This section seeks to explain why this should be by considering the factors likely to affect participation in a voluntary land diversion scheme of the ESA, set-aside and FWGS type.

The extent to which farmers participate in such a scheme is expected to depend upon factors that are conveniently placed under two main headings: economics and attitudes. Under the economic head, the first thing that MAFF has to do is to set the target number of holdings (or target area) that it seeks to attract into the scheme. There will then be a payment rate (£ per hectare per annum) that makes entry financially attractive at the target holdings. It seems highly likely that MAFF is able to gauge this payment rate with some accuracy. It does after all have considerable information on the profitability of different types of farming in different areas and it also took advice from academic agricultural economists and others in gauging appropriate payment rates. However the payment rate that makes entry financially attractive at the target holdings is not the rate that needs to be set if attitudes are other than neutral and strongly held. Thus, if farmer attitudes to the scheme are in general favourable, a lower payment rate (than the one that makes entry financially attractive at the target holdings) may be set since some at least of the farmers who are financially disadvantaged by joining may opt to enter. Similarly, a higher payment rate may be needed to counter a generally hostile attitude. The payment rate that makes entry financially attractive at the target holdings therefore needs to be modified to allow for farmer attitudes. However it seems highly likely that MAFF was unable to do this in significant degree. This is not at all surprising: all the schemes were new and there was little understanding of how farmers would view them. It seems likely therefore that MAFF set the payment rate for each scheme to make entry financially attractive at the target holdings, without allowance for farmer attitudes. Thus, in practice, if farmer attitudes to a scheme are generally favourable, target entry is expected to be exceeded; whereas if attitudes are generally unfavourable, target entry is expected not to be achieved.

Consider now the determinants of farmer attitudes. Attitudes may be determined essentially by the type of scheme: that is, farmers react to the idea and the generality of the scheme. In this event, they may view some schemes with favour and others with hostility. On the above arguments, target entry is expected to be exceeded if attitudes to the scheme are generally favourable but not to be met if attitudes are generally unfavourable.

However some schemes may not, by their nature, elicit a strong response from farmers. Attitudes to the scheme type are then neutral or only weakly held. In this situation, farmers' views are likely to develop in relation to the scheme details, that is the requirements and constraints that entry entails and, importantly, the payment rate offered. If MAFF has designed a high entry scheme, this package of details will need to make entry attractive to a majority of farmers. The farming press, the National Farmers' Union (NFU) and other opinion-formers are then likely to be supportive in discussing and presenting the scheme since it offers something for most farmers. As such, a favourable attitude is likely to develop. In contrast, if MAFF has designed a low entry scheme in which the package of details is attractive to only a minority of farmers, the opinion-formers are likely to see the scheme as marginal and unhelpful to most farmers so that an unfavourable attitude develops. Thus, if attitudes are determined by scheme detail, target entry is expected to be exceeded in schemes designed to secure a high entry since a favourable attitude is likely to develop; but not to be met in schemes designed to secure the participation of a minority of farmers.

These arguments and conclusions are summarised in Figure 7.1 which also places the real schemes. Thus, the AIS, the last of the long line of schemes designed to encourage increased productivity and production, helped farmers to do what most of them wanted to do: to farm more effectively. Farmers are expected to be favourably disposed to this type of scheme so that the AIS appears on the top line of Figure 7.1. In contrast, the FWGS discourages farming and encourages the planting of trees. On the assumption that most farmers want to be farmers and not foresters, farmer attitudes to schemes of this type are expected to be unfavourable so that FWGS appears on the second line of Figure 7.1. Set-aside and ESA schemes encourage farmers to continue farming but in a restrained way. Farmers are unlikely perhaps to strongly support, nor to strongly oppose, the idea of such schemes. Rather they wait and see what is on offer and what others are saying before forming a view so that attitudes are determined by scheme details. Most of the ESA schemes are, as noted above, high entry so that a favourable attitude is expected to develop (the third line of Figure 7.1). In contrast, set-aside is a low entry scheme. A generally unfavourable attitude is therefore expected to develop so that set-aside appears on the bottom line of Figure 7.1.

In summary, therefore, farmer attitudes to voluntary land diversion schemes may be determined primarily by scheme type or by scheme detail. Attitudes determined by scheme type may be generally favourable as in the case of the AIS or generally unfavourable as in the case of the FWGS. Attitudes determined by scheme detail are favourable in the case of high entry schemes, such as ESAs, but are unfavourable in the case of low entry schemes such as set-aside. On the assumption that MAFF

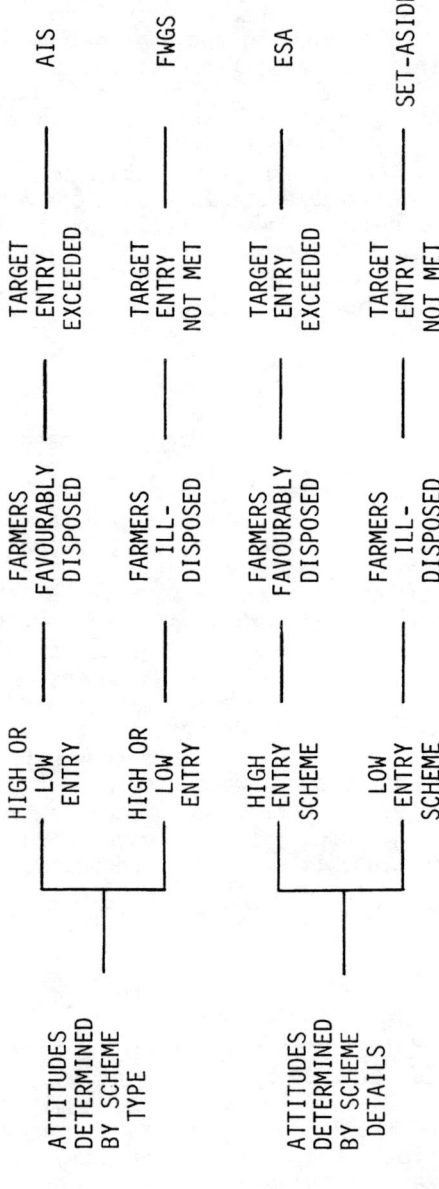

As drawn, the model assumes that farmer attitudes are not allowed for in setting payment rates so that the target entry is exceeded if attitudes are favourable but is not met if attitudes are unfavourable. If attitudes are allowed for in setting payment rates, the target entry is secured at a low cost if farmers are favourably disposed to the scheme (which is therefore cost-effective); and at a high cost if farmers are ill-disposed.

Figure 7.1 Participation model for voluntary land diversion schemes

was unable to allow for the effect of attitudes in setting payment rates, target entry is expected to be exceeded if attitudes are favourable (AIS and ESAs); but is not expected to be met if attitudes are unfavourable (set-aside and FWGS). These expectations are supported by the participation levels sought and achieved as reviewed above.

Exploring the model

Uses of the model

The model summarised in Figure 7.1 therefore offers an explanation as to why target participation has been achieved in ESA schemes but not in relation to set-aside and FWGS. It may also be used to predict the likely success of extensification schemes that may be introduced in the future. Thus, the recently announced schemes designed to reduce the output of beef and sheep encourage restrained farming so that attitudes are likely to develop in relation to the package of details (MAFF, 1990c). If the details make entry attractive to a majority of the eligible farmers, the scheme is likely to be viewed with favour and the target participation met. If, in contrast, the details make entry attractive to a minority of the eligible farmers, the scheme is likely to be seen as marginal and unhelpful to most farmers and target participation is unlikely to be met.

The model may also be used to suggest how to make schemes more successful in terms of participation. Thus, it has been argued that set-aside is currently unsuccessful because farmer attitudes develop in relation to scheme details which are unattractive to most farmers. Clearly, the target participation for a low entry set-aside scheme could be secured by offering a relatively high payment rate to counter the hostile attitudes. But that would produce an expensive scheme. In contrast, an attempt could be made to design a cost-effective low entry set-aside scheme by reinforcing farmer attitudes to the idea of set-aside. Thus, farmer attitudes to set-aside, which in the main involves fallowing land, probably tend to be favourable but not strongly held (see below) so that in practice attitudes develop, as has been argued, in response to scheme details. However, if MAFF were to mount a campaign proclaiming the merits of fallowing as good agricultural practice and lauding those who enter set-aside as responsible and progressive, stressing their contribution to surplus reduction and to improving the public's perception of farming, a more strongly held favourable attitude to the type of scheme might develop. In that event, set-aside would move from the bottom line to the top line in Figure 7.1 so that even a low entry scheme would be successful.

The difficulties in securing the target entry in a cost-effective way are even greater if farmers are ill-disposed to the scheme type, as was suggested to be the case for the FWGS. Then, hostility to the idea of the scheme must be broken down or substantially weakened. Attitudes are then determined by scheme details and a successful high entry scheme as might be usefully introduced under the Countryside Commission's Community Forest Programme is then readily developed. But to produce a successful low entry woodland scheme, as with the FWGS, not only requires the breaking down of a basically hostile attitude but its replacement with a favourable one. This is likely to be extremely difficult, if not impossible, to achieve. One approach however may be to include operations to which farmers are in general hostile in a package of operations that is viewed in overall terms with favour. In this way, less attractive operations may gain support by association. In short, farmers may be more encouraged to embark on an operation to which they are in general hostile if that operation is presented not as a free-standing scheme but as part and parcel of a scheme involving several or many operations most of which are viewed with favour. If this argument is correct, the FWGS might be more successful if incorporated with the FCGS which encourages a wide range of agricultural and conservation oriented practices.

Clearly the same argument applies to low entry schemes in general, including set-aside as discussed above and the various schemes operated by the conservation agencies, such as the recently introduced stewardship scheme (Countryside Commission, 1991). These schemes currently suffer since they are seen as attractive to relatively few farmers so that unfavourable attitudes develop. If however they were part of an overall package that offered something to most farmers, a more favourable attitude might develop in relation to the component parts. That land seems to have been induced more readily out of arable production through the ESA than the set-aside scheme may perhaps provide evidence in support of this effect. These explanations, predictions and suggestions for designing more cost-effective schemes do of course depend on the model's probity. Some attention to the model's underlying assumptions is therefore desirable.

Assumptions made in developing the model

Four assumptions were made in developing a model. First, it was assumed that MAFF is able to determine with reasonable accuracy the payment rate that makes entry financially attractive at the target holdings. Second, it was assumed that MAFF knows little about the favourability of farmer attitudes to ESAs, set-aside and farm woodlands so that attitudes were not allowed for in setting payment rates to the schemes. Third, farmers are assumed to react to the idea of some schemes and to the details of others so that farmer attitudes are determined by scheme type or by scheme detail. And fourth, it was assumed that attitudes determined by scheme detail develop in response to what others (the farming press, National Farmers' Union and other opinion-formers) are saying about the scheme. None of these assumptions seems unreasonable but all merit further exploration.

Is the allocation of schemes to the model correct?

Further assumptions were made in allocating the four schemes to the model as shown in Figure 7.1. The correctness of this allocation may be tested in a number of ways. One possibility would be to check in the farming press and other sources how farmers reacted to the announcement of the schemes. Thus, was there a strong early reaction; which aspects of the scheme were most discussed; and so on?

Another possibility is to check directly through interview and attitude surveys how farmers view each of the schemes. A preliminary indication is given by Potter and Gasson (1987) who surveyed 145 predominantly arable holdings in various parts of England and Wales to gauge inter alia the likely level and pattern of uptake under a range of voluntary land diversion schemes. To this end, the farmers were presented with three schemes being a one or two-year fallowing of cereal land (the cereal scheme); a five-year conversion of cereal land to permanent pasture with management and stocking restrictions to enhance conservation interest (the grassland scheme); and the planting of broadleaved woodland on land presently in a productive farming use (the woodland scheme). One aspect of the study explored farmers' willingness to entertain each of these three hypothetical schemes, the results of which are reproduced in Table 7.4 (after Potter and Gasson, 1987). Table 7.4 also records estimates of the strength of respondents' attitudes and the favourability of those attitudes to each of the three schemes. Thus respondents classed by Potter and Gasson as "willing" or as "opposed" hold stronger views than those classed as "neutral" or "reluctant". Arguably the views of those classed as "willing" or as "opposed", being strongly held, are determined essentially by scheme type while the views of those classed as "neutral" or "reluctant", being weakly held, are more likely to be determined by scheme details. As Table 7.4 shows, Potter and Gasson's data indicate that 23% of farmers had strong views about the cereal scheme; 35% about the grassland scheme; and 69% about the woodland scheme. Similarly, farmers favourably disposed to each of the three schemes may be indicated by the number who are willing (to participate in the scheme) plus the number who are neutral (since they showed no hostility and typically discussed practical details). Then, as Table 7.4 again shows, some 80% of farmers are favourably disposed to the cereal scheme but only 65% of the grassland

Table 7.4
Attitudes to cereal, grassland and woodland schemes

	Cereal	Grassland	Woodland
Number of respondents	123	118	116
% willing	17	15	15
% neutral	63	53	8
% reluctant	14	12	23
% opposed	6	20	54
% holding strong view about scheme type	23	35	69
% favourably disposed to scheme type	80	68	23

All data are taken from Potter and Gasson (1987) which includes full descriptions of their hypothetical cereal, grassland and woodland schemes (see also text). The categories describing the extent to which farmers are prepared to entertain these schemes are also fully described in Potter and Gasson (1987) as:
willing, keen, interested, prepared to consider joining;
neutral, no comment, discussed only practical details;
reluctant, would join only if obliged to do so; and
strongly opposed, scheme not acceptable, would not comply.

Those falling in Potter and Gasson's fifth category (not necessarily unwilling but not eligible or cannot suggest a figure) are not included in the above Table.

scheme and only 23% to the woodland scheme. Thus, Potter and Gasson's data suggest that: in the case of the cereal scheme (and to a lesser extent the grassland scheme) farmers are in general well disposed to the scheme type although attitudes are likely to be determined by scheme details; whereas attitudes to the woodland scheme are strongly held and are typically unfavourable. While there are differences, Potter and Gasson's cereal, grassland and woodland schemes provide good approximations for respectively UK set-aside, ESA schemes and the FWGS. Their survey therefore provides preliminary support for the allocation of schemes to the model as in Figure 7.1

Finally, the allocation of schemes to the model may be explored by considering the financial position of entrants and non-entrants. Thus, a scheme that is viewed unfavourably is likely to be characterised by the non-entry of some who would be financially advantaged by joining. In contrast, a scheme that is viewed favourably is likely to be characterised by the entry of some who are financially disadvantaged by joining. Schemes that are viewed favourably therefore encourage farmers to do things that are not financially sensible. This observation supports the conservationists' contention that the progression of grant schemes culminating with the AIS in the mid-1980s and to which, as argued earlier, farmers are likely to have been well disposed, encouraged the agricultural improvement of areas, some of substantial conservation interest, for little if any agricultural benefit.

Note

1. Being the Ministry of Agriculture, Fisheries and Food (MAFF) in England; the Welsh Office Agriculture Department (WOAD); the Department of Agriculture and Fisheries for Scotland (DAFS); and the Department of Agriculture for Northern Ireland (DANI). The schemes discussed in this chapter are administered by all four departments although reference is made, as a shorthand, primarily to the work of MAFF.

References

Brotherton, D.I. (1990), 'Initial participation in UK set-aside and ESA schemes', Planning Outlook, vol. 33, pp. 46-61.

Brotherton, D.I. (1991), 'What limits participation in ESAs?' Journal of Environmental Management, vol. 32, pp. 241-249.

Countryside Commission (1991), Countryside Stewardship, The Commission, Cheltenham.

House of Commons (1989), House of Commons Parliamentary Debates, Session 1988-89, Official Reports (Hansard), vol. 146, 7 February, cols. 589-590 and 605-606, HMSO, London.

MAFF (1987), Farm Extensification Scheme, Consultation Paper, MAFF, London.

MAFF (1988a), John MacGregor Launches Farm Set-Aside Scheme, News Release 225/88, MAFF, London.

MAFF (1988b), Farm Woodlands: 'Next Generation Scheme' Launched by John MacGregor, News Release 351/88, MAFF, London.

MAFF (1988c), 26,000 Farmers Respond to Land 'Set-Aside' Scheme, News Release 418/88, MAFF, London.

MAFF (1989a), Environmentally Sensitive Areas, HMSO, London.

MAFF (1989b), Environmentally Sensitive Farming a Huge Success, says John MacGregor, News Release 234/89, MAFF, London.

MAFF (1989c), Ten Million Trees will Grow from Scheme, says Minister, News Release 262/89, MAFF, London.

MAFF (1989d), Farmers Urged to Apply Early for Farm Woodland Scheme, News Release 343/89, MAFF, London.

MAFF (1990a), Set-Aside: Third Year Take-Up, News Release 397/90, MAFF, London.

MAFF (1990b), Repeat Applications Allowed under Farm Woodland Scheme, News Release 261/90, MAFF, London.

MAFF (1990c), Beef and Sheep Pilot Extensification Schemes, News Release 392/90, MAFF, London.

MAFF, DAFS, DANI and WOAD (1988), Agricultural Statistics United Kingdom 1986, HMSO, London.

Potter, C. and Gasson, R. (1987), Set-Aside and Land Diversion: the View from the Farm, Set-Aside Working Paper No. 6, Wye College, University of London, Ashford.

8 Soil characteristics of reverted farmland in upland mid-Wales

JOHN GERRARD

INTRODUCTION

The upland areas of Britain have witnessed many phases of reclamation and improvement. The latest of these occurred in the post-second world war period when a rise in the availability of production-based agro-subsidies was accompanied by an increased turnover of rough grazing to improved pasture (Parry, 1982). This process had dramatic effects in the uplands and, partly as a result of criticism expressed by the conservation lobby and concern at over-production, many subsidies were withdrawn.

Consequently, large areas of the British uplands are now reverting back to rough pasture. Studies in the United Kingdom (e.g. Porchester, 1977; Parry et al., 1982-5; and Parry and Sinclair, 1985) have gone some way towards establishing the areal extent of reclamation and reversion, but changes that take place in the soil after reclaimed land is allowed to revert, have been subject to fewer studies. Recent policy changes mean that reversion is likely to be more widespread than at present, and therefore it is important to know the detailed soil characteristics associated with land reversion, should the margins of agriculture change once again and land undergo secondary reclamation. Reclamation should have changed the soil but there is little information on the nature and persistence of such changes. It was to provide such information that this study in Mid-Wales was conducted.

BACKGROUND TO LAND USE CHANGE

The depression of the 1930's encouraged an agricultural change from arable to grass and the proportion of land under the plough reached a nadir (Stamp, 1962; and Parry, 1982). Some researchers, notably Stapledon (1936), realised the potential of some marginal land and proposed that better utilisation by converting this rough grazing to improved farmland would aid settlement in the depopulating rural areas. Experiments at Cahn Hill, near Aberystwyth, demonstrated that when hill grassland, which had never been sown, was ploughed, manured and reseeded, it resulted in an immense increase in its grazing value (Tansley, 1949). Thus, the outbreak of the Second World War led to over 1 million acres of old grassland going under the plough.

Upland farming has always been the poor relation in British agriculture, accounting for over one third of the agricultural area but producing only about 7% of its output. The plan for the further expansion of agriculture, announced in 'Food from our own Resources' (Command 6020, 1975), indicated that increased output from the uplands was integral to this desired expansion but would necessitate land improvement on a large scale (Green, 1976). Productivity may be increased in a number of ways. The existing sward can be improved by controlling and diversifying grazing, by fertilizing or by killing weeds with selective herbicides. Alternatively swards may be replaced with those of a higher production potential, by applying seeds of better grasses, together with fertilizers or by cultivation to break up the vegetation mat and redistribute minerals within the soil profile (Newbould, 1985). Any of these procedures will cause changes in the soil.

Once soil has undergone some degree of conversion and so long as the inputs are continued, the soil will tend to develop along a pathway towards the characteristics of improved farmland (as shown in Figure 8.1). Once inputs are discontinued, the soil will develop along a pathway towards its original moorland form. Whether the soil retains its original form or whether it reaches equilibrium at some higher capability status is one key issue that is addressed in this study. If the soil does not regain the characteristics of its original moorland form, but remains at a higher productive potential level, this will be important for future land use planning. If this land should once more be in demand for reclamation, it will be beneficial to distinguish between soils of these areas and soils of areas classed as possessing a lower agricultural potential.

EFFECT OF LAND USE CHANGES ON SOIL

Throughout history soil has been altered by cultivation, drainage, irrigation and the grazing of livestock. But, in spite of this, man as a soil modifier has yet to be incorporated fully into pedology (Yaalon and Yaron, 1966). It is usually

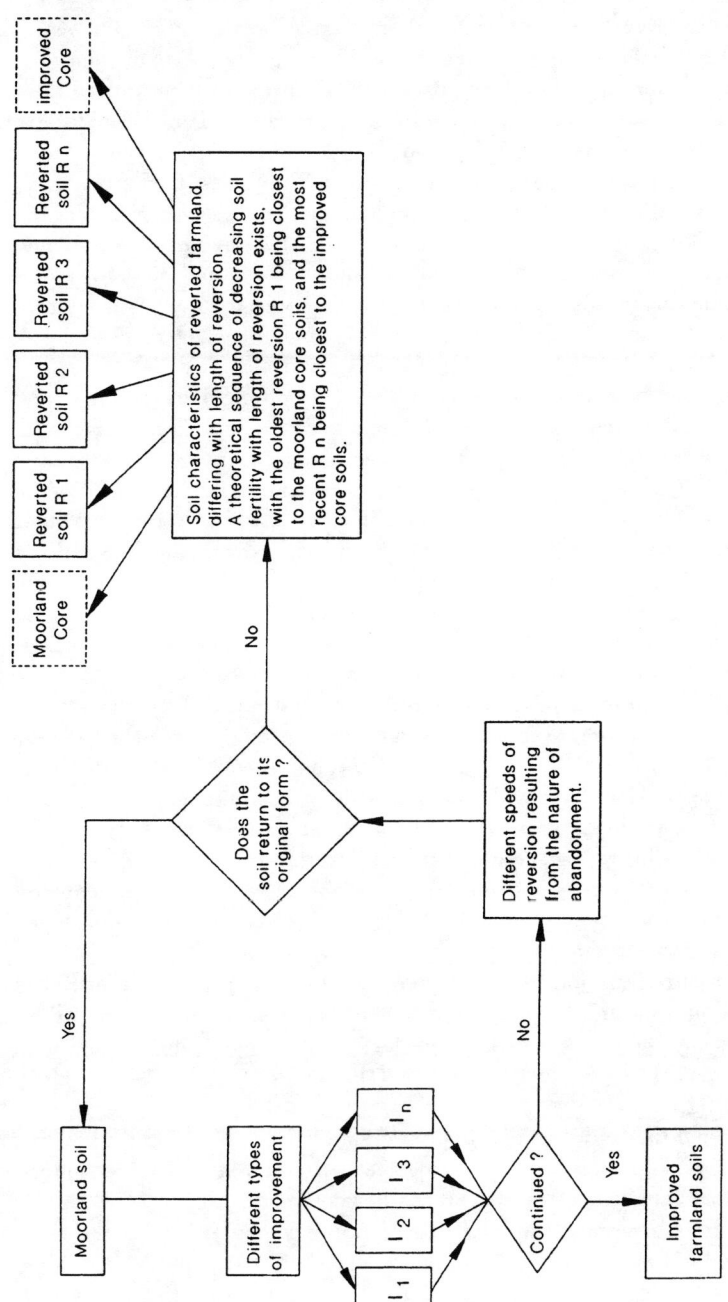

Figure 8.1 The theoretical pathways of upland soil development

man's destructive role that has been stressed (e.g. Albrecht, 1956) but man's actions are also beneficial. Aderikhin et al (1960) have stressed that when soils are correctly used for agricultural purposes there is an improvement in all their physical, chemical and agronomical properties. Conry (1970, 1972a, 1972b) has demonstrated this on many soils in Ireland.

There have been a number of studies directed towards the problem of increasing grassland productivity in upland areas (e.g. Davies, 1967; and Newbould, 1985) and towards an assessment of the wider environmental conditions of upland land use (e.g. Munro, 1973; MacEwen and Sinclair, 1983; and Countryside Commission, 1984). There have, however, with some exceptions, been fewer studies of the relationships between upland management and soil changes (e.g. Floate, 1977; Ball, 1978; and Riley and MacLeod, 1980.

Upland areas receive more water than they lose through evaporation and transpiration. If this excess water does not run off or percolate down through the soil it may encourage peat formation. However, in percolating soluble constituents are washed out and the soil becomes impoverished and acid. The vegetation becomes dominated by acid-tolerant species, whilst worms and other organisms find conditions difficult and disappear. Soils in this condition have little ability to support worthwhile grazing vegetation. The differing influence of climatic factors on soil type is presented in Figure 2. To achieve any real degree of success, farmers must adopt methods to ameliorate, or in more drastic cases, reverse the natural soil-forming processes in marginal areas.

Soil processes leading to peat and podzol formation need to be changed to produce brown earths. Improvement procedures have been documented by many workers (e.g. Newbould, 1974, 1985; Floate, 1977; and Davies, 1980). Often the most effective method is to provide the soil with an adequate supply of bases, especially lime. This encourages the growth of 'better' grasses, which decompose more rapidly, reducing acidity and allowing earthworms and other soil organisms to mineralise the litter, permit strong root development and create a deep soil with well-incorporated mull humus. This, in turn, creates a well-developed granular or crumb structure giving good conditions for moisture movement, aeration and root penetration. Lime is often used in conjunction with fertilizers for, if used alone, it can cause impoverishment (Thompson and Troeh, 1978). Studies stressing the fundamental need for this treatment in improvement programmes have been made by Reith and Robertson (1971, 1973) and by Bennett et al. (1968).

If the soil is not too acid it can be improved simply by oversowing the existing sward with seeds of low-fertility demanding species. But this is usually confined to Molinia dominated grass swards or heather-dominated shrub vegetation ie 'open' at the base as opposed to 'close' turf-forming communities. In the latter case it is usual to remove the existing plant material either by intensive grazing, cutting and burning or in extreme cases by deep ploughing. But heavy soils

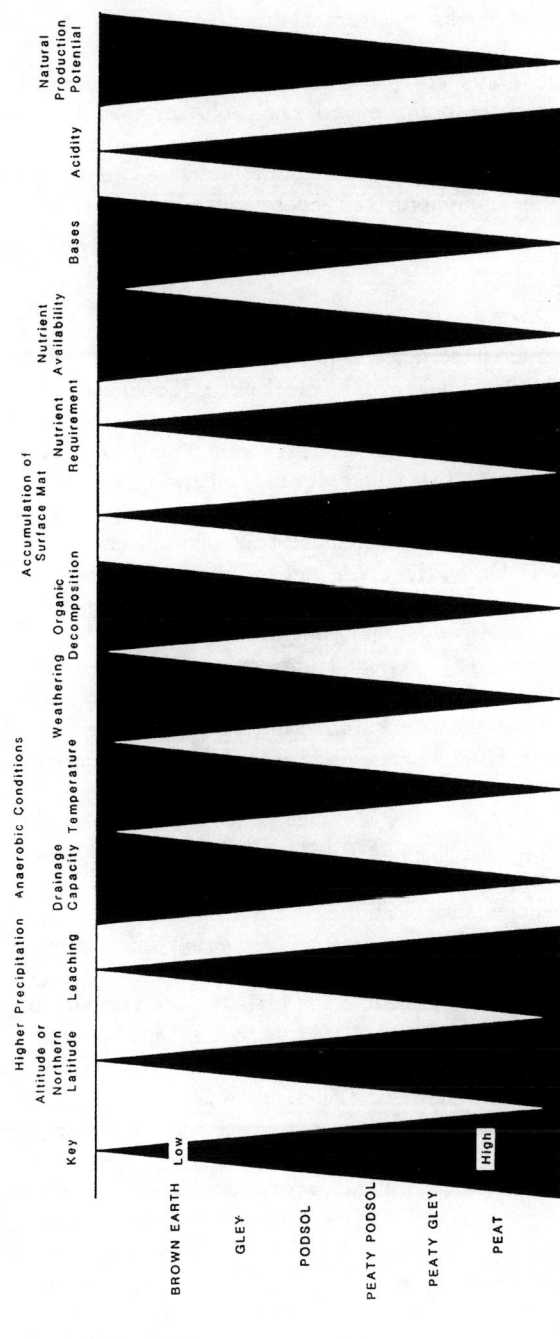

Figure 8.2 Soil type and climate-based factors

often possess a system of cracks which act as drainage channels and which may be sealed by ploughing, leading to increased waterlogging.

Drainage of hill soils is often costly and difficult. If drainage is carried out and land is allowed to revert the drains soon become blocked and the soil rapidly returns to a waterlogged condition. On most hills there is such a variation in land that it is more economic to select the naturally drained areas for treatment leaving the wetter areas unimproved. Such endeavours lead to a mosaic reclamation pattern.

REVERSION EFFECTS

Reversion will occur if the importance of good management and the maintenance of fertility after initial establishment is overlooked (Copeman, 1978). Soil changes in reverted arable land differ between moist and dry sites. On reverted moist sites there appears to be a slight increase in organic matter in upper soil layers. Organic carbon content also increases in comparatively old reverted land indicating humus enrichment. Deterioration of drainage channels can create reducing conditions leading to increased mobility of heavy metal ions and further acidification of the soil. On nutrient deficient soil on old reverted land there is often a slight decline in nutrient content. Large discharges of nutrients may also occur from reverted areas especially phosphorous and potash.

Soil changes under reverted grassland appear to be different to those on reverted arable sites although some moist reverted arable soils may be similar to grassland soils with respect to content of inorganic substances, the form of humus and pore volume. On reverted meadowland with uncontrolled drainage the pore volume appears to increase as a function of the age of reversion and the pores gradually fill with water, eliminating the meadow plants which were originally present. Few investigations have revealed any dependence between age of reversion and pH although the largest C/N ratios are found on the oldest areas (European Economic Community, 1980).

It is difficult to generalise because of the great variety of local conditions of slope, aspect, geology, altitude and climate of the reverted sites examined. However, without generalisation sensible soil classification becomes impossible and each location must be treated as an individual. Also, many of the investigations have been either very cursory or the soil information has been merely an adjunct to another study such as an analysis of vegetation succession. However, there have been a few studies in the United Kingdom that have specifically investigated soil changes on reverted land.

Allenby and Gerrard (1988), reporting on vegetation and soil differences across farmland and enduring moorland on Anglezarke Moor, Lancashire, found quite large contrasts between soils. Higher pH values, nitrogen content and electrical conductivity characterised soils on reclaimed land. Differences were less marked between soils on land that had reverted at different times. Acidity increased with length of reversion but electrical conductivity and nitrogen content showed no systematic change, even on land that had reverted over a hundred years previously. This indicates that some soil changes initiated by land improvement can persist for an appreciable period of time. Crompton (1953) noted that in areas of rough grazing on derelict farms in east Lancashire, the soil profile exhibited several inches of very acid surface mat with Nardus stricta, Deschampsia flexuosa and sedges, yet beneath the mat were remains of an old top-soil often over one foot deep.

A similar study has been conducted on Dartmoor on land most of which had reverted prior to 1800 (Gerrard, 1982). The effect of reclamation was to change humic brown podzols and ironpan stagnopodzols to the more cultivable brown podzolic soils. Drainage had been increased, any hardpans destroyed and organic matter more evenly distributed with depth. History of reversion shows that the once-improved soils gradually revert back to the ironpan stagnopodzols or humic podzols which dominate most of the uncultivated parts of Dartmoor. However, after 200 years, reversion processes have not been completed and soils still show the effects of improvement.

The most detailed study of soil changes resulting from reclamation and subsequent reversion has been that of Maltby (1979) on Exmoor. The immediate effects of reclamation was an inversion and mixing of the upper soil profile. There was also an increase in surface stoniness and bulk density values. One of the most significant immediate changes was the increase in microbial numbers (Maltby, 1975). Contemporary change towards the original moorland condition is suggested by a dense root mat and high organic carbon layers at the top of the profile. A further feature of reverted sites was the lack of intensive worm activity, resulting in a less effective circulation of translocated materials and a gradual build up in the fermentation layer and an unhindered remineralisation of iron in the top horizon.

Thus some consistent soil changes occur following reclamation and subsequent reversion. The majority of such studies have concentrated on land that was improved some time ago and has suffered quite longterm reversion. There is little information about land that has been reclaimed more recently and also reverted for short periods. Thus, the Mid-Wales study, now to be discussed, with its unequalled time series data on reclamation and reversion, provides a unique opportunity to establish the scale of soil changes. A fuller analysis of the results of this study can be found in Phillips (1989).

METHODOLOGY

The increasing concern for the uplands has resulted in a number of publications such as 'The Future of Upland Britain' (Tranter, 1978), 'New Life for the Hills'

(MacEwen and Sinclair, 1983) and 'The Upland Landscapes Study' (Sinclair, 1983). The Countryside Commission funded study into changing land use in the Cambrian Mountains (Parry and Sinclair, 1985) has provided the data base for the Mid-Wales study. Data on land use change was obtained for seven dates: 1948, 1964, 1970, 1978, 1980, 1983, 1986. The data have also been extended back in time by using the 1935 Land Utilization Survey, Ordnance Survey Sixth Edition one inch maps (1947) and the First Edition six-inch survey. This has produced a mosaic of land use histories, an example of which is shown in Figure 8.3. This mosaic formed the basis of the sampling scheme. Symbols for land use history refer to the periods of reclamation and reversion since 1948. The number 1 refers to improved land, 2 to reverted land or moorland core. Thus the land use history represented by 2211111 shows that the land was in an improved state in 1948 until 1983 when it was identified as reverted. The extent of reversion is shown in Table 8.1. Between 1948 and 1986, 8,831 ha of reversion occurred of which more than half was reclaimed again. Indeed 60% of all land that reverted between 1978 and 1980 had been reclaimed by 1983. More than 4,000 ha remain moorland today.

Table 8.1

Enduring and temporary reversion of improved farmland to rough pasture 1948-86, Cambrian Mountains

Period	Enduring reversion		Temporary reversion		Total reversion
	ha	% total	ha	% total	ha
1948-64	459	40.1	686	59.9	1,145
1964-70	1,054	37.8	1,733	62.2	2,787
1970-78(1)	1,256	45.4	1,513	54.6	2,769
1978-80(2)	312	35.0	579	65.0	891
1980-83	1,039	88.5	135	11.5	1,174
1983-86	65	100.0	0	0.0	65
Total	**4,185**	**47.4**	**4,646**	**52.6**	**8,831**

Notes: 1. Includes some reversion between 1970-80
2. Includes some reversion between 1978-83

Source: (Parry, 1987)

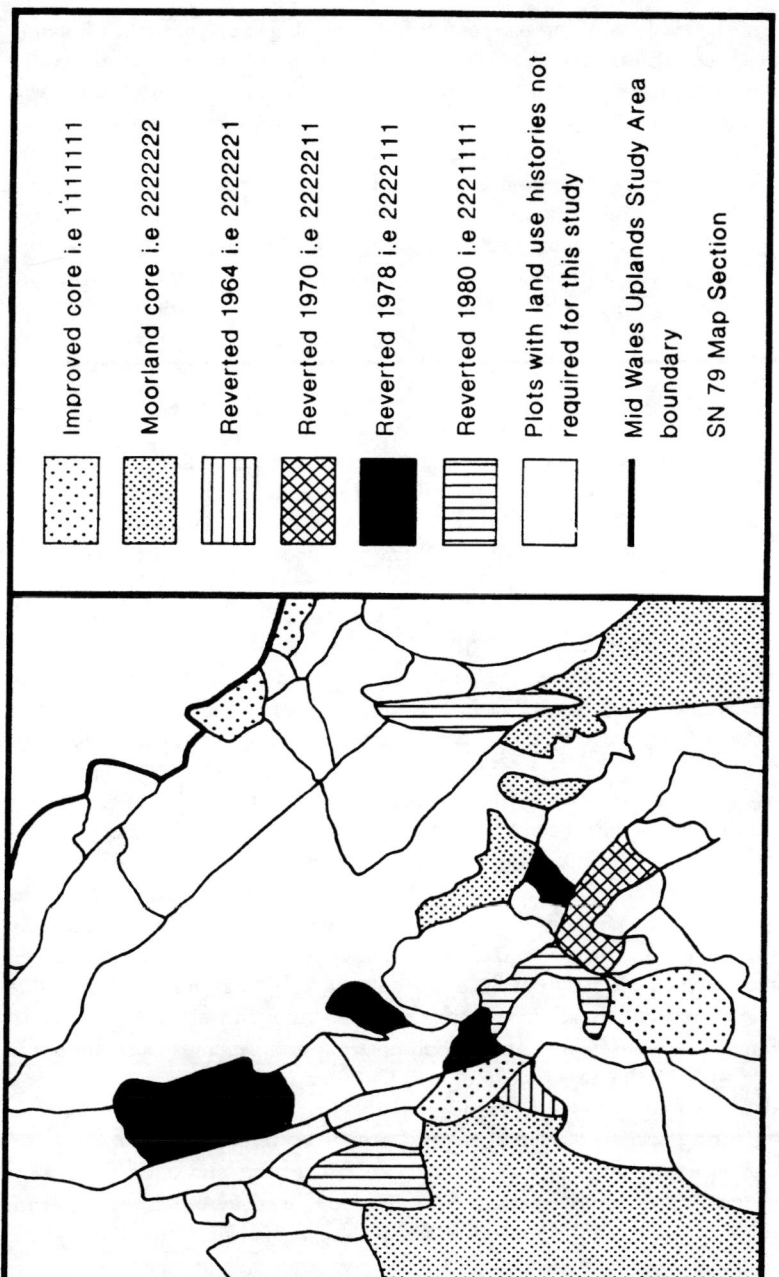

Figure 8.3 A characteristic mosaic of land-use histories

The use of side-by-side or transect studies has been extensive in soil and vegetation research in order to achieve a representative sample and yet involve the smallest possible environmental variation. The overall aim of this study was to isolate reversion as the main soil-forming factor. Sites were sampled, where possible, along transects with differing land use histories composed of different periods of reversion as well as moorland and improved areas to act as controls (Fig. 8.4). This enables changes in soil characteristics caused by different lengths of reversion to be compared with control sites in areas possessing similar soil types initially. The results presented here are from 8 sites at Llanwrthwl, south of Rhayader, and at 17 sites at Glaspwll, near Machynlleth. Soil was sampled, at 10 cm intervals, from the faces of soil pits at the various sites.

RESULTS

It was apparent from the soil profiles that there were major differences between moorland core and improved sites, even if these sites had been improved for only a short time. Soils of the moorland core were ferric stagnopodzols typical of the Hafren series, possessing thick, up to 10 cm, Om or Ah horizons of dark brown stoneless semi-fibrous peat overlying a greyish brown, mottled Eg horizon of variable thickness (Rudeforth et al., 1984). These horizons are followed by a strong brown slightly stony sandy silt or clay loam. All soil of sites that had been reclaimed for at least one period possessed characteristics of either typical brown earths of the Denbigh series or typical brown podzolic soils of the Manod series. Such soils possessed neither a true organic horizon nor eluviated horizons.

Analysis based simply on profile characteristics can be misleading. Thus a number of properties have been examined. In order to simplify the interpretation sites have been grouped into categories that summarise the length of time, prior to 1986, that they have been reclaimed or allowed to revert. Thus sites in the list of four reclaimed periods were identified as reclaimed in 1986, 1983, 1980, and 1978. Sites listed as reverted for three periods were known to have reverted some time between 1978 and 1980. The data have been summarised in Table 8.2. Some consistent trends can be discerned in line with earlier discussions. Organic matter decreases in the upper soil horizons and becomes more uniformly distributed with depth on reclamation, with the trend reversing on reversion. Soil pH follows the well established trend of increasing with reclamation and then declining during periods of reversion. Soil properties related to pH and organic content, such as organic carbon, exchangeable hydrogen and cation exchange capacity react in a similar way. The rise in base saturation values with reclamation is notable as is the quite sharp drop again when the sites revert. Nitrogen content appears to decline with reclamation and increase again only after lengthy reversion.

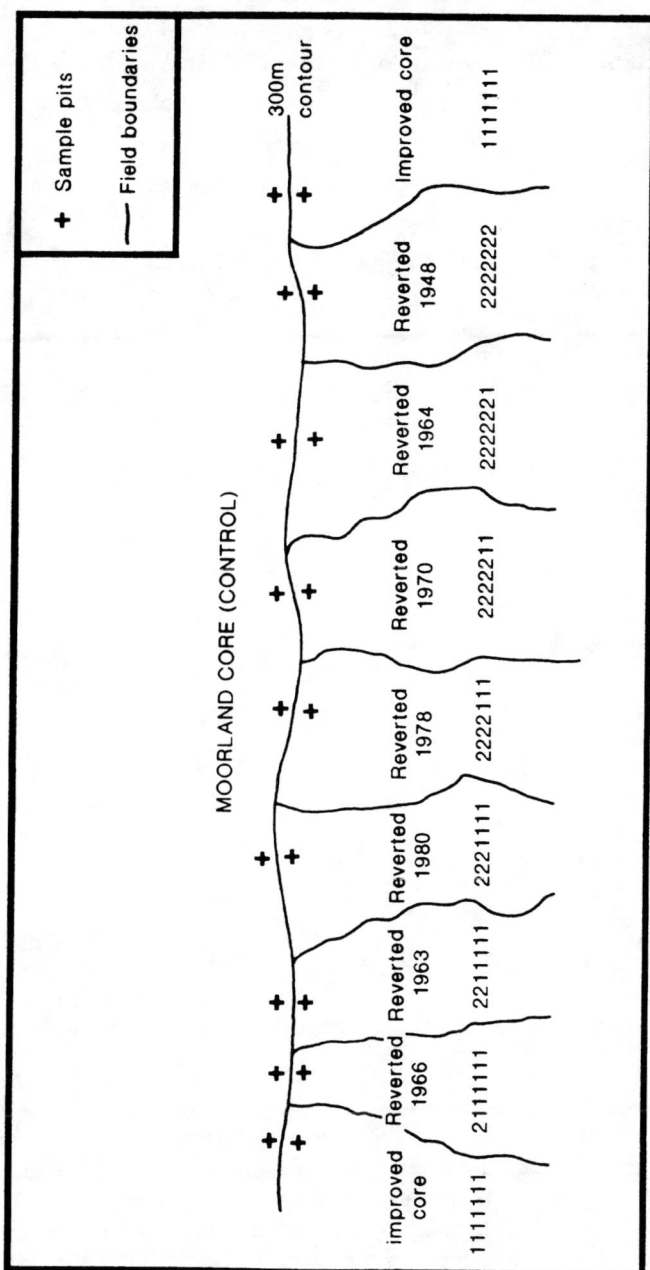

Figure 8.4   The optimum soil/land-use transect

Table 8.2

Arithmetic means, standard deviations and coefficient of variation for the moorland control sites at Glaspwll

	DEPTH cm	n	ARITHMETIC MEAN	STANDARD DEVIATION	COEFFICIENT OF VARIATION %
Loss on ignition	10	8	10.8	3.609	33.3
	20	7	10.2	1.627	15.9
	30	7	7.5	0.834	11.1
pH	10	8	4.5	0.207	4.5
	20	7	4.6	0.075	1.6
	30	7	4.7	0.139	2.9
% Carbon	10	8	4.5	1.647	36.2
	20	7	4.2	0.749	17.5
	30	7	3.0	0.374	12.3
% Nitrogen	10	8	0.4	0.077	16.9
	20	7	0.3	0.068	20.0
	30	7	0.2	0.051	21.5
Carbon/nitrogen ratio	10	8	9.9	3.130	31.6
	20	7	12.7	1.496	11.7
	30	7	3.1	1.683	12.7
Cation exchange capacity	10	8	37.5	7.910	21.0
	20	7	29.1	6.904	23.6
	30	7	23.9	8.379	35.0
Exchangeable hydrogen	10	8	9.4	2.015	21.4
	20	7	8.4	1.820	21.6
	30	7	6.7	1.330	19.8
Total exchangeable bases	10	8	6.9	1.050	15.1
	20	7	7.0	0.838	11.9
	30	7	6.0	0.760	12.5
Percentage base saturation	10	8	18.7	2.346	12.5
	20	7	24.8	4.229	17.0
	30	7	30.2	18.900	62.4

Rank order correlation coefficients have been calculated between the more important soil properties and the number of periods of reclamation that sites at Rhayader have experienced. Thus land which has been reclaimed continuously since 1948 has been ranked highest (1) with unreclaimed land being ranked lowest (8). The correlation coefficients are shown in Table 8.3. Some of the coefficients are comparatively high indicating not only that there are differences between reclaimed and unreclaimed land but that relationships can be established with length of reversion.

Table 8.3

Spearman rank correlation coefficients between soil properties and number of periods of reclamation

	10 cm	DEPTH 20 cm	30 cm
Loss on ignition	-.714	-.012	.810
% nitrogen	-.818	.036	.045
cation exchange capacity	-.690	.071	.993
Exchangeable hydrogen	-.765	-.274	-.036
% base saturation	.798	-.051	-.756
Carbon/nitrogen ratio	.631	-.122	.910
Total exchangeable bases	.417	.363	-.107

It is not surprising that many of the good correlations are with properties at the 10 cm level. Surface horizons will be most affected by cultivation practices. All correlations for the 20 cm level are extremely poor but become higher again at 30 cm depth. The reasons for this are not clear but may be related to the mixing of material and improved drainage conditions. At the 10 cm level there are negative correlations between length of reclamation and loss on ignition, nitrogen content, cation exchange capacity, exchangeable hydrogen and liming requirement. There are positive correlations with percentage base saturation and C/N ratios. At the 30 cm level there are positive correlations with loss on ignition, cation exchange capacity and C/N ratios and a negative correlation with percentage base saturation.

The use of unreclaimed moorland core sites as control plots is essential to the soil sampling in this research, in order to provide a base line upon which to compare sites of differing reversion dates. The survey at Glaspwll provided 8 moorland control sites and these have been examined statistically to reveal how consistent the moorland core is a unit of soil. The arithmetic mean, standard deviation and coefficient of variation for the soil properties are presented in Table 8.4.

Table 8.4

A summary of soil properties grouped according to number of continuously reclaimed or reverted periods prior to 1986

	DEPTH	RECLAIMED PERIODS (before 1986)				REVERTED PERIODS (before 1986)			MOORLAND CORE
		2	4	6	7	3	4	6	
Loss on	10	7.7	6.9	10.0	8.2	13.6	10.8	7.8	11.2
ignition	20	6.5	6.2	6.3	6.3	9.2	7.5	7.8	9.9
	30	32.0	5.2	4.7	4.6	8.0	4.7	4.6	6.7
pH	10	5.3	5.4	5.9	4.7	4.7	4.9	4.1	4.4
	20	5.3	5.5	6.1	4.5	4.8	5.0	4.0	4.6
	30	5.2	5.4	6.2	4.6	4.9	4.4	4.3	4.7
	10	3.1	2.8	4.2	3.3	5.8	4.6	3.2	4.7
% carbon	20	2.6	2.4	3.3	2.5	3.8	3.0	3.2	4.1
	30	14.3	2.0	2.6	1.7	3.3	1.8	1.7	2.7
	10	0.44	0.35	0.36	0.38	0.36	0.41	0.41	0.50
% nitrogen	20	0.25	0.27	0.25	0.32	0.31	0.23	0.40	0.34
	30	0.19	0.20	0.23	0.15	0.21	0.21	0.22	0.22
Carbon/nitrogen	10	7.1	7.8	11.7	8.7	16.2	11.0	7.7	9.7
ratio	20	10.3	9.0	13.1	7.8	12.4	13.3	7.9	11.9
	30	75.0	9.9	13.6	10.9	11.3	8.3	7.7	11.9
Cation exchange	10	30.4	27.6	38.3	29.6	39.9	41.2	31.2	38.2
capacity	20	30.4	24.6	28.6	26.9	31.2	31.5	25.5	29.6
	30	24.7	25.7	29.2	20.8	34.9	21.7	17.8	22.1
Exchangeable	10	5.6	3.8	3.4	7.1	11.7	5.7	10.5	10.1
hydrogen	20	4.2	2.8	3.4	7.2	9.2	6.3	10.3	8.6
	30	4.1	3.9	3.4	5.5	3.4	4.7	6.4	6.6
Total exchangeable	10	9.0	8.2	8.4	6.2	7.1	5.4	4.8	6.7
bases	20	7.1	7.0	8.0	5.6	7.1	6.0	4.8	6.4
	30	5.7	7.0	7.1	4.3	7.5	5.0	4.9	5.8
Percentage base	10	29.6	29.7	28.4	21.1	17.8	16.9	15.4	17.6
saturation	20	23.3	25.4	31.9	21.1	22.8	20.7	18.9	23.8
	30	23.0	27.3	29.6	22.4	21.5	23.1	27.5	30.5

The data can be plotted on scattergraphs to illustrate the dispersion of moorland control values around their means. Scattergraphs also represent moorland core as a unit and permits comparison of reclaimed and reverted sites against moorland sites as shown in Figures 8.5 to 8.7. Figure 8.5 illustrates loss on ignition, pH and exchangeable hydrogen. Loss on ignition shows some variation from the mean moorland values, decreasing with depth, but this probably reflects the unfavourable decomposition conditions in the uplands. The pH scattergraph shows the ideal distribution of reverted and reclaimed values. The grouping of all sites that have undergone at least one period of reversion are clustered around the control mean, whereas reclaimed plots are placed above the mean. It is interesting to note that mean pH values increase with depth, possibly indicating leaching or that the organic matter at the surface releases humic acids which suppress pH, and below the surface the mineral soil releases salts which encourage pH. Exchangeable hydrogen shows a trend for reclaimed sites to be below the mean values, and the decrease in mean value with depth is linked to the organic matter content of the soil.

Figure 8.6 illustrates carbon, nitrogen and C/N ratio. Carbon and nitrogen are linked to organic matter content, carbon showing that the reclaimed sites generally fall below the mean, whereas nitrogen is similar but shows much closer grouping of the results. The C/N ratio represents the opposite of organic content, for the higher the ratio the more decomposition is taking place. Figure 8.7 shows cation exchange capacity, total exchangeable bases and base saturation. Cation exchange capacity averages decrease with depth and again are linked with organic content. Total exchangeable bases show much closer groupings of the reverted sites around the moorland means. Base saturation is a useful measure of leaching, and long term improved sites are generally above the mean values, whereas reverted and moorland sites are grouped around the means, and the increase with depth indicates that leaching is taking place.

CONCLUSIONS

Soil is extremely variable, not only from site to site but also within individual profiles thus it is difficult to make general statements. But some trends are detectable. Distinct profile differences exist between moorland core/reverted sites and sites that have undergone reclamation. Higher mean loss on ignition and associated cation exchange capacity occur on reverted sites, together with lower total exchangeable bases and percentage base saturation values and pH. These results are essentially similar to those reported by other workers. Ultimately general statements or even 'models' of land and soil capability may be established which will be of use in the planning of future use of these marginal upland areas. Land capability maps usually indicate that reverted land and moorland core are of identical value. This is usually untrue. Reverted farmland

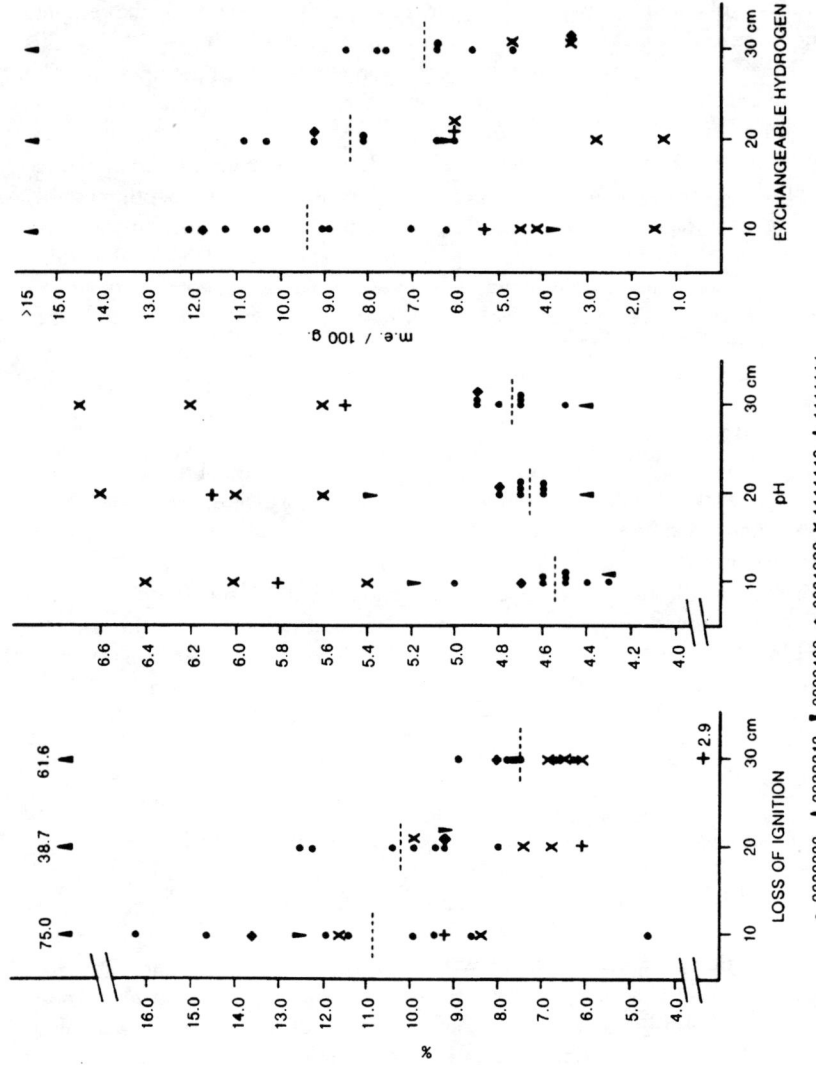

Figure 8.5 Scatter diagrams for (a) loss-on-igniton; (b) pH; (c) exchangeable hydrogen

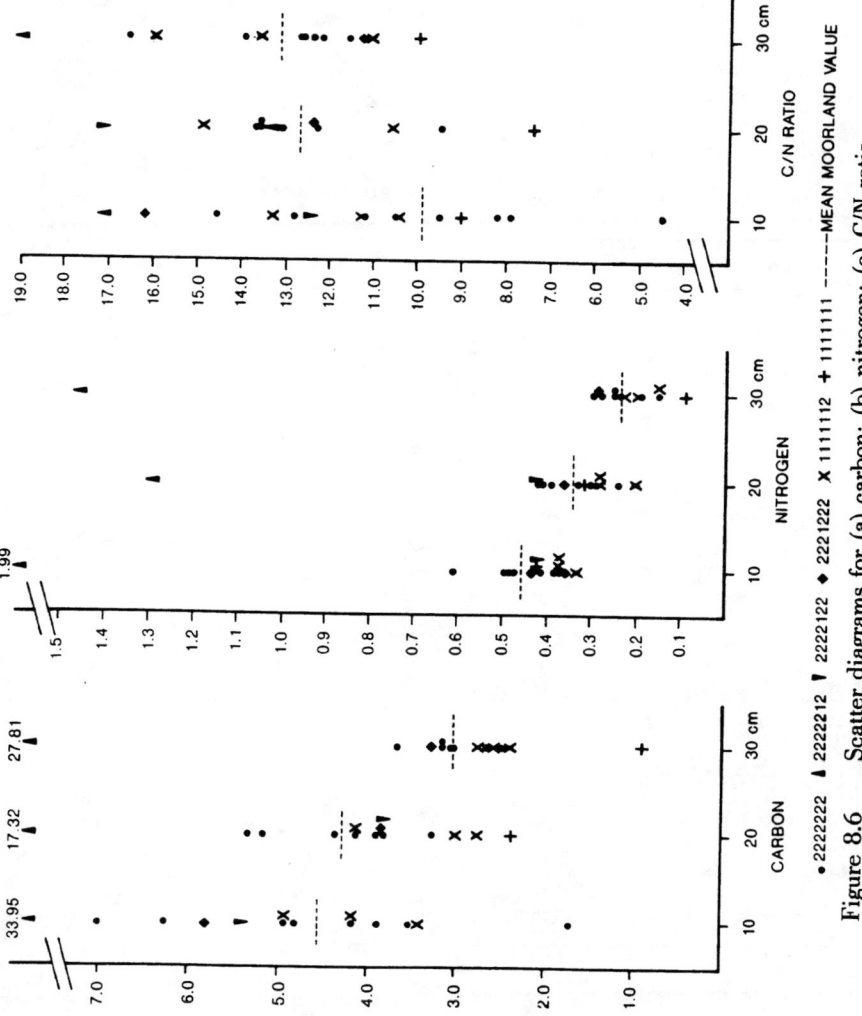

Figure 8.6 Scatter diagrams for (a) carbon; (b) nitrogen; (c) C/N ratio.

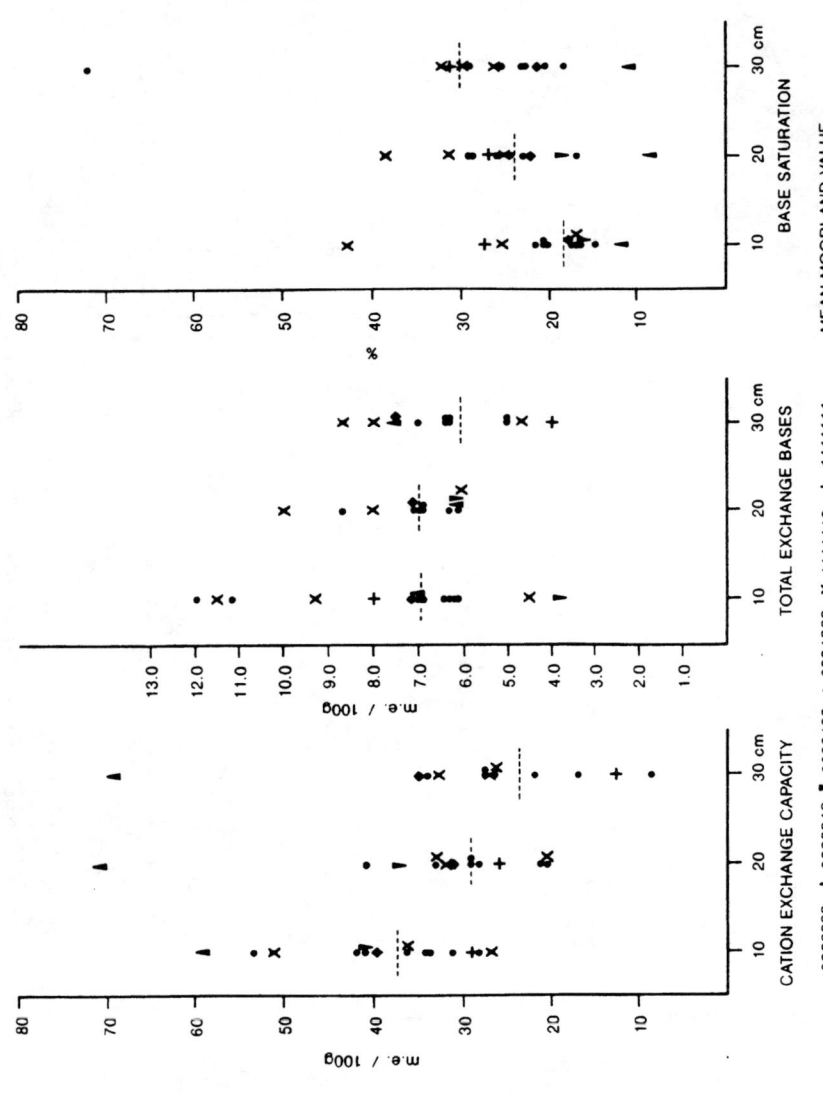

Figure 8.7 Scatter diagrams for (a) cation exchange capacity; (b) total exchangeable bases; (c) percentage base saturation

has both a different ecological value and a higher agricultural potential. This distinction should be included in future land capability mapping. This would ensure that better quality reverted land is given due consideration in future management schemes.

REFERENCES

Aderikhin, P.G., Tikhova, Ye.P., Kulakov, V.P. and Deglyareva, N. Ya. (1960), 'Changes in the podzolic soils of the Murmansk Region under cultivation', Soviet Soil Science, 4, pp. 379-383.

Albrecht, W.A. (1956), 'Physical, chemical and biochemical changes in the soil community', in W.L. Thomas (ed.), Man's role in changing the face of the Earth, Chicago, University of Chicago Press, pp. 648-673.

Allenby, P.L.M. and Gerrard, A.J. (1988), Soil and vegetation characteristics of reverted farmland on Anglezarke Moor, Lancashire, School of Geography, University of Birmingham, Working Paper Series, no. 45.

Ball, D.F. (1978), 'The soils of Upland Britain', in E.B. Tranter (ed.), The future of Upland Britain, Centre for Agricultural Strategy, Reading, pp. 397-416.

Bennett, R.J., Russel, W.D. and Watkin, J.E. (1968), 'Lime and phosphate treatments for reclamation of heather moorland', Journal of the British Grassland Society, 23, pp. 34-39.

Conry, M.J. (1970), Man's role in soil profile modification and formation in Ireland, unpub. Ph.D. thesis, University College, Dublin.

Conry, M.J. (1972a), 'Pedological evidence of man's role in soil profile modification in Ireland', Geoderma, 8, pp. 139-146.

Conry, M.J. (1972b), 'The reclamation of mountain soils and attendant profile and land-use changes', Scientific proceedings, Royal Dublin Society, Series B, 3, pp. 137-157.

Copeman, G.J.F. (1978), 'Some agronomic problems and aspects for Upland Britain', in E.B. Tranter (ed.) The future of Upland Britain, Centre for Agricultural Strategy, Reading, pp. 14-21.

Countryside Commission (1984), A better future for the Uplands, The Commission, Cheltenham.

Crompton, E. (1953), 'Grow the soil to grow the grass: some pedological aspects of marginal land improvement', Agriculture, 60 (7), pp. 301-308.

Davies, H. (1967), 'Influence of soil and management on the botanical composition of 20-years old reclaimed hill pastures in Mid-Wales', Journal of the British Grassland Society, 22, pp. 141-147.

Davies, T.H. (1980), 'Hill land improvement', ADAS Quaterly Review, 36, pp. 47-59.

European Economic Community (1980), Effects on the environment of the abandonment of agricultural land, Information on Agriculture, The Community, London.

Floate, M.J.S. (1977), 'British hill soil problems', Soil Science, 123, pp. 325-331.

Gerrard, A.J. (1982), Soil characteristics of reverted farmland: A pilot study from Dartmoor, Surveys of Moorland and Roughland Change, Department of Geography, University of Birmingham, no. 13.

Green, F.H.W. (1976), 'Recent changes in land use and treatment', Geographical Journal, 142, pp. 12-26.

Command 6020 (1975), Food from our own resources, HMSO.

MacEwen, M. and Sinclair, G. (1983), New life for the hills, Council for National Parks, London.

Maltby, E. (1975), 'Numbers of microorganisms as ecological indicators of changes resulting from moorland reclamation on Exmoor, U.K'., Journal of Biogeography, 2, pp. 117-136.

Maltby, E. (1979), 'Changes in soil properties and vegetation resulting from reclamation on Exmoor', Welsh Soils Discussion Group, 20, pp. 83-117.

Munro, J.M.M. (1973), 'Potential pasture production in the uplands of Wales', Journal of the British Grassland Society, 28, pp. 59-67.

Newbould, P. (1974), 'The improvement of hill pastures for agriculture: A Review, Part I', Journal of the British Grassland Society, 29, pp. 241-247.

Newbould, P. (1985), 'Improvement of native grassland in the uplands', Soil Use and Management, 1, pp. 43-49.

Parry, M.L. (1982), 'The changing use of land', in R.J. Johnston and J.C. Doornkamp (eds.), The changing geography of the U.K., London, Methuen, pp. 13-36.

Parry, M.L. (1987), Mid-Wales Upland Study: update to 1986, unpublished report to the Countryside Commission, Cheltenham.

Phillips, J.P. (1989), The soil characteristics of reverted farmland in the Mid-Wales Uplands, upub. M.Sc. thesis, University of Birmingham, England.

Parry, M.L., Bruce, A. and Harkness, C.E. (eds.) (1982-5), Surveys of Moorland and Roughland Change, Department of Geography, University of Birmingham.

Parry, M.L. and Sinclair, G. (1985), Mid Wales Uplands Study, Countryside Commission, Cheltenahm.

Porchester, Lord (1977), A study of Exmoor, HMSO, London.

Reith, J.W.S. and Robertson, R.A. (1971), 'Lime and fertilizer requirements for the establishment and growth of grass on deep peat', Journal of Agricultural Science of Cambridge, 76, pp. 89-95.

Reith, J.W.S. and Robertson, R.A. (1973), 'The nutrient requirements of herbage on deep acid peat', Journal of Agricultural Science of Cambridge, 80, pp. 425-434.

Riley, H.C.F. and MaCleod, D.A. (1980), 'Grass production studies in the uplands of north-east Scotland, I. The effects of soil parent material, altitude and soil major group', Grass and Forage Science, 35, pp. 115-122.

Rudeforth, C.C., Hartnup, R., Lea, J.W., Thompson, T.R.E. and Wright, P.S. (1984), Soils and their use in Wales, Soil Survey of England and Wales, Bulletin no. 11, Harpenden.

Sinclair, G. (1983), The Uplands Landscapes Study, Environment Information Services, Narberth.

Stamp, L.D. (1962), The Land of Britain: Its Use and Misuse, London, Longmans.

Stapledon, R.G. (1936), A survey of the agricultural and waste lands of Wales, London, Faber and Faber.

Tansley, A.G. (1949), Britain's Green Mantle, London, George Allen and Unwin.

Thompson, L.M. and Troeh, F.R. (1978), Soils and soil fertility, New York, McGraw-Hill.

Tranter, E.B. (1978), The future of Upland Britain, Centre for Agricultural Strategy, Reading.

Yaalon, D.H. and Yaron, B. (1966), 'Framework for man-made soil changes - an outline of metapedogenesis', Soil Science, 102, pp. 272-277.

9 Britain's new forests: Public dependence on private interest?

KEVIN BISHOP

Over the last few years there has been a growing move towards creating new multi-purpose woodlands in Britain. There are, for example, plans to create a new national forest in the Midlands; Community Forests around major conurbations in England and Wales; a new central Scotland woodland between Edinburgh and Glasgow and proposals to recreate the native Caledonian forest in Scotland. These proposals can be linked to: changes in national forestry policy, structural shifts in agriculture with the prospect of surplus agricultural land, increasing pressure for recreational opportunities and the evolving role of rural planning and countryside management, all of which are being increasingly influenced by a growing social and political awareness of environmental issues.

New Forests in the Countryside around Towns

Fairbrother (1970) was one of the first authors to explicitly suggest surrounding major cities in Britain with 'tree belts' although Howard's (1898) concept of Garden Cities included an element of tree planting. Fairbrother envisaged 'tree belts' as:

> ....*more than urban decoration - continuous woodland screens planned and planted as a whole, flowing round our urban areas in irregular masses, sensitive to the land-use and contours of the ground and their outlines defined to harmonise with the open landscape....Tree belts would have their own*

> *identity as sylvan areas, small but definite stretches of woodland, boundaries belonging equally to the rural and urban landscape, separating but also reconciling the town and country.*
>
> (Fairbrother, 1970, p.309)

In more recent years the Countryside Commission (for England) has taken the initiative. In 1987 the Commission, following a major review of countryside recreation policy, published "Policies for Enjoying the Countryside" (Countryside Commission, 1987a). As part of this new emphasis to provide and manage appropriate access to wider areas of countryside, the Commission identified a need for "major new forests on the edge of our large cities" (p.20) the aim being that these forests would become "important recreational assets" (p.20). The Countryside Policy Review Panel, appointed because of the "compelling need to examine most carefully the rapidly changing rural scene in England and Wales" (Countryside Policy Review Panel, 1987, p.3), outlined the "considerable potential for establishing new woods within the urban fringe and managing existing ones better" (p.29). The theme of new woodlands was also adopted in the Countryside Commission's policy statement on "Forestry in the Countryside" (Countryside Commission, 1987b). In this policy statement the Commission stated that "the starting point for public support for forestry should be to maximise all potential benefits to the nation" (p.7), as such, forestry policy should be based on the following multiple-objectives:

- production of a national supply of timber as a raw material and as a source of energy;
- offer an alternative to agricultural use of land;
- contribute to rural employment either in timber industries or through associated recreation developments;
- create attractive sites for public enjoyment;
- enhance the natural beauty of the countryside, and;
- create wildlife habitats.

(Countryside Commission, 1987b, p.7)

To illustrate the move towards multi-purpose forestry the Countryside Commission proposed two new initiatives: the creation of forests around some of our major conurbations and the establishment of a new forest in the English Midlands.

Community Forest Concept

Following the publication of "Forestry in the Countryside", the Forestry Commission joined the Countryside Commission in developing and launching the concept of Community Forests (see: Countryside Commission, 1989a and 1989b). The Community Forest programme, formally launched in July 1989, now consists of three lead projects: south Tyne and Wear/north east Durham (Great North Forest); south Staffordshire (Forest of Mercia) and east London (Thames Chase), followed by a second tier consisting of a further eleven possible forests (see figure 9.1). The nine second tier English Community Forests were formally launched on 14 February 1991. The decision on the proposed Community Forests in Wales has been delayed by the formation of the new Countryside Council for Wales.

Figure 9.1 Community Forest Programme in England and Wales

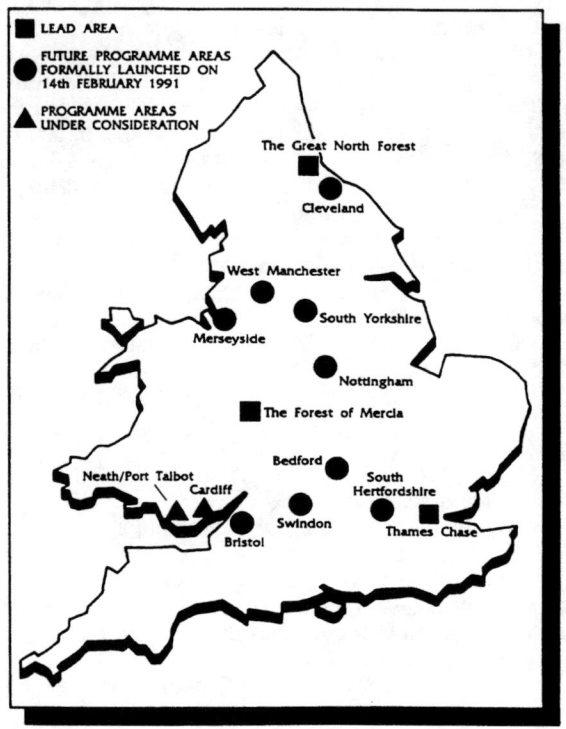

(Bishop, 1991)

Community Forests are to be multi-purpose forests "designed, developed and managed to provide for the community's leisure needs" (Taylor, 1989, para. 4). Each forest will cover an area of approximately 10-15,000 ha, within which 30-60 per cent of the land will be planted, predominantly though not exclusively, with broadleaved trees. The vision is not of continuous forest but a network of community woodlands and other landscape features, such as farmland, heathland, meadows and water features. Existing literature concentrates on explaining the 'Community Forest vision' (Countryside Commission, 1989a and b) and provides guidance on preparing a Community Forest plan (Countryside Commission, 1990a). Little has been written about how this vision will be implemented. However, large-scale changes in landownership are not envisaged (Countryside Commission, 1989a and 1989b; Kirby, 1989 and Minter, 1989). Instead the main approach will be to discuss with landowners and occupiers the business opportunities that might be available to them from diversifying, in whole or part, into leisure and forestry, with private landowners encouraged to use existing grant schemes to create and manage their own woodland areas. This represents a continuation of the voluntary approach that has underpined previous countryside management initiatives (Bishop, 1990). In the three lead areas project teams have already been established, funded jointly by the Countryside Commission and relevant local authorities for an initial period of three years, with member and officer level steering committees. These teams are responsible for compiling a non-statutory community forest plan which will outline the aims of the scheme and how it is to be implemented (Countryside Commission, 1990a).

The New National Forest in the Midlands

The other current multi-purpose forest initiative in England is the Countryside Commission's concept of a new forest in the Midlands. It is proposed that the forest would cover an area of 150 square miles, containing a framework of woodland within which would be situated a variety of land uses: "perhaps only half of the area might eventually become woodland of one kind or another" (Countryside Commission, 1989c). The vision is based on the New Forest in Hampshire and should not be confused with the Community Forest concept, being more of a national rather than regional or local initiative:

> *Imagine a forest as large as the Isle of Wight set in the Heart of England....a subtle blend of woodland, open spaces, farmland and communities....a place where people from all over the country will be able to enjoy themselves and delight in the wildlife....a leisure resource that will help to stimulate economic enterprise and create jobs....a ready-made source of home-grown timber....a green carpet that will put new life into derelict land and fresh vigour into a declining agriculture industry. That is the Countryside Commission's vision of the national forest it is proposing to create in the Midlands.*
> (Countryside Commission, 1990b)

In contrast to the Community Forest concept, which was launched without any public consultation, the Countryside Commission prepared a consultation document on the "New National Forest for the Midlands" (Countryside Commission, 1989c) which sought the views on where, from a short list of five possible sites the forest should be located, how it could be achieved and then subsequently managed.

Figure 9.2 New National Forest Area of Search

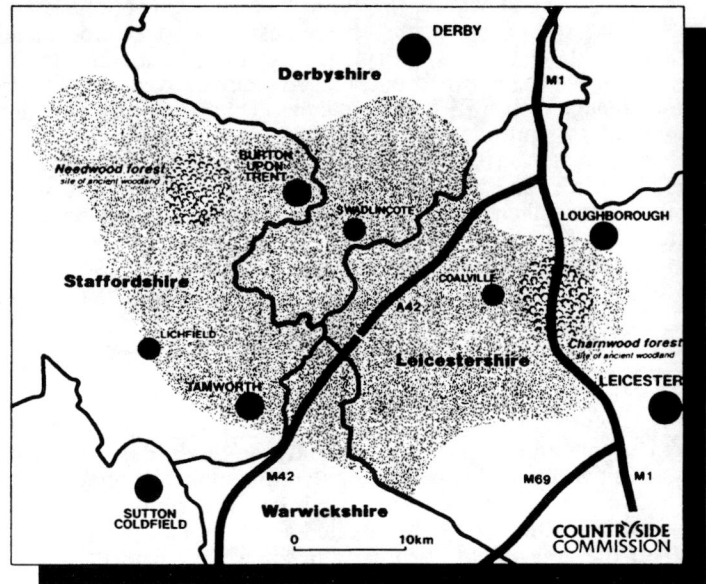

(Countryside Commission, 1990b)

Following this consultation exercise the Needwood/Charnwood area was selected between Leicester and Burton-on-Trent (see figure 9.2) and a project team assembled to compile a forest business plan. As with the Community Forest concept, the emphasis is on voluntary participation:

> *There will be no compulsory purchase of land to establish the new national forest: rather the scheme will open up new opportunities for farmers, both owner-occupiers and tenants. A package of measures will be put in place to encourage farmers and landowners to plant and manage trees.*
> (Countryside Commission, 1990b)

Central Scotland Woodlands

Almost simultaneous to the Community Forest and Midland Forest proposals was the launch, by the Scottish Office, of Central Scotland Woodlands:

> *An exciting new woodland environment is to be created...stretching from the Campsies to the foothills of the Pentlands...from the eastern fringes of Glasgow to the western fringes of Edinburgh...sweeping from the valley of the Forth to the valley of the Clyde.*

(Scottish Office, 1989)

The woodlands would be "a truly multi-purpose asset for all the community - and for wildlife and leisure too" (Scottish Office, 1989). Central to the concept is economic regeneration by environmental improvement. Three main types of woodland are envisaged:

> **Community Woodlands**, close to urban areas, will be planned from the outset to provide access to an attractive rural haven of peace and quiet on the very doorstep of the local community.
>
> **Amenity Woodlands** will be specifically designed to improve the landscape and environment not only near where people live and work, but also throughout the area on better quality land.
>
> **Productive Woodlands** are at the heart of any truly multi-purpose forest, providing the raw materials for man's use in ways that respect the environment but still bring prosperity and jobs to the area as a whole. Located generally on poorer land in the more remote parts of the area they will be mainly coniferous, providing timber that industry demands. Careful landscaping and public access will still be important, but timber production will be the main purpose".
> (Scottish Office, 1989)

The concept of Central Scotland Woodlands has arisen from other woodland/tree planting initiatives aimed at improving the landscape of the Central Belt between Edinburgh and Glasgow (Bishop, 1990), although the scale of the latest proposal is substantially larger than any of the previous projects. To implement the concept of Central Scotland Woodlands a new limited company, Central Scotland Woodlands Ltd., has been established by the Scottish Office with an annual budget of £2.5 million for the next 20 years. This funding includes an element of Woodland Grant Scheme money from the Forestry Commission, recreation facility provision and amenity tree planting grants from the Countryside Commission for Scotland, as well as, core funding from the Scottish Office. Central Scotland Woodlands Ltd. is proposing a more pro-active approach to woodland creation than at present envisaged for Community Forests or the new national forest with land acquisition by the company and woodland creation facilitated by development schemes, as well as by voluntary planting.

European Blueprints

The blueprints for these new forest proposals, particularly the Community Forests, are the recreational forests found around many European cities (Countryside Commission, 1989a), for example, the Amsterdamse Bos, the German Stadwalds, Oslo's Oslomarka and the Vestkoven on the edge of

Copenhagen. These European forests all benefit, or have benefited, from substantial public sector support. For example, a plan to create the West Forest Park (Vestkoven) on the fringe of Copenhagen, was produced under the direction of the Danish ministries of Environment and Planning, Culture and Agriculture, and implemented by public sector acquisition of land on the open market ,with 50 per cent of the costs funded by central government. The Dutch Randstadgroenstructuur is another example of the more interventionist approach of our European counterparts to land use and landscape change. The Randstad area in Holland can be regarded as a big metropolis including within it the cities of Amsterdam, Rotterdam, the Hague and Utrecht. Unlike other such areas the centre of the Randstad consists of open agricultural land covering approximately 160,000 ha, the so-called 'green heart' (Van Gessel, 1988). Pressures upon this agricultural area from changes in European agricultural policy and urban expansion led to the formulation of plans in the 1970s to safeguard the open land or green heart of the Randstad area. The Randstadgroenstructuur envisages a strong green buffer between the various urban areas and the green heart. The green buffer will consist of extensive forests and recreation areas to absorb urban recreational pressure and protect agricultural land from such pressure.

In drawing up the plan, the Randstad was subdivided into three landscape groups 'consolidation', 'adaptation' and 'restructuring' areas each with its own distinct policies. 'Restructuring areas' were generally identified close to cities and were given priority for landscape improvement in the plan. In 'adaptation areas' small-scale and scattered urban and green uses are being fitted into the existing landscape structure, agriculture is to be stengthened and existing landscape features reinforced by development of complimentary small forest and recreation projects. Retention of existing land uses receives priority in the 'consolidation area' which mostly equates to the green heart. The Randstadgroenstructuur is being implemented by provincial authorities who can acquire land on the open market. As well as creating new forest/recreation areas the plan is also concerned with creating viable farm units through a process of farm amalgamation and restructuring. The Dutch government is making a significant contribution towards the costs of implementing this plan having committed over £120 million, at current exchange rates, to land acquisition and forest creation.

Public Dependence on Private Interest

The new forest proposals in Britain are based on the assumption that: new multi-purpose woodlands will benefit the community at large by enhancing the landscape; provide new environments for recreation and wildlife; attract development; and help to mitigate the 'greenhouse effect' (as shown in figure 9.3). The aim is to demonstrate, through the successful integration of these objectives, a model of sustainable land use (Countryside Commission, 1989c).

Figure 9.3   Proposed Benefits of Multi-purpose Woodland

(Bishop, 1990)

The majority of benefits associated with new multi-purpose woodland creation are for the public at large and also non-monetary. Yet the newly established project teams responsible for implementing these proposals (with the possible exception of Central Scotland Woodlands Ltd.) are heavily reliant on private interest to achieve forest creation. An interview and questionnaire survey of agricultural, developer and mineral landowners/occupiers in three case study areas (Tyne and Wear, Bristol and Hertfordshire) was undertaken by the author to ascertain the extent to which such landowners/occupiers might participate in new forest creation. The surveys were concerned with the way farmers, developers and mineral companies acquire and use land, the format of these ownership rights, the factors that influence land management and attitudes of these landowners/occupiers towards multi-purpose woodland creation. The research concentrated on private landowners and occupiers because, from the scant information available (Northfield, 1979; Pacione, 1990), they appear to own most of the land surface of Britain. For example, 80 per cent of the area designated for the 'Forest of Mercia' is in private ownership and only 15 per cent of the land within the 'Great North Forest' is publicly owned. Also, private landowners cannot be forced to comply with government policy to the same extent that public authorities can be.

The Farmers' Perspective

Over the past four years government policies towards agriculture have changed dramatically as a result of a combination of factors including: agricultural over-production; the environmental impact of intensive agriculture; and the rising costs of a support policy that could no longer be justified in a climate of increased environmental awareness. As a result, farmers are now faced with a plethora of schemes that are aimed at curbing agricultural production. The majority of these schemes provide, in varying formats, payments for tree planting/woodland creation. Forestry has been identified as the main alternative use for surplus agricultural land. For example, according to the House of Commons Agriculture Committee (1990) "Forestry is likely to be the most extensive alternative land use: it has the potential to offer an attractive balance between commercial viability and environmental enhancement". Despite the fact that the impact of these new schemes is unclear, they are envisaged as playing an important role, together with changes in forestry policy, in the creation of new multi-purpose forests (Countryside Commission, 1989a, 1989b and 1989c). There is, however, no history of farm woodland creation in Britain indeed, in contrast, there is a legacy of farm woodland neglect, so woodland planting must be viewed as an innovation. An interview survey of 120 farmers in the three study areas thus attempted to examine the factors that influence farm woodland adoption and diffusion (Bishop, 1990). The vast majority of respondents interviewed (over 90 per cent) were not interested in new woodland planting. For example, the farmers interviewed were unlikely to plant more than 30 ha of woodland in total, representing only 0.28 per cent of the area in the survey. This widespread disinterest in new woodlands as a form of farm diversification results primarily from the long term commitment and unsure financial returns from forests as shown in figure 9.4. These are contrary to the requirements of the majority of farm businesses involved in diversification or planning to diversify. This disinterest appears to be deep rooted, for example, only 16 per cent of respondents were able/willing to supply a hypothetical annual grant level that would prompt them to plant trees on their land. Farm woodlands were perceived by most of the farmers interviewed as a conservation luxury and not as a viable alternative farm enterprise. This lack of interest in woodlands also applied to existing farm woods which were rarely viewed as an integral part of farm management. Of the 102 individual woodland areas included in the survey only 16 were actively managed, although these 16 woods were spatially significant - accounting for 71 per cent of the woodland area included in the survey.

Figure 9.4 Reasons for not Planting new Farm Woodlands

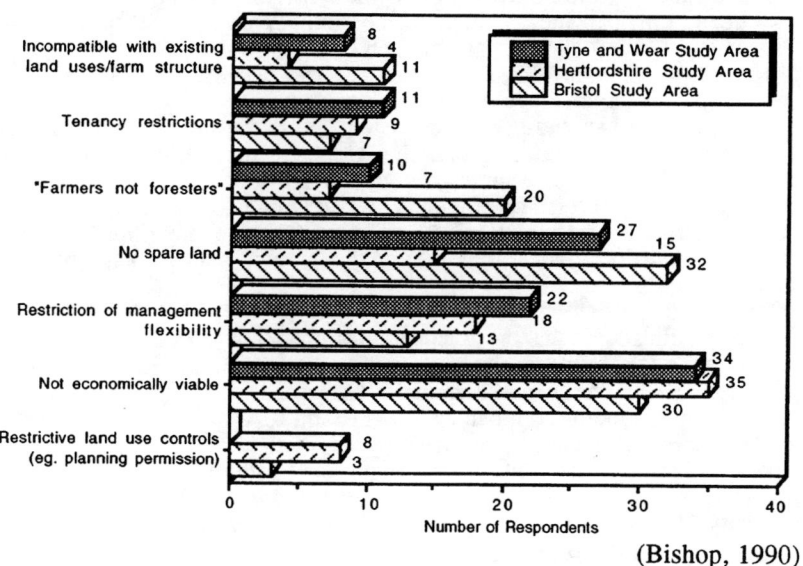

(Bishop, 1990)

The reasons for not wishing to plant new woodlands, as shown in figure 9.4, suggest possible reforms to environmental policy, such as, complete removal of woodlands from the planning system to avoid any perceived threat of Tree Preservation Orders preventing felling. But such changes alone are unlikely to result in large-scale woodland planting. Farm woodland creation is unlikely to be adopted as an alternative land use because of: the differences between woods and other agricultural crops; the lack of integration of existing farm woods into farm businesses; the lack of a marketing structure for timber; the long time span before any return on capital invested and the non-market nature of some woodland creation benefits, increased amenity value for example.

The Developers' Perspective

As well as affecting the farming community, recent changes in rural land policy also have important implications for the nature and form of future development schemes (Bishop, 1990). The prospects of surplus agricultural land, footloose employment and retailing, and the increasing demand for leisure and recreation facilities - both formal and informal - have led to an increasing number of greenfield development proposals. As Elson (1987) notes, an important aspect of these developments is the associated landscape. For example, planned developments of this kind often involve the creation of green environments as both a marketing tool and as part of a package designed to increase the chances of obtaining planning permission. The 'greening' of development schemes has not been confined to leisure, retail, industrial and business developments, new private housing schemes have also been shown to include areas of community and recreation provision (Elson and Garbutt, 1989), and on a larger scale, the private new towns proposed by Consortium Developments Ltd. (1985a and 1985b) also contained substantial 'green' areas. An interview and questionnaire survey of a sample of house builders and various property developers was also undertaken by the author to examine the land acquisition aspect of the development process. The survey covered the scope for positive management of land held for future development, for example, by creating woodland landscapes as an interim land use. The attitudes of developers towards environmental improvement as part of the development package was also surveyed.

The results illustrated that the practice of land banking (acquisition of land for future use) was widespread amongst those surveyed. Examples were provided of land banks in excess of 10,000 ha, and the length of ownership prior to development commencing was found to vary from an average of seven years to a maximum of 50 years. These results indicate that development interests could have a significant role in the creation of new forests because of the size of their land holdings and also because the majority of their land holdings are in the urban fringe where Community Forests are proposed.

Woodland creation, of any format, on land held for future development was however dismissed as unrealistic by all forms of property developer. Although examples were quoted, of tree planting undertaken in advance of development to enhance chances of obtaining planning permission, interim use of land held for future development is normally however a continuation of existing use. In contrast, woodland creation/tree planting was viewed by the majority of companies as sterilising future development options. The scope for woodland creation as an interim land use and ultimate mature landscape setting for future development is further restricted by the discernible trend, illustrated in the survey, towards increased use of options and conditional contracts to acquire an interest in land without planning permission, rather than outright acquisition of the freehold. Management of land acquired under options or conditional contracts remains the responsibility of the freeholder/occupier, with developer influence minimal until planning permission is forthcoming. The survey of developers thus indicated more potential for woodland creation in association with development rather than in advance of it. Although multi-purpose woodland areas had not been created as part of a development scheme by any of the companies surveyed this appears to be a result of planning authorities not considering such features to be suitable elements of a planning gain package rather than companies being fiercely opposed to woodland creation. A possible constraint to woodland creation is also the problem of long term management, a problem likely to be exacerbated where developments are sold and the developer no longer retains any management commitments, as in most housing developments.

The Mineral Perspective

The extraction of minerals has a catalytic effect on the landscape. Unlike other forms of development, mineral extraction is normally a temporary use of land and upon cessation of extraction the land can be restored either to its former use, to a new use or just abandoned. As a result of changing rural policies, there is now a need to consider non-agricultural after-uses of mineral workings, particularly forestry and amenity uses. A survey of both mineral planning authorities and mineral companies by the author, in the selected case study areas, was undertaken to determine the factors and policies that govern acquisition of land rights by mineral companies and the scope for restoration of mineral workings to multi-purpose woodland.

Figure 9.5 Factors Affecting the Restoration of Mineral Workings

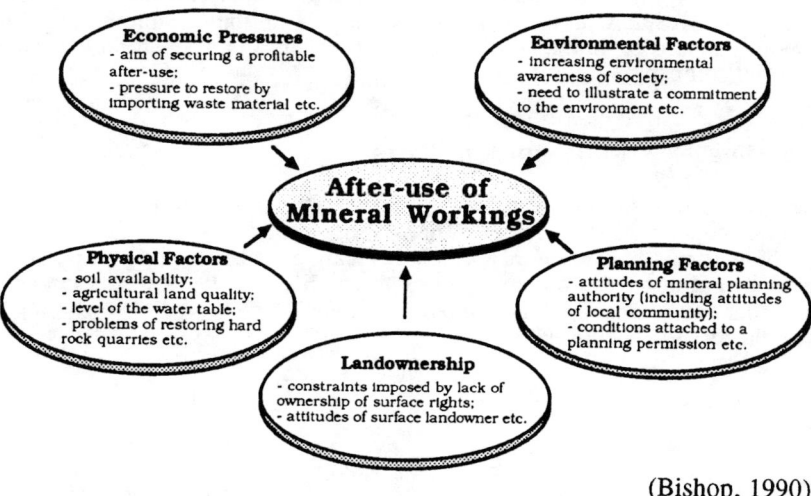

(Bishop, 1990)

The factors that affect the restoration of mineral workings were found to be many and varied (as shown in figure 9.5). From the interviews with mineral companies it would appear that restoration schemes are initiated by mineral companies with mineral planning authorities determining the final scheme. Although no examples of reclamation to multi-purpose woodland were encountered, the results of the survey suggest that there is scope for restoration of mineral workings to a woodland after-use. The lack of past examples of reclamation to woodlands is primarily a result of planning policies that emphasised the need to restore agricultural land to its previous use, which often engendered a stereotyped approach to the compilation of restoration plans, rather than any economic or physical reasons for not planting new woodlands on former mineral sites. One of the principal constraints to multi-purpose woodland, amenity and/or conservation reclamation is the ownership of surface rights. Where the mineral company has freehold ownership of the surface they can exercise almost complete autonomy in the choice of after-use, but when the surface rights are owned by a third party, the mineral company often occupies an intermediate position between the landowner and the planning authority. All of the companies interviewed stated that agricultural landowners tended to want mineral workings restored to agricultural land that was easy to farm. This constraint is likely to increase in significance because the survey also revealed that mineral companies are increasingly avoiding the outright acquisition of the surface freehold, preferring to acquire the necessary rights to mineral extraction by means of option agreements. Other potential constraints to the creation of multi-purpose woodland after-use, identified in the survey, include: lack of expertise and familiarity with restoration to multi-purpose woodland and other amenity uses; a perception that restoration to an amenity after-use is more expensive than restoration to agriculture; and the problem of long term management. Unlike restoration to agriculture, amenity after-uses such as multi-purpose woodlands could result in a net annual loss, especially in the early establishment years. Also, there is no identifiable market for amenity land uses, unlike agricultural land which can always be sold by the mineral company.

Creating New Multi-purpose Forests

The case study surveys of private landowners/occupiers undertaken by the author indicate that sole reliance on existing grant structures and voluntary participation is unlikely to result in large-scale tree planting on private land. The format of tree/woodland planting that is likely to be achieved under a voluntary system is illustrated in table 9.1 together with possible constraints that the research identified.

Table 9.1
Format of and Possible Constraints to Voluntary Woodland Creation

Types of Landowner/ occupier	Format of tree/woodland planting	Possible problems/constraints
Agricultural	Limited woodland planting associated with: • improvement of the landscape of 'hobby' farms; • planting to establish or increase the sporting value of a farm; • planting as part of a farm diversification scheme, for example, landscaping of a caravan site. Farmers may be more willing to voluntarily consider creation of 'wooded margins' as a form of extensification rather than creation of actual woodlands.	• Economics - long term nature of forestry investments is often incompatible with the short term need to diversify the farm business. • Lack of woodland management experience. • Landownership arrangements - not just the distinction between owner-occupier and tenant but also the influence of development and mineral interests in the form of options and conditional contracts which increase land use uncertainty. • Green belt policies - ambitious farm diversification plans, which often include tree/woodland planting proposals, may conflict with green belt policies. • Tree planting may be perceived as sterilising development potential and removing associated 'hope' value.
Developer	Possibility of tree planting in advance of development to increase chances of obtaining planning permission limited to land where the developer has necessary control over surface rights. Possibility of woodland creation as part of a planning gain package. This possibility is likely to be greatest for business park and leisure developments where the value of a green environment is already a marketing factor.	• Landownership/land acquisition arrangements. • Incompatibility of tree planting with construction/development. • Perception that tree planting in advance of development reduces chances of obtaining planning permission. • Costs of and practical problems of continued management.
Mineral	Possibility of occasional planting in advance of mineral extraction, where the mineral company controls the surface rights, to provide landscape buffer around future workings. Tree planting for landscaping purposes as part of a planning condition. There is scope for restoration to a multi-purpose woodland after-use, but this is likely to be limited to sites where the mineral operator owns the surface freehold and will not become widespread unless companies perceive this after-use as: • increasing chances of obtaining planning permission; • being cheaper than restoration to agriculture; and/or, • enhancing the company's 'green' credentials.	• Landownership/mineral working arrangements - trend away from freehold acquisition of surface rights reduces mineral operator's and planner's ability to determine after-use. • Possible lack of familiarity with restoration to non-agricultural uses. • Physical problems of restoration (especially hard rock quarries). • Attitudes/policies of mineral planning authorities, in particular, continuation of policies requiring restoration to agriculture. • Problem of continued site management after reclamation, need to illustrate that restoration to multi-purpose woodland may not be more expensive than restoration to agriculture.

One of the key constraints to woodland creation identified in the surveys was the problem of obtaining the necessary property rights. The surveys demonstrated that property rights over land are being divided into more complex forms of user and occupier rights. The traditional distinction between owner occupation and tenancy ignores the apparent increasing significance of non-agricultural interests in land which manifest themselves in terms of option agreements, conditional contracts and other innovative forms of tenurial arrangements. The presence of these non-agricultural interests and more complex division of property rights hinder the prospects for woodland creation by increasing land use uncertainty.

If voluntary participation, encouraged by existing grant structures, proves insufficient to implement the various new forest proposals, as the surveys suggest, then the various project teams will have to consider a number of other measures aimed at promoting woodland creation including: *enhanced grant levels* or other fiscal incentives; *demonstration woodlands*; *open market land acquisition* and *positive use of the planning system* .

The research indicated that provision of *enhanced grant levels* are unlikely to result in the creation of new woodland areas if unlimited public access is required. For example, only 19 out of 118 'farmers' interviewed were able or willing to provide a hypothetical annual grant bid level that would prompt them to plant trees on their land. However, consideration should be given to grant-aiding non-traditional forms of woodland creation which may be more compatible with the aims and requirements of farmers planning to diversify. For example, short rotation coppice reduces the time lag between investment and harvesting and more closely resembles a farm crop than other forms of woodland planting. Another idea worth further development is that of 'wooded margins'. The concept of wooded margins would be an extension of conservation headlands and has already been applied in the Countryside Premium Scheme (Countryside Commission, 1989c) where it constitutes one of the management options. Newly planted woodland strips along existing hedgerows, or as part of a field rationalisation programme may be more advantageous than isolated woodland planting for a number of reasons including: creating enhanced wildlife corridors and linking rights of way to provide wooded walks. Such planting may also be more compatible with farming than isolated woodland creation perhaps providing a form of extensification. Results from the first operative year of the Countryside Premium Scheme illustrate that the wooded margin has been the third most popular management option, resulting in the creation of 401 ha of wooded margins from applications by 41 farmers (Bishop, 1990).

The feasibility of developing *demonstration woodlands* on working farms should also be explored. The farm interview survey revealed that farmers tend to diversify into activities with which they are familiar or they have seen to be successful on other farms. A demonstration woodland scheme would attempt to illustrate through demonstration and practical advice the advantages of woodland establishment and could be extended to include schemes involving restoration of mineral workings and interim uses for future development sites.

Local authority *acquisition of land* for new woodland creation, as suggested by the Countryside Policy Review Panel (1987), appears extremely remote given limited public sector funds. However, Forestry Commission acquisition of land as part of the creation of new multi-purpose forests remains a possibility. To-date, Forestry Commission land acquisition has been concentrated in upland areas where land prices are lowest - primarily a function of the marginal economics of coniferous afforestation. If the non-market benefits likely to accrue from Community Forests and the New National Forest in the Midlands are taken into account then there is an obvious case for the Forestry Commission to consider purchasing/leasing strategic parcels of land as part of the implementation programme.

Positive use of the planning system appears to be one of the most feasible mechanisms for implementing these various new forest initiatives because it is not reliant on public sector resources. This option would entail planning authorities revising their development plan policies and more widespread acceptance of environmental improvements through planning gain. Development plan policies should be used to promote forestry as an interim, as well as more permanent, land use. For example, in certain areas of Merseyside forestry is being promoted as an interim use for vacant industrial land with the objective of promoting economic restructuring by environmental improvement and providing an economic use for the land (St. Helens and Knowsley Groundwork Trust, 1988). Mineral planning authorities would also have a role to play, preparing reclamation strategies/guidelines that are based on the desirability of certain after-uses rather than waiting for mineral companies to submit restoration plans.

Central to the concept of positive planning would be the use of planning agreements and conditions to secure environmental objectives. West Lothian District Council and Hertfordshire County Council provide examples of the types of planning policy that could be adopted to promote woodland creation. West Lothian District Council are considering allowing release of land for 'lowland crofting' in association with woodland planting and access arrangements (West Lothian District Council, 1991). Policies to allow this form of development have been written into the draft version of the Calders Area Local Plan (West Lothian District Council, 1990). Hertfordshire County Council are including a policy on planning gain for woodland creation, aimed at creating a Community Forest north of London, in their structure plan review. The policy is based on the footprint principle enshrined in Planning Policy Guidance Note 2 "Green Belts" (Department of the Environment, 1988). No new development would be permitted but re-development or re-use of existing buildings will be permitted within the green belt where the development: makes a significant contribution to the Community Forest; involves proposals for woodland planting, nature conservation and public access; and is designed to minimise environmental impact (Hertfordshire County Council, 1990). For example, re-development of agricultural buildings which might not have been permitted could now be granted planning permission if the landowner enters into an agreement to afforest specified areas of the farm and allow public access.

The use of planning gain to achieve Community Forest or other woodland creation is not without problems. For example, it could bring woodland creation into conflict with the aims of green belt designation (Council for the Preservation of Rural England, 1991). More specifically, with the Hertfordshire policy, there are problems of landowners and occupiers erecting 'agricultural buildings', which currently rarely require planning permission, to maximise the re-development value of holdings. The policy may also lead to increased land fragmentation as landowners sell off most of their holdings to minimise the area to be afforested whilst retaining re-development potential.

The research also identified important roles for the project teams in terms of: provision of advice and long-term management. The project teams should work in partnership with local authorities and other related bodies to provide advice on farm diversification, planning gain and restoration of mineral workings, with the emphasis on illustrating the practical benefits of tree planting/woodland creation. For example, with mineral workings the project teams could aim to fulfil a role similar to that of the Agricultural Development Advisory Service for agricultural after-uses providing, in partnership with the Forestry Commission, technical guidance on restoring sites to multi-purpose woodland. As well as performing an advisory role the project teams should be equipped or the Forestry Commission enabled to deal with day-to-day management of multi-purpose woodland sites within the new forests. This role would overcome the problem identified in the research of long-term management of old mineral sites restored to an amenity after-use. Management could be undertaken in return for purchasing the former mineral site for a nominal fee or grant of a long-term lease at a peppercorn rent. The costs of management could be funded by sponsorship from the mineral company who would benefit from having their name associated with a 'green' project and be able to use the site as an example to planning authorities of their commitment to good reclamation. This management function could also be extended to other woodland areas, especially those provided as 'planning gain'.

Conclusion

The various new forest proposals that have been launched during recent years are heavily reliant on private interest because of the pattern of British landownership yet offer very little incentive to private landowners to participate in new woodland creation. Indeed, the idea of woodland creation, especially when linked to increased public access to the countryside, is a complete anathema to many private landowners.

The scale and nature of these new forest proposals distinguishes them from previous countryside initiatives, such as the New Agricultural Landscapes project (Westmacott and Worthington, 1974 and 1984; Hamilton and Woolcock, 1984), and means that new mechanisms for implementing environmental policy must be developed. Sole reliance on the voluntary approach that has underpined previous countryside management initiatives is unlikely to result in the format or level of forest creation envisaged. Whilst enhanced fiscal incentives may increase the level of woodland planting, acquisition of strategic land parcels to form core woodland areas for informal recreational use should not be ruled out and the contribution of appropriate enabling development will need to be considered. These new forest proposals mark an important change in countryside policy away from a protective ethos concerned with minimising the environmental impact of an expansionist agricultural sector to creating new landscapes on surplus agricultural land for the twenty first century. The process of implementation will not be easy nor rapid and it is to be hoped that the practical difficulties of and long time span associated with woodland creation will not result in declining public and political support.

References

Bishop, K. D. (1990), 'Multi-purpose Woodlands in the Countryside around Towns', unpublished Ph.D. thesis, University of Reading, Reading.

Bishop, K. D. (1991), 'Community Forests: Implementing the Concept', The Planner, vol. 77, pp. 6-10.

Consortium Developments Ltd. (1985a), 'The Plan for Small New Country Towns', Consortium Developments Ltd., London.

Consortium Developments Ltd. (1985b), 'Tillingham Hall: Outline Plan', Consortium Developments Ltd., London.

Council for the Preservation of Rural England (1991), 'Community Forest Charter', Council for the Preservation of Rural England, London.

Countryside Commission (1987a), 'Policies for Enjoying the Countryside', Countryside Commission CCP 234, Cheltenham.

Countryside Commission (1987b), 'Forestry in the Countryside', Countryside Commission CCP 245, Cheltenham.

Countryside Commission (1989a), 'Forests in the Community', Countryside Commission CCP 270, Cheltenham.

Countryside Commission (1989b), 'Forests in the Community', Countryside Commission CCP 272, Cheltenham.

Countryside Commission (1989c), 'A New National Forest in the Midlands (Consultation Paper)', Countryside Commission CCP 278, Cheltenham.

Countryside Commission (1990a), 'Advice Manual for the Preparation of a Community Forest Plan', Countryside Commission CCP 271, Cheltenham.

Countryside Commission (1990b), 'The New National Forest', Countryside Commission CCP 328, Cheltenham.

Countryside Policy Review Panel (1987), 'New Opportunities for the Countryside', Countryside Commission CCP 224, Cheltenham.

Department of the Environment (1988), 'Planning Policy Guidance Note 2: Green Belts', HMSO, London.

Elson, M. J. (1987), 'The Urban Fringe - Will Less Farming Mean More Leisure?', The Planner, vol. 73, pp. 19-22.

Elson, M. J. and Garbutt, J. (1989), 'Recreation and Community Provision in Areas of New Private Housing', Housing Research Foundation, Amersham.

Fairbrother, N. (1970), 'New Lives, New Landscapes', Architectural Press, London.

Hamilton, P. and Woolcock, J. (1984), 'Agricultural Landscapes: An Approach to their Improvement', Countryside Commission CCP 169, Cheltenham.

Hertfordshire County Council (1990), 'A Community Forest for North London and South Hertfordshire: Approved Bid to the Countryside Commission', Hertfordshire County Council, Hertford.

House of Commons Agriculture Committee (1990), 'Land Use and Forestry, Second Report, Volume1', House of Commons Paper 16-1, Session 1989-90, HMSO, London.

Howard, E. (1898), 'Garden Cities of Tomorrow', Attic Books (1989 reprint), London.

Kirby, M. (1989), 'Greening the Green Belts: The Community Forest Concept', Country Landowner, vol. XLIII, pp. 24-25.

Minter, R. (1989), 'Urban Forestry: The Coming of Age', Timber Grower, no. 113, pp. 16-17.

Northfield Committee Report (1979), 'Report of the Committee of Inquiry into the Acquisition and Occupancy of Agricultural Land', Cmnd. 7599, HMSO, London.

Pacione, M. (1990), 'Development Pressures in the Metropolitan Fringe', Land Development Studies, vol. 7, pp. 69-82.

Scottish Office (1989), 'Central Scotland Woodlands', Scottish Office, Edinburgh.

St. Helens and Knowsley Groundwork Trust (1988), 'New Uses for Vacant Industrial Land', unpublished report prepared for Knowsley Metropolitan Borough Council by St. Helens and Knowsley Groundwork Trust, St. Helens.

Taylor, G. (1989), 'The National Community Forests Programme and the South Tyne and Wear/North East Durham Community Forest', Countryside Commission, Newcastle.

Van Gessel, P. (1988), 'Randstadgroenstructuur', Ministry of Agriculture and Fisheries, The Hague, Netherlands.

West Lothian District Council (1990), '<u>Calders Area Local Plan (Draft Version)</u>, West Lothian District Council, Linlithgow.

West Lothian District Council (1991), '<u>Lowland Crofting Handbook (Draft Version)</u>, West Lothian District Council, Linlithgow.

Westmacott, R. and Worthington, T. (1974), '<u>New Agricultural Landscapes</u>', Countryside Commission, Cheltenham.

Westmacott, R. and Worthington, T. (1984), '<u>Agricultural Landscapes: A Second Look</u>', Countryside Commission CCP 168, Cheltenham.

10 Countryside in revolt: Rural response to a proposed hazardous waste facility

OWEN FURUSETH

Introduction

The traditional image of rural America is a clean, healthy countryside far removed from the pollution of urban centers. Although this imagery has always been somewhat tainted by the reality of functional rural landscapes; e.g. extractive industries and forestry, the recent environmental history of the USA has debunked the myth of bucolic rural America. A growing body of anecdotal and substantiated data disclose widespread environmental contamination and risk from toxic contaminants.

Ironically, the most recent Federal government regulations and programs designed to control pollution and clean up existing hazardous waste facilities have created growing rural protest. This opposition is based, at least, in part on the perception that current environmental initiatives are biased against rural communities. Rural areas see themselves becoming the dumping grounds for industrial refuse. The irony is that urban areas enjoy the economic benefits provided by sophisticated manufacturing activities, while rural communities are left to dispose of the hazardous and toxic residuals. Few jobs are created and environmental risks are magnified.

Every year American industry generates 125 billion pounds of non-nuclear toxic waste, and by some estimates 90 percent of these materials are disposed of improperly. Accordingly, the passage of the Resource Conservation and Recovery Act in 1976 (RCRA) has been hailed by environmentalists as landmark legislation. This act set in motion a series of policy actions and regulatory programs which, for the first time, controlled the disposal of hazardous wastes in the USA. Although RCRA designated the US Environmental Protection Agency (EPA) as the lead organization for implementing the waste disposal policy, most of the regulatory and operating responsibilities of the act fall to the state governments.

Viewed in the abstract, government oversights and control over private sector handling of toxic and hazardous materials is popular and necessary; but public support and adulation quickly fade when state governments begin to identify communities where hazardous waste disposal facilities can be located. The siting of hazardous waste disposal facilities has emerged as one of the most controversial environmental issues in the United States. Growing awareness of past environmentally abusive disposal practices has led to an organized public outcry against the proposed location of all types of waste handling facilities. Today, the 'not-in-my-backyard' (NIMBY) syndrome, as it has been termed, is undoubtedly the largest obstacle to the siting of new facilities.

Given current siting problems, one popular approach to minimize opposition to new facilities is to search for sites in rural communities, preferably in economically distressed or disadvantaged areas. This strategy posits overcoming community resistance, not by addressing and resolving siting issues or community concerns, but by offering attractive financial incentives to overlook them. The underlying assumption is that rural areas, especially disadvantaged communities with large numbers of poor and minority residents, are less able to mount effective political resistance. Moreover, these communities are more likely to succumb to the temptations of financial incentives. Recent history suggests that this strategy has worked. For example, a report prepared for the U.S. Congress found that hazardous waste facilities in the US tend to locate in jurisdictions with predominantly low income, black populations. (U.S. General Accounting Office, 1983, p. 1).

However, the events surrounding the State of North Carolina's attempt to find a host community for a regional hazardous waste disposal facility over the past 24 months, suggest a shifting in the relationship between the state and the rural community with respect to the disposal of hazardous materials. The docility and accommodation that urban based decision-makers had come to expect from rural communities did not exist. Initial opposition to the proposed facility grew into the most important environmental policy issues in North Carolina's history. In the course of events, scattered rural opposition grew into a statewide political force. A neo-populist political movement was born; and eventually, the state abandoned its proposal.

This chapter recounts the events surrounding North Carolina's experiences and examines the development of the rural opposition to the hazardous waste facility with emphasis on the populist elements which evolved. Those issues which dominated the policy making process are also presented. Finally, the wider implications of environmental neopopulism on rural restructuring in the USA are discussed.

Institutional Setting

The Resource Conservation and Recovery Act of 1976 (RCRA) requires each state government to develop a 'capacity assurance plan'. These plans spell out how and where non-nuclear hazardous materials will be disposed. The intent of this requirement is to insure that states which are the source of wastes, take responsibility for safely disposing of these wastes. Within RCRA there was an October, 1989 deadline. By this date, each state was required to provide for the management of its hazardous waste for the next 20 years. Although individual states could devise their own intra-state plans, the EPA strongly encouraged states to join with nearby jurisdictions to create multi-state regional hazardous waste disposal systems.

North Carolina businesses and industries annually generate 2.8 billion pounds of hazardous waste. Most of this waste is produced in the urbanized counties of the state. For example, the largest county, Mecklenburg, produces over half of North Carolina's hazardous waste materials. On-site treatment is the most widely practiced disposal option. However, 5 percent (176 million pounds) of the hazardous waste is shipped out-of-the state for disposal. The largest quantity goes to incinerator and landfilling operations in South Carolina (102 million pounds) and Alabama (7 million pounds).

North Carolina Hazardous Waste Treatment Commission

In 1984 facing pressures from the EPA to meet its RCRA obligations, the State established the North Carolina Hazardous Waste Treatment Commission (Treatment Commission). The assignment of the Treatment Commission was to identify and solicit 'volunteer' communities interested in hosting the location of intra-state hazardous waste disposal facilities. Beyond providing State assurances of plant safety and protection for the surrounding areas from pollution, the Treatment Commission offered the host community financial incentives from transfer payments and tax revenues. These bonuses were intended to mitigate any negative social externalities and insure the hazardous waste facility would be an economic asset.

Despite the enticements no local government agreed to host the facility. During the five years it existed, the Treatment Commission carried on discussions with government leaders in three jurisdictions, Edgecombe, Jones, and Hertford Counties all in the east of the state as shown in Figure. 10.1. All three of the potential counties fit the profile for likely hazardous waste host jurisdictions: rural; poor; and a majority black population. In each instance public opposition to hosting a hazardous waste facility forced local governments to withdraw from the dialog.

Senate Bill 324

Faced with increased Federal government pressure to develop hazardous waste treatment capacity, the North Carolina Legislature overwhelmingly passed Senate Bill 324 in May 1989. This bill completely changed the rules and conditions surrounding hazardous waste disposal policy in North Carolina. First, the Hazardous Waste Treatment Commission was not only renamed the North Carolina Hazardous Waste Management Commission (Waste Commission) but was also made quite different from its predecessor. It was, for example, empowered with broader and more significant powers, including the responsibility to develop criteria for selecting a site or sites for hazardous waste facilities and choosing suitable locations for hazardous waste management facilities. Second, the bill also allowed the Governor to authorize the establishment of essential hazardous waste facilities. The language and intent of Senate Bill 324 was thus clear, with the state options to overcome local government's reluctance to host a hazardous waste facility. Simultaneously, the State government was preempting local opposition by removing local government's traditional authority in land use and development decisions.

A third and equally important change contained in Senate Bill 324 was the scale of the hazardous waste disposal operations envisaged with the legislation requiring North Carolina to join a regional and inter-state hazardous waste disposal schemes. Following negotiations the State agreed to participate in a regional hazardous waste processing and disposal program with Alabama, Kentucky, South Carolina and Tennessee. Under the terms of the agreement, North Carolina agreed to build or permit a private operator to construct a 50,000 tons per year

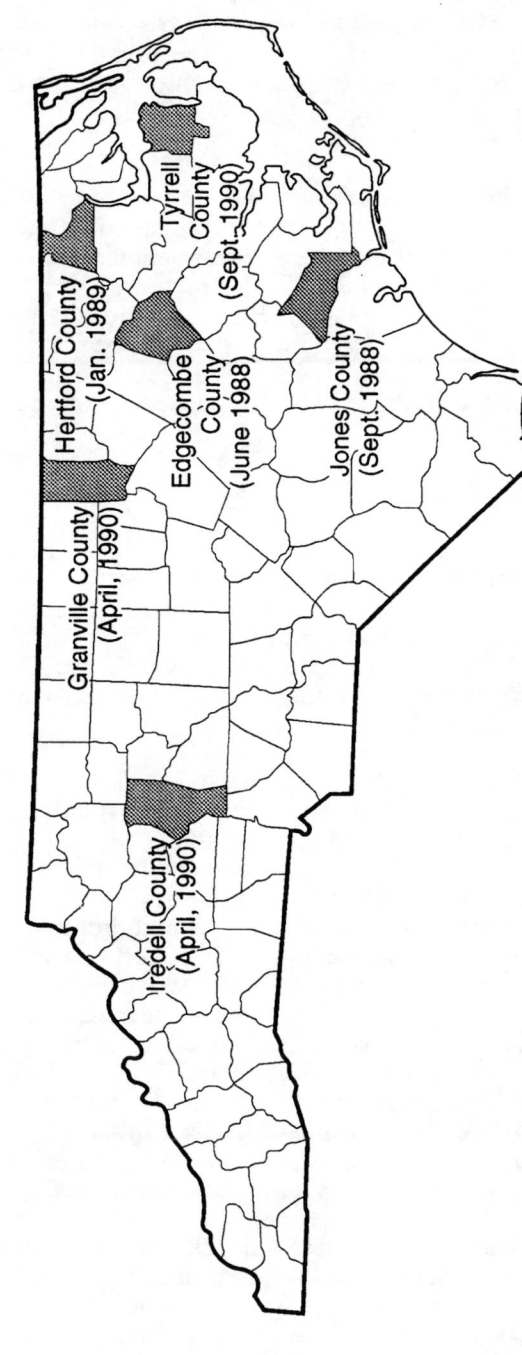

Figure 10.1 Counties Involved in the Hazardous Waste Disposal Facility Site Selection Process

hazardous waste incinerator; a 15,000 tons per year solvent distillation and recovery unit, and a 10,000 tons per year ash disposal facility, e.g. landfill. According to the agreement, these hazardous waste disposal facilities must be in operation by December 1991, or the State would be disqualified from the interstate program.

North Carolina's shift in locational decision-making was thus reasonable and in line with the policy approaches taken by other state governments since the efforts of the former Treatment Commission had not been producing the desired results. In this respect, North Carolina was not alone. By the late 1980's, NIMBY opposition had stymied hazardous waste disposal programs in many parts of the USA. Those states which were making the most significant progress toward RCRA capacity assurance goals were those adopting state preemptive decision frameworks.

Site Selection Process

The Waste Commission began its work with very little opposition. Critics were geographically scattered, most were ineffectual, and opposition was primarly limited to environmentalists. As the Waste Commission narrowed the list of eligible places to build the hazardous waste facilities, communities remaining as potential hosts however became increasingly uneasy.

The site location factors and criteria established by the Waste Commission generally followed accepted regulatory standards. The legislative guidelines required that hydrological and geological variables; environmental and public health factors; natural and cultural resources; local land uses; transportation resources; aesthetics; availability and reliability of public utilities; and availability of emergency response personnel and equipment be utilized as site selection criteria. Most locational criteria were based on scientifically derived standards, for example, potential sites could not be in the 100 year floodplain nor within the hurricane storm surge or inundation area. However, other standards were less objective. The Legislature prohibited the location of the facility within municipal boundaries except on existing industrially zoned land. This criteria combined with a 350 acre minimum parcel size standard established by the Waste Commission, effectively eliminated most urban areas from consideration as hazardous waste sites.

In late 1989, the Waste Commission began screening potential hazardous waste disposal facility sites. Initial public response to the presentation of site criteria and maps showing potential host communities, as measured by attendance at public hearings, was widespread indifference. Only 1035 people attended 12 public forums held by the Waste Commission throughout the state between November 1989 and March 1990. Clearly, at this juncture, the hazardous waste facility was still a minimal threat to most North Carolinians.

By April 26, 1990, the screening process had removed all but two percent of the state land area from siting consideration. In the course of the filtering process, the Waste Commission had eliminated all but 18 'potentially acceptable, high priority' sites from an original list containing 2851 eligible parcels as shown in Figure 10.2. Only two of these candidate sites were located in urban counties generating large amounts of hazardous materials. Four days later, the Waste Commission selected a 1,400 acre parcel in Iredell County and a 940 acre parcel in Granville County in the north and west part of the state as shown in Figure 10.1. At the same meeting, ThermaKEM Incorporated, a private waste disposal company was chosen to build and operate the facility.

Public Protest Expectations

These Waste Commission decisions created the expected public protest from citizens and property owners in Granville and Iredell Counties. Most observers expected the opposition to quickly subside. As in other states, concern about environment contamination is a secondary consideration to voters and politicians. There had never been a viable statewide environmental cause; green politics were not a part of the state lexicon.

What is more important to North Carolinians is economic growth. Industrial recruitment and job creation are powerful themes in the state and local political arena. When economics are weighed against environment, invariably the former is selected. The need to locate a hazardous waste facility somewhere in North Carolina was the message from the capitalist interests. In press releases and public relations efforts, these interests warned that without such a facility North Carolina factories would be closed, new businesses would avoid relocating in the state, and jobs would be lost. The decision of the Waste Commission was publicly endorsed by the State Republican Party, the North Carolina Citizens for Business and Industry, a pro-business lobbying group, the North Carolina Textile Manufact ring Association, the North Carolina Furniture Manufacturing Counci. the National Federation of Independent Business, and the North Carc na Chemical Industry Council.

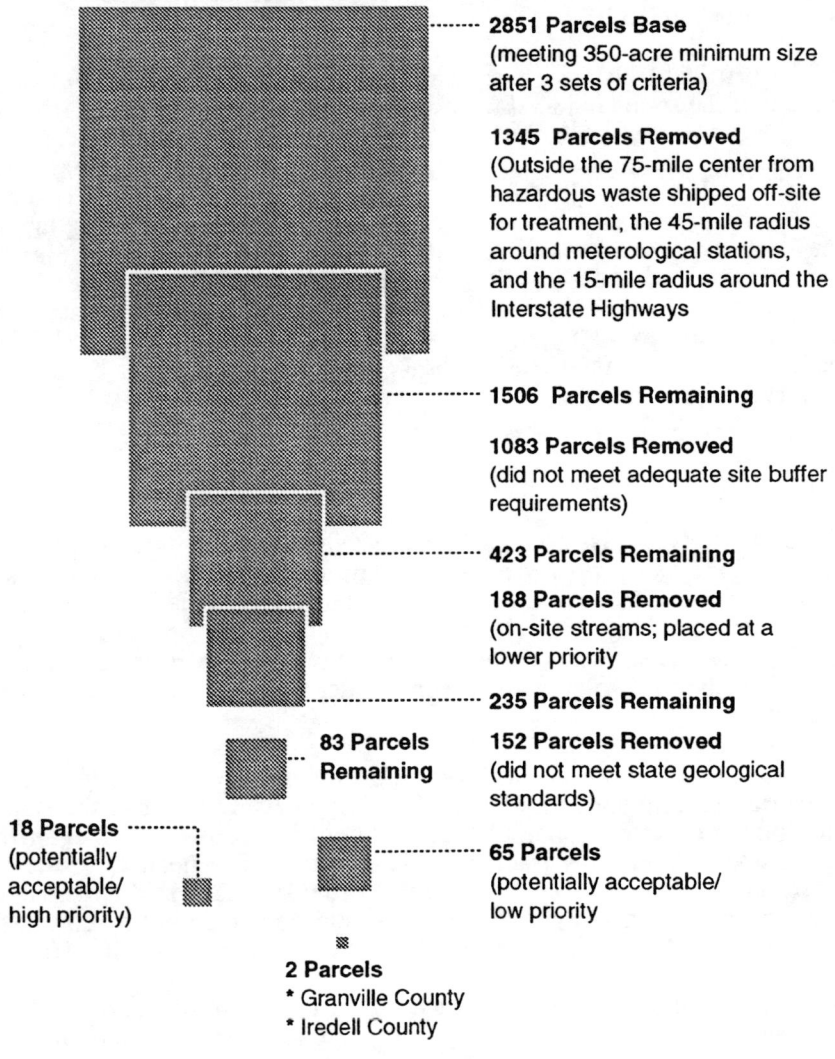

Figure 10.2 Screening Process for Selecting Hazadous Waste Sites

Additionally, the site selection process had the strategic effect of reducing potential active opposition by proposing two small rural areas. Neither Granville nor Iredell County had a reputation for political activism. Both were viewed as ideologically conservative. Granville County has 38,345 residents, with blacks comprising 39 percent of the population. The economy of the county is heavily agricultural. The estimated farm earnings in 1990 were $58,000,000. Tobacco is overwhelmingly the most important crop, generating $25,000,000 in farm income.

Iredell County has 82,931 residents. Blacks make up 16 percent of the population. The county ranks among the top agricultural counties in the state. Iredell farmers are the state's largest producers of eggs, milk, and beef cattle. Total agricultural production generated $85,000,000 in farm earnings in 1990.

The decision matrix created by the State, along with the social and economic milieu of North Carolina, weighed strongly for the quick siting of the hazardous waste facility. The conventional logic was that the concerns and protests of farmers and landowners in two small rural areas were clearly overshadowed by the greater economic good associated with this facility. However, the assumptions behind this premise were no longer viable.

Hazardous Waste Facility Under Attack

Over the next eight months, the Waste Commission's recommendations and the State's implementation efforts fell into disarray. Fundamental to the failure were two factors. First, the unwillingness of the public, especially the rural residents of Granville and Iredell Counties to acquiesce to the power of the State. Although faced with the enormous resources of the State and its allies, the opponents never conceded. By portraying their fight as a 'David versus Goliath' contest, they were able to use the State's larger resources to their advantage. A second factor was the lack of public confidence in the 'correctness' of the state's decision to participate in a regional hazardous waste program. Despite assurances by members of the Waste Commission and the State government that the waste incinerator was needed, many North Carolinians doubted the State's position.

Contributing to public doubts was the state government's poor record for punishing air and water pollution violators. Repeatedly, public discussions focused on whether the State would or could fulfill its pledge to protect the health of residents near the proposed hazardous waste facility. The selection of ThermaKEM to build and operate the hazardous waste facilities did not help the effort. The company had a weak environmental record at waste incineration plants in other states, including South Carolina.

Populist Roots

Although criticism of the hazardous waste facility eventually spread statewide, the opposition to the facility was focused in Granville and Iredell counties. In both communities, 'grass roots' citizen opposition groups quickly organized and remain in place today. While both are independent they have cooperated and coordinated their activities.

Newby's analysis of agrarian political movements provides a context and framework for these groups. As he notes, agrarian movements often reflect the protest of a colonial region against the economic or political dominance of a metropolitan region (Newby, 1978, p. 12). As the conflict surrounding the hazardous waste facility evolved, it increasingly emerged as a rural versus urban conflict. The view among opponents was that the State and supporting urban interests were sacrificing Granville and Iredell counties for their economic needs.

At the same time, the issue created a stronger social cohesion within the affected rural communities, serving to minimize conflict and social distance between local groups. Landowners and workers, old residents and newcomers, blacks and whites all worked together to stop the facilities.

An analysis of the opposition groups and their activities finds a marked similarity with an earlier protest movement, populism. Populism was a powerful American political and economic protest movement beginning around 1890. It was primarily agrarian, developing out of the Farmers Alliances and People's Parties. Geographically, populism was focused in the Southeastern and Western states.

The appeal of populism was primarily to rural folk, especially farmers, small capitalists, and workers. The ideological basis for the movement was premised on the notion that an elite had taken control of the monetary and political affairs of the State; the populist remedy was to restore the State back into the hands of the plain people. Like Marxists, populists questioned income distribution and economic privilege but their enmity was not focused upon class rather on a small clique of "big business" manipulators.

The populists approach to problem solving or policy making was for small, simpler solutions rather than complex policies. Their outlook gave preference to home based solutions as opposed to external approaches to problem solving. Populist ideology was tinged by isolationism.

In temperament, populism merged elements of religiosity with politics. Populist politicians and political meetings were lively and emotional. One commentator noted "(a) typical populist gathering resembled nothing so much as a camp meeting."

Neo-Populist Opposition

Many populist elements and characteristics were reincarnated in the Granville and Iredell hazardous waste facility opposition groups. These neo-populists, like their predecessors perceive their efforts as championing the interests on plain people fighting to restore the rights and privileges of citizens and local governments. Throughout the conflict the opposition groups portrayed the State as a corrupted entity under the control of big business especially out-of-state corporate interests.

Both opposition groups were rural based and evolved in a 'grass roots' fashion. Early leadership positions were occupied by farmers and small business persons. Women and blacks were active in decision-making. The Iredell group, for example, was initially organized by farmers, accountants, doctors, homemakers and a doctor. Although each group received technical support and advice from environmental groups, most notably Greenplace, control of the campaign against the hazardous waste plans remained with local leaders.

From the outset, a central theme of the hazardous waste opponents was that the waste disposal facilities represented a threat to agricultural resources and most importantly to the rural ethos. Although the public demonstrations and protest activities were geographically focused on the impact of the waste facilities on the Granville and Iredell sites and the externalities to the surrounding landscape, the waste incinerator evolved into a metaphor for more fundamental issues. It epitomized the growing tension between rural and urban fractions within North Carolina.

The public protest and demonstrations by hazardous waste facility opponents were large, colorful and emotionally charged. For example, an article in *The Charlotte Observer* reporting on a protest march in Salisbury noted:

> The parade...filled with waving children, chanting adults, wailing fire trucks and an assortment of floats... took 50 minutes to wind through the city. Some parade organizers estimated the crowd of marchers and spectators at 4,000 to 5,000. rowan County Sheriff Bob Martin said the 200-unit procession was a mile long... Farmers rode tractors. Their children rode on a flatbed truck carrying a large banner that read, "1,679,500 Breeder Chickens, Approximately 1,000 employees, 72,283 Turkey Production"... One float carried a likeness of Gov. Jim Martin with a noose around his neck (Williams, 1990b).

The linkage between the hazardous waste facility and the destruction of rural lifestyles were omnipresent in almost every action by the opponents. The images appearing in the media were small yeoman farmers protecting their land. Writing about a confrontation between state staff and protestors in Iredell, *The Charlotte Observer* reported:

> Escorted by a convoy of N.C. Highway Patrol troopers -- along with a crowd-control dog -- a handful of engineers and geologists traveled the winding back roads to meet people who own the land that the state wants to test. They wanted permission to get on the property for preliminary studies.
>
> Each time, they were turned away. Protestors blocked driveways, sang "America the Beautiful" and chanted "Not here, not there, not anywhere!"...Mike Bennett gathered fellow protestors at the rusted chain stretching across the driveway... He turned to the pack of state troopers. "We're just out here protecting our farms and our families." (Williams, 1990e)

As publicity about the Granville and Iredell County protests and legal actions increased over the Summer months, statewide agricultural and rural interest groups joined the opposition. In July, North Carolina Secretary of Agriculture, James Graham, a conservative politician, denounced the proposed hazardous waste facility at a public hearing. Graham labeled the incinerator an attack on North Carolina agriculture. Following this action, the Department of Agriculture began openly cooperating with the incinerator opponents. By Fall all major farm organizations publicly supported the Iredell and Granville groups.

In the face of increasing public sympathy for incinerator opponents, the state's two largest and most influential newspapers, *The Charlotte*

Observer and *The* (Raleigh) *News and Observer* moved to marshall public support for the hazardous waste facility. Beginning in the summer, the editorial writers of both newspapers questioned the responsibility and validity of waste facility critics. In one instance, Jerry Shinn, Associate Editor of *The Charlotte Observer*, wrote a commentary warning that a small group of Iredell County farmers were putting their own self interests ahead of the economic fortunes of the State. On another occasion, after an unusually boisterous protest march in Granville County, *The News and Observer* scolded the demonstrators for their attacks on Governor Martin and went on to warn:

> The protestors have no serious solution to the hazardous waste problem, of course. They ignore the reality of the need to deal with it, and reject Mr. Martin's reasonable assertion that North Carolina cannot continue to produce hazardous waste and ship it to other states... He is trying to do the right thing (Editorial Staff, 1990a).

Support for the hazardous waste facility by the Charlotte and Raleigh newspapers was symbolic of a rural-urban schism on the issue. Both papers represented the interests of urban oriented capitalists. Neither paper seriously considered the opponent's claims that the site selection process was biased toward a rural location decision nor that the rural community would be destroyed. In one particularly inflammatory incident, *The Charlotte Observer* editorial cartoon portrayed incinerator critics as hypocritical rural buffoons as shown in Figure 10.3. In the minds of many opponents, this reaffirmed *The Observer's* urban biases in favor of the incinerator.

Policy Collapse

Under its original schedule the Management Commission was scheduled to make a final decision on either the Granville or Iredell sites at a July 1, 1990 meeting. Because of public protests and the resulting political considerations the decision was postponed. The delay proved costly.

During the next five months, the neo-populist opponents of the plan garnered a growing share of public support. Public marches, news conferences, and even a free videotape "public information" program kept the campaign highly visible. In the Fall legislative election, campaign candidates throughout North Carolina were forced to take public positions on whether to proceed with the hazardous waste facilities.

Figure 10.3 Reproduced with Permission of Kevin Siers, *The Charlotte Observer*

Simultaneously, the State and the Waste Management Commission were losing public support and confidence. A committee of the Natural Resource Council (1989) warned that one of the most serious problems facing public officials in these situations is establishing credibility. The public tends to 'judge the messenger as well as the message' (p. 119). Public perceptions of deceit, misrepresentation, coercion, the self-serving framing of information, and actual or perceived professional incompetence or impropriety are important influences on the way information is evaluated.

At times it seemed that the State was totally oblivious to the problems of risk related communication. On many occasions the Commission changed its rules and procedural guidelines in order to avoid controversy or speed along the site selection process. In July, for example, the Commission dropped the requirement that the waste facility have direct access to a four laned road when it opened. At the same meeting it changed "public hearing notification" rules; effectively allowing the Commission to move locations and reschedule public hearings on short notice. Governor James Martin, also proved to be a damaging ally when he was quoted at a press conference saying the hazardous waste facility was safe, but that he would not like to live next door to one. The action and comments of the State tended to confirm the charges of critics that the locational decision-making process was flawed. The activities of the Waste Management Commission and Governor were easy targets for the neo-populist ideology of their critics.

The integrity of the locational process was seriously tainted in September when a local government official in Tyrrell County expressed an interest in hosting the hazardous waste facility. A small, economically disadvantaged jurisdiction, located in coastal North Carolina, as shown in Figure 10.1, Tyrrell was interested in the jobs, tax revenues, and added incentives. These included a state funded four-laned road and 'possibly a doctor.' The Waste Management Commission was embarrassed when it was pointed out that the County did not qualify to host the hazardous waste facilities under the State guidelines. Nevertheless, the Governor and Waste Commission were prepared to select Tyrrell as the host county. Local public protest quickly ended Tyrrell's interest in the project. According to the County magistrate, 'Nobody else in the United States wants it. So now it's Let's give it to Tyrrell County. They can keep their junk in Raleigh and Mecklenburg County. Don't bring it here' (Riley 1990b).

Defeat of the Plan

On December 13, the North Carolina Council of State, composed of the Governor, Lt. Governor, and the eight State Commissioners, voted to block construction of the hazardous waste facility. Two months later, North Carolina was removed from the regional hazardous waste agreement. The grueling ordeal for State officials and citizen opponents was over.

Although the vote ended the saga of siting a regional hazardous waste facility in North Carolina, the events of 1990 have had a profound impact on citizen-State relationships. In the future it is highly unlikely that legislators or state policy-makers will take for granted the acquiescence of citizens in matters of environment, health, and property rights. This is particularly true in instances where there is a public perception of significant risk or where potential impacts are widespread. The State's traditional top-down decision-making model is under challenge by a changing political and social climate, including neo-populism. The State is also on notice that inadequate or incompetent government responses are no longer acceptable excuses to citizens. In the past, policy failures were simply explained away as human error or resource inadequacies. In the future, citizen activism is likely to force the State to be more accountable for its actions.

Finally, the events around the hazardous waste facility site selection process have provided a new sense of empowerment to rural North Carolinians. While rural communities may be disadvantaged in comparison to urban areas, they need not sacrifice their human and natural resources in order to compete economically. Nor is it necessary for rural communities to accept urban areas castoffs for the good of the larger state. These lessons seem to have spread. In the short period since the hazardous waste facility vote, several other rural North Carolina communities have exhibited a growing assertiveness in dealing with urban oriented economic interests.

A Concluding Observation

The events and neo-populism framework presented in this paper refer to the North Carolina experience. However, evidence from other states indicate that North Carolina is not an anomaly. Throughout the USA rural areas are undergoing similar transformation. In particular, communities are becoming sensitive to the impacts of environmentally disruptive and destructive economic activities on local conditions. Currently, rural protests and political activism against State dominance, such as in North Carolina, are scattered and episodic; however, they are a harbinger for larger scale restructuring during the remainder of this decade.

References

Associated Press (1990a), 'Granville Incinerator Vote Near, But Foes Fight To The Last', *The Charlotte Observer*, December 9, p. 5B.

Associated Press, (1990b), 'Tests for Incinerator Halted', *The Charlotte Observer*, October 12, p. 2B.

Associated Press (1990c), 'Waste: It's Business As Usual, Site Selection Process Won't Wait for Courts to Decide Lawsuits', *The Charlotte Observer*, August 12, p. 9B.

Barrett, R. (1990a), 'Granville Site is One of Two on Incinerator List', *The News and Observer*, May 2, 1A.

Barrett, R. (1990b), 'State Had Dropped Tyrrell as Potential Site', *The News and Observer*, Sept. 14, p. 11A.

Boyce, F.A. (1990), 'Officials Don't Alter Waste Plans Much, Despite Criticism', *The Charlotte Observer*, July 31, p. 5D.

Committee on Risk Perception and Communication, Natural Research Council (1989), *Improving Risk Communication*, National Academy Press, Washington, D.C.

Cutter, S.L. and Solecki, W.D. (1989), 'The Pattern of Airbirone Toxic Releases in the United States', *Professional Geographer*, vol. 41, pp. 149-161.

Davis, C.E. and Lester, J.P. (1989), 'Federalism and Environmental Policy', in J.P. Lester (ed.), *Environmental Politics and Policy, Theories and Evidence*, Duke University Press, Durham, pp. 55-74.

Dresher, J. (1990), 'Rulings Don't Faze N.C.: It May Skip Waste-Site Testing', *The Charlotte Observer*, July 12, p. 5D.

Editorial Staff (1990a), 'An Ugly Form of Protest', *The News and Observer*, October 23, p. 12A.

Editorial Staff (1990b), 'But It Has To Go Somewhere', *The Charlotte Observer*, July 8, p. 2D.

Editorial Staff (1990c), 'Council Flunks Test', *The News and Observer*, December 16, p. 6J.

Editorial Staff (1990d), 'N.C. Running Out of Options', *The Charlotte Observer*, December 16, p. 5D.

Granville County Agricultural Extension Service (1990), *Farm Income Estimates, Final Report,* Agricultural Extension Service, Oxford, North Carolina.

Hazardous Waste Management Commission (1990a), 'Hazardous Waste in N.C.', in *An Introduction to Hazardous Waste Management in North Carolina*, State of North Carolina, Raleigh.

Hazardous Waste Management Commission (1990b), *Q & A...About Hazardous Waste*, State of North Carolina, Raleigh.

Hazardous Waste Management Commission (1990c), *Summary, Site Selection Process of the Hazardous Waste Management Commission*, State of North Carolina, Raleigh.

Hazardous Waste Management Commission (1990d), *Temporary Rules of the North Carolina Hazardous Waste Management Commission*, State of North Carolina, Raleigh.

Hazardous Waste Management commission (1990e), 'What is the HWMC?', in *An Introduction to Hazardous Waste Management in North Carolina*, State of North Carolina, Raleigh.

Henderson, B. (1990), 'Support Is Sought for Incinerator Site', *The Charlotte Observer*, August 25, p. 2C.

Horan, J. (1990a), 'Commission Under Gun to Beat Incinerator Deadline', *The Charlotte Observer*, October 11, p. 6B.

Horan, J. (1990b), 'Council of State Blocks Incinerator', *The Charlotte Observer*, December 14, p. 1A.

Horan, J. (1990c), 'Counties Chosen In Closed Session As Possible Chemical-Waste Sites', *The Charlotte Observer*, May 2, p. 1C.

Horan, J. (1991), 'N.C. Back at Square One', *The Charlotte Observer*, February 3, p. 2B.

Iredell County Agricultural Extension Service (1990), *Farm Income Estimates, Final Report*, Agricultural Extension Service, Statesville, North Carolina.

LaClau, E. (1977), *Politics and Ideology in Marxist Theory*, Humanities Press, London.

Legislative Commission on Toxic Substances and Hazardous Waste (1987), *Hazardous Waste Facility Siting a National Survey*, New York State Legislature, Albany.

McKenna, G. (1974), *American Populism*, G.P. Putnam & Sons, New York.

Minter, J. (1990), 'Exuberant Marchers Protest Incinerator in Salisbury Trek', *The Charlotte Observer*, July 15, p. 3D.

Newby, H. (1978), 'The Rural Sociology of Advanced Capitalist Societies', in H. Newby (ed.), *International Perspectives in Rural Sociology*, John Wiley & Sons, New York, pp. 3-30.

Nugent, W.T.K. (1963), *The Tolerant Populists, Kansas Populism and Nativism*, University of Chicago Press, Chicago.

Oppel, R. (1990), 'Incinerator Must Go Somewhere', *The Charlotte Observer*, July 21, p. 2C.

Patterson D. (1990), 'Resignations Urged', *The Charlotte Observer*, September 6, p. 6C.

Pomatu, G. (1986), 'A Common Heritage: The Historical Memory of Populism in Europe and The United States', in H. Boyte and F. Riessman (eds.), *The New Populism, The Politics of Empowerment*, Temple University Press, Philadelphia, pp. 30-40.

Riley, S. (1990a), 'Hazardous-waste site incentives tempt officials in Tyrrell', *The News and Observer*, Sept. 14, p. 1A.

Riley, S. (1990b), 'Waste proposal not winning converts in Tyrrell', *The News and Observer*, September 15, p. 1B.

State of North Carolina (1989), North Carolina *Administrative Code, Chapter 18 N.C. Hazardous Waste Management Commission*, State of North Carolina, Raleigh.

United States General Accounting Office (1983), *Siting of Hazardous Waste Landfills and Their Correlation with Racial and Economic Status of Surrounding Communities*, U.S. General Accounting Office, Washington, D.C.

United States General Accounting Office (1987), *Hazardous Waste Uncertainties of Existing Data*, U.S. General Accounting Office, Washington, D.C.

Williams, P. (1990a), 'Chemical-Waste Plant Isn't Farmer's Idea of Bumper Crop', *The Charlotte Observer*, June 27, p. 1B.

Williams, P. (1990b), '1,400 Protest Potential Iredell-Rowan Waste Site', *The Charlotte Observer*, May 8, p. 2D.

Williams, P. (1990c), 'Iredell, Rowan Sue N.C. Commission Over Choice of Hazardous Waste Site', *The Charlotte Observer*, May 9, p. 5B.

Williams, P. (1990d), 'Judge Says Waste Official May Have Conflict of Interest', *The Charlotte Observer*, July 12, p. 5D.

Williams, P. (1990e), 'Protesters Block Land, Win Waste Site Round', *The Charlotte Observer*, June 26, p. 1A.

Williams, P. (1990f), 'Waste Officials OK Rules That Could Hinder Opponents', *The Charlotte Observer*, July 24, p. 2B.

Williams, P. (1990g), 'Waste Protest Is a Portrait of Grass Roots', *The Charlotte Observer*, July 24, p. 1A.

York, J. (1990), 'Waste Site Opponents Keep Fast Company In Racing's Earnhardt', *The Charlotte Observer*, August 17, p. 1B.

11 Nitrates in water: The politics of pollution regulation

SUSANNE SEYMOUR AND GRAHAM COX

Agriculture and Environmental Regulation

Farming practices pose some of the more acute practical and conceptual challenges for social scientists and policy makers concerned with environmental regulation. This is in part because of the progressively more intrusive impact which highly intensive methods of production make upon the environment. Additionally, the extensive and fragmented nature of the industry means that prevailing regulatory models, formulated to tackle problems of a different nature in other non-agricultural sectors, can often have only a limited application (Lowe, 1988).

The intrinsic character of agriculture, therefore, calls into question one of the key principles embodied in prevailing models of regulation, namely a presumption in favour of treating pollution and damage to the environment as unwanted externalities of the production system. But the distinction between the internalities and externalities of production, which is, in any case, often only a convenient fiction, ceases to be in any way appropriate in relation to agriculture as soon as environmental concerns are accorded a serious status.

For example, as an extensive land use, the activities associated with agriculture produce not only marketable goods but also, at one and the same time, distinct rural environments. Indeed, rural environments, as aspects of processes of production, are in a perpetual state of creation and re-creation. Agricultural goods and the rural environment must thus be seen - to use the term favoured by economists - as in a relationship of 'joint supply'. But even this term, with its implied notion of separateness is redolent of the language of internalities and externalities whose appropriateness must be questioned (Lowe et al., 1990).

Such thinking is, of course, central to the approach adopted in *Blueprint for a green economy* (Pearce et al., 1989) which has recently been so dramatically propelled to the forefront of Government thinking on environmental matters in Britain. The view advanced by Pearce and his colleagues is that policy should be based on a process of identifying what consumers would be prepared to pay to enjoy environmental 'goods', and accept by way of compensation for environmental 'bads'. They argue that environmentally sensitive policies - both present and across generations - are best pursued by generating appropriate market signals based on the prices so ascribed. The case is, at first sight, a persuasive one: not least because the ambition to assess and monetize degrees of concern is accompanied by the presumption that the effort - and it must, inevitably, be a very considerable one - can deliver the sort of precision that policy makers value.

Although an effective means of communicating information, markets can only provide knowledge which is readily available. Not surprisingly, therefore, environmental problems are often the consequence not specifically of market failure but of a lack of understanding of the implications of an economic decision at the time it was taken. Nitrate pollution is a case in point where assigning responsibility for the damaging consequences of past and present actions is notoriously difficult. In such circumstances the techniques of cost-benefit analysis provide no way, in themselves, of generating an acceptable definition of the public interest: although any assessment must, whether implicitly or explicitly, embody such a concept. Indeed, it is important to recognise the characteristic limitations of that discourse. Crucially, it consistently occludes the political nature of decisions being taken and purports to offer technicist solutions to problems framed precisely so as to be amenable to its procedures. Debate tends, therefore, to be concerned predominantly with matters of regulatory technique rather than the broader objectives of policy.

In treating questions which are of a fundamentally ethical nature, involving, for example, distributional issues and questions of intergenerational equity, processes are involved which are essentially socio-political (Bowers, 1990). To suppose that such decisions can be resolved through translation into some species of economic calculus is bound to be something of a pretence which blurs a key distinction. For as Sagoff (1988) has noted, this confuses preference with ethical judgement since the soundness of ethical judgement is not equivalent to willingness to pay, however relevant economic information might be to the making of a good argument. It is precisely the argument of the proponents of such methods, of course, that it is only willingness to pay which counts, since it is only what we are willing to pay for that we will actually do. The case is forcefully presented and, as such, demands a critical response which goes beyond the technical confines of neo-classical economics.

Environmental goals, Sagoff argues, do not necessarily stem from self interest, from our willingness as consumers to pay in markets. They are related rather to our sense of who we are and our preparedness to act on our beliefs so that they may find their way, as public values, into legislation. Environmental goals presuppose shared values which have to be argued on their merits and that essentially political process is very different from the exercise of hypothetically pricing our interests at the margin.

Private and public preferences must be seen as conceptually distinct. Public 'preferences' express what most people believe is best for the community as a whole rather than their own wants or desires. Thus, in arguing for or against a public policy they seek creatively to develop and change the views of others rather than merely register already existing views. That process is necessarily public whereas 'The genius of cost benefit analysis is to localize conflict among affected individuals and thereby to prevent it from breaking out into the public realm' (Sagoff, 1988, p. 97).

Apart from problems of applying externality arguments to agriculture, prevailing models of regulation which assert that the regulatory effort should seek to internalise the true social costs of production are typically also subverted by the present treatment of agriculture. Policy processes in agriculture have tended to overturn this 'polluter pays' principle and there are particular reasons for expecting it to be a policy sphere in which political processes will continue to dominate (OECD, 1989).

In particular, governments have begun to recognise that the production of marketable goods simultaneously recreates the rural environment. Accordingly, measures have been introduced which combine efforts both to constrain production and generate certain conservation benefits. But we are, nevertheless, some way from achieving an integrated approach to production and environmental regulation in agriculture and the progress that has been made has involved paying farmers not to pollute or otherwise harm the environment. The character of these policies has stemmed in large part from the particular view that has been taken of property rights (Bowers, 1988, p. 166) and there are strong reasons for supposing that such considerations will continue to prevail whatever the formal acknowledgement given to the 'Polluter Pays Principle' (PPP) (Cox, Lowe and Winter, 1988a), and despite recent EC and OECD assertions that agricultural activity should in no way be seen as exempt from this principle.

The PPP is also a principle whose grounds of application are always likely to be both 'local' and keenly questioned. In relation to nitrate pollution, there are several other reasons for also supposing that the prospects for its effective implementation in Britain are limited. What little evidence there is suggests that formal regulation of increasing farm pollution raises a range of particularly intractable administrative, compliance and enforcement difficulties (Lowe, *et al.*, 1990 and Hawkins, 1984). More than any other, perhaps, the issue of diffuse nitrate pollution exemplifies these difficulties and shows why efforts to resolve them are so contested. The newly established National Rivers Authority (NRA), for example, does not yet appear to have a regulatory strategy to deal with diffuse farm pollution on a day-to-day basis.

We are, however, in a period characterised by the effective suspension of many hitherto distinctive features of the British system of policy-making for environmental regulation: new precedents are being set. Under diverse pressures, including those from the environmental lobby and the European Community, and under the impact of privatization, a profound shift in the style of British regulation is occurring (Haigh 1989; Lowe and Flynn, 1989). It involves a move from a largely informal and decentralised approach to an increasingly formal, legalistic and centralised one. The transition is having a profound effect in the agricultural sector, not least because here the style of regulation has traditionally been informal and decentralised and, in many respects, largely voluntary. Whereas in 1983, David Vogel, in seeking to draw contrasts between Britain and the United States, was able to point to British experience as demonstrating that it is 'possible for a pluralist democracy to regulate business reasonably well without making the regulatory process into an ideological, political and legal battleground' (Vogel, 1983, p. 90), the situation has now changed. In 1987, the House of Commons Select Committee on the Environment, for example, called for a 'far more interventionist and regulatory approach to farm pollution'. The issue of agriculture and nitrate pollution is already undermining Vogel's assessment.

It is not hard to understand why. Pointing to the relationship between regulation and political culture, Vogel accounted for the differences between Britain and the United States in terms of the former's highly respected civil service, its business community disposed to place a high value on acting 'responsibly' and a public not unduly suspicious of business-government co-operation. As far as relations between the state and agriculture are concerned, however, those conditions no longer obtain. There is now a deep scepticism about the ability of the Ministry of Agriculture, Fisheries and Food (MAFF) to have sufficient regard to the interests of consumers. Indeed, in the wake of a decade of relentless criticism of the farming industry for its profligate demands upon public resources, the deleterious impact of its activities on the countryside and the disturbing implications of its practices for food safety, the accumulation of anomalies has precipitated a crisis situation in which policy making is more than usually fraught.

Competing Understandings of Nitrate 'Pollution'

Nitrate 'pollution' of drinking water in Britain is presently formally defined in the terms set by the European Community as any level of concentration over 50mg per litre. The Drinking Water Directive, agreed by all member states in 1980 and brought into force in 1985, provided the definition of nitrate pollution but, above all, it was lobbying by the environmental group, Friends of the Earth (FoE), along with the privatization of water, which transformed nitrates in water into an issue with a high and sustained political profile.

Prior to the Directive, UK water suppliers worked to an upper limit of 100mg of nitrate per litre of water for the general population, in line with the 1970 World Health Organization (WHO) recommendations and the expert opinion of government medical advisors. This was, however, very much an advisory level and water containing higher nitrate concentrations was not specifically labelled as 'polluted'. The effective halving of the limit has meant that drinking water supplies which would have been defined in 1979 as 'safe' were, by 1985, having to be redefined as 'polluted'. Nonetheless, this change must itself be set in the context of varying WHO limits throughout the 1960s and 1970s when the upper limit for nitrate ranged from 45 to 100mg per litre. Whilst these fluctuations occurred in the assessment of safe levels of nitrate in water, actual concentrations were rising in the UK water supply, particularly in aquifers. As early as 1974 some sources exceeded 50mg per litre of nitrate and a number of boreholes were taken out of use (Hill, et al., 1989, p. 232).

Despite having agreed to the stricter limits in 1980 and having acquiesced in their implementation, the UK Government has contested the validity of the level. Indeed, in 1987 the House of Commons Select Committee on the Environment suggested that the Department of the Environment ask the EC for a re-examination of the nitrate pollution level. This scepticism is shared by a powerful set of interests. The Government's Chief Medical Officer was joined by farmers, the fertilizer manufacturers and representatives of water industry in regarding the Drinking Water Directive as embodying an essentially arbitrary level. These groups see no risk to the population from either infant methaemoglobinaemia (blue baby syndrome) or stomach cancer at levels of nitrate up to 100mg per litre in drinking water. They do, however, advise that infants under one year should not consume water containing more than 50mg of nitrate per litre.

These groups are notable for describing the issue in ways which characterise supporters of the 50mg per litre limit as irrational, and they seek, in particular, to question the scientific status of the arguments they advance. Thus, in 1986, ICI complained that 'no scientific basis' had been given for the halving of the limit and they emphasised, moreover, that 'no reference was made to new medical advice' (ICI, 1986, p. 3). The Fertiliser Manufacturers Association (FMA), meanwhile, went even further in evidence presented to the Association of Agriculture (1988). In a letter dated 17 June 1988, it pointed out that:

> "Whether the levels presently experienced in this country form 'pollution' is a matter of controversy . . . there are grave doubts whether the law is based on a sensible evaluation of the risks associated with such low levels of nitrate in water."

Outlining the National Farmers' Union (NFU) viewpoint, the then Deputy President C. David Naish similarly stated late in 1987 that he believed 'the EC limit of 50mg is too low for UK conditions . . .

It was set arbitrarily and without any scientific base . . . Research simply does not support the *fear* that high-nitrate water may be linked with stomach cancer.' (NFU, 1987, p. 4 (our italics)) Whilst acknowledging the nitrate issue, the NFU feel that 'it is greatly exaggerated' by what they choose, somewhat disparagingly, to refer to as 'the European standards-setting exercise'. It is an exercise which they believe has set 'over-rigorous standards which cannot be justified under UK conditions'. The Regional Water Authorities (RWAs) also saw no need to abandon the 100mg per litre standard in favour of what they regarded essentially as a 'scientifically unsound' level. As David Baldock reports, the water authorities held the 50mg per litre standard to be 'the product of a Community decision making process lamentably vulnerable to emotive and ill-informed influences', and they expressed considerable embarrassment that the Department of the Environment (DoE) had agreed to it (Baldock, 1988, p. 24). A leading water authority spokesman on the nitrate issue, Dr Brian Croll from the Anglian region (along with Severn Trent the area most severely affected by the nitrate issue), in an interview in *The Surveyor* in 1987, rejected claims that health is threatened by nitrate concentrations of between 50 and 100mg per litre, and accused the environmental group, FoE, of 'making too much fuss' about the EC level, adherence to which would be an extremely costly undertaking for the water suppliers (22 October). It is worth noting, perhaps, that the arguments advanced by these interests are more than somewhat disingenuous given that in many areas there was considerable difficulty in meeting the previous less stringent standards.

Environmental groups, the most prominent of which has been FoE, have been alone in consistently supporting the 50mg limit. They stress, in particular, that it is sensible to err on the side of caution in the light of what they consider inconclusive and scant evidence relating both to stomach cancer and the debilitating effects of sub-clinical blue-baby syndrome. They also emphasise the detrimental ecological impact of rising nitrate levels. In taking such a view they are strongly supported by the government's own statutory conservation agency, the Nature Conservancy Council (NCC). In a letter dated 10 September 1988, an NCC official expressed the opinion that even the current EC nitrate level is 'too high for the well-being of wildlife' (Association of Agriculture, 1988).

Explanations of Nitrate Pollution and Identification of 'Polluters'

Just as interested parties question the level of concentration at which nitrate is defined as 'polluting', so too do they demonstrate a striking lack of consensus in the matter of identifying the causes of rising nitrate levels in water. Such discrepant explanations are, of course, more easily sustained in a context characterised by an historical dearth of government resources for research into the problems of nitrate leaching. This contrasts markedly with the well-funded nature of research into nitrate nutrition. The research gap has certainly exacerbated what would, in any case, have been a highly contentious issue. It is, then, a relatively easy matter for the agro-chemicals industry, farmers, the water industry and the Government to lend their weight to one set of causal factors whilst environmental groups typically favour others. There is no compelling weight of evidence which can be cited in any attempt to foreclose debate. The situation is, in Kuhnian terms, one of rather obvious paradigm conflict with competing parties mobilising contrasting resources in pursuit of their more general ends.

The debate over the main causes of nitrate pollution is, of course, integrally linked to the identification of 'nitrate polluters' and most of the groups involved in the nitrate debate have an interest in espousing 'cause of leaching' explanations which play down their responsibility as 'polluters'. It is in the identification of responsibilities and solutions that the alliance between government, the fertilizer manufacturers, the farming lobby and the water industry tends to fragment. We will first of all outline the scientific debate and then go on to explore its influence amongst the wider set of interests.

The scientific debate

Government agricultural scientists Scientists from the government's Agriculture and Food Research Council (AFRC) experimental stations have been particularly influential in establishing the scientific parameters of the nitrate debate. At the forefront has been the AFRC Institute of Arable Crops Research at Rothamsted; indeed, in an exclusionary gambit familiar in scientific controversies, Tom Addiscott, one of the chief researchers involved, has claimed a monopoly of scientific credibility in relation to the issue. In response to the Association of Agriculture debate he welcomed the 'opportunity of putting forward the scientific side of a very complex problem', and dismissed most of the 'opinions' expressed which he felt 'seem to have been based more on emotion than fact and have tended to greatly over-simplify the issue' (Association of Agriculture, 1988).

In particular, Rothamsted has pursued and publicized research which denies that inorganic fertilizer applications contribute anything but the most insignificant amounts to nitrate leaching and indictes organic farming as far more polluting than conventional practice. Findings of experiments undertaken at Rothamsted from 1980-1984 emphasise that on average 'only 1.3%' of the inorganic fertilizer applied in spring was in the soil in the following autumn in a form susceptible to leaching (Macdonald *et al*, 1989, p. 407). This claim that such a low level of leaching is the appropriate one is, however, highly selective since it fails to report direct spring leaching. Neither does it refer to the cumulative effects of the introduction of increasing supplies of nitrogen from outside the system. Nevertheless, the Rothamsted view emanates from an institution which enjoys impeccable scientific credentials in the world of agricultural research.

These scientists have also placed a great deal of emphasis upon manure as more highly polluting than inorganic nitrogen and stress a number of reasons why this is so. They argue that it is less uniform in nitrate content, giving less accuracy in application and, in the case of farmyard manure, it is often applied in autumn when leaching rates are highest and plant uptake of nutrients lowest. Researchers at Rothamsted claim that 'during autumn the plots given farmyard manure can contain 100kg/ha **more** nitrate-nitrogen that is vulnerable to washing out than those given chemical fertiliser', and have concluded that 'the organic plots therefore constitute the greater risk' (Rothamsted, 1988, pp. 2-3). Representatives of the organic farming movement, however, have complained that on a well-run farm manures would never be applied at high rates to bare, arable land as in the Rothamsted experiment (Dudley, 1990, p. 90).

The ploughing of permanent pastures and grass leys has also been labelled a major polluting activity by agricultural scientists. Indeed, organic farming has been condemned for incorporating such stategies, together with the growing of nitrogen-fixing legumes. However, here there is conflicting evidence from within the agricultural research community itself. Experiments at another government research station at North Wyke have revealed that although leaching losses rise to a peak of 100-150kg when the ley course of the organic rotation is ploughed, this is followed by very low leaching levels, down to 5kg/ha, in the remaining years. The conclusion drawn by Nigel Dudley, formerly of the Soil Association which represents Britain's organic movement, is that 'annual average leaching losses of as low as 20kg/ha are achievable in a correctly-managed organic system' (Dudley, 1990, pp. 89-90).

Water industry scientists Scientists from the Water Research Centre (WRc) have produced a nitrate leaching model which, in contrast to the Rothamsted research, assumes a linear relationship between the use of inorganic fertilizers and nitrate leaching. For some time this caused conflict between the two groups of scientists. Now, however, a leading water industry expert on nitrates, Dr Andrew Skinner (of Severn Trent NRA), concedes that the water industry has been guilty of shorthand in the past by stating that fertilizers were causing the nitrate problem. The confusion appears to be a product of both lack of information and communication. Firstly, the WRc model is essentially a geological leaching model, and whilst research carried out by the WRc and the British Geological Survey (BGS) suggests that linear modelling of nitrate movement through geological structures is reasonably accurate (BGS, 1986), the same could not be claimed for the movement of nitrate through the soil. In fact, the WRc and Rothamsted have concentrated on separate elements of nitrate leaching. The water industry has modelled nitrate movement in geological strata while the agricultural scientists have been responsible for modelling nitrate leaching in the soil. Thus, the water scientists have been reliant upon their agricultural colleagues at Rothamsted for soil nitrate leaching information to feed into their geological model. Nevertheless, because of a dearth of basic data on soil nitrate leaching and poor co-ordination between hydro-geological and agricultural research it would appear that the soil leaching data fed into the WRc's model has, in the past, been oversimplified. All these factors have contributed to a WRc model which has been criticized because it draws an unwarranted direct correlation between inorganic nitrate use and nitrate leaching. However, despite this simplification identified in the WRc model, the impetus to establish the first study to investigate in practice the protection of groundwater supplies from nitrates came from the water industry and Dr Skinner. The resulting *Hatton study* provided the model for the Government's own feasibility assessment of treatment and protection measures (Department of the Environment *et al.*, 1988 and DoE, 1988).

Intensive farming Where conventional agricultural scientists and their colleagues in the water industry come to some sort of consensus, albeit more loudly voiced by the latter, is that nitrate leaching is exacerbated by intensive agricultural practices. While agricultural scientists accept the role played by intensive agricultural practices in nitrate leaching, they emphasise the benefits of intensification. The water industry, on the other hand, is rather less inclined to defend intensive agriculture and has condemned its detrimental impact on water quality.

While the range of evidence presented by scientists suggests it is probable that only a small proportion of inorganic nitrogen directly leaches from the soil (much less than the 50% suggested by FoE), there is evidence that it is the *indirect* effects of inorganic fertilizer application which have led to nitrate pollution problems. Such causal relationships defy straightforward presentation. Inorganic fertilizer application constitutes an additional input of nitrogen from outside the system, and the increased production this has allowed has resulted in a greater volume of crop residues, which are vulnerable to breakdown and leaching, being left in the soil after harvest. In addition, with the availability of cheap inorganic nitrogen supplies which may be applied in spring, there has been little incentive to conserve soil nitrogen in the autumn, either by planting cover crops, or by sowing winter crops at an early date.

Amongst considerable dissensus it is, nonetheless, important to note that there is general agreement that almost all inorganic fertilizer applied in the autumn leaches out of the soil and, indeed, this practice has not been recommended by the Ministry of Agriculture's Agricultural Development and Advisory Service (ADAS) since 1985. Although most farmers have only abandoned the practice in the past ten years, some are still applying autumn nitrogen and, until recently, the representatives of chemical companies dealing directly with farmers were still advising its use. The continuing effects of a practice, albeit one in decline, are thus presently serving to complicate further an already perplexing issue.

Environmental groups

Environmental groups have identified inorganic nitrogen fertilizer application as the principal reason for rising nitrate levels. They have interpreted the coincidence of rising concentrations of nitrate in water sources and the massive post-1945 rise in the use of manufactured inorganic fertilizers as causally significant and as proof, therefore, of the direct leaching of the latter. Friends of the Earth (FoE), in a 1988 briefing paper on nitrates, asserted that only 'about half of the nitrogenous fertilizer added to the soil is taken up by the growing cereal plant', and went on to claim that the 'remaining fertilizer is either leached downwards into the groundwater or lost in surface run-off, in both cases it will reappear in rivers and streams'. In advancing such claims the environmental groups have often used terms such as '*artificial* nitrogenous fertilizers' (our italics), thereby implying that inorganic nitrogen is 'unnatural' and alien, believing that their arguments will gain credence from these pejorative associations (FoE, 1988, p. 1).

However, in concentrating their early campaigns on the contribution of *direct* leaching of inorganic fertilizers to the nitrate problem, environmental groups may have compromised their own arguments for action: in particular for their favoured scheme of a tax to cut nitrogenous fertilizer use (FoE, 1988). If they had argued for the nitrogen tax because it would lead to less intensive farming and thus less nitrate leaching their logic would not have been so obviously flawed, nor their remedial policies so easily dismissed.

Fertilizer manufacturers

The fertilizer manufacturers have drawn upon, and in some cases funded, the research carried out by conventional agricultural scientists. In contrast to the 50% leaching rate suggested by FoE, they assert that inorganic nitrogen makes an insignificant contribution to leaching, and that most nitrate leaches from the soil's store of organic nitrogen, augmented by organic fertilizers and the ploughing of permanent pastures. In particular, they have been at pains to stress the essentially 'natural' properties of nitrate. Thus, the FMA ran an advertisement carrying the message 'We've been blamed for putting nitrate in water. Here's why that's not entirely fair.' In this they presented nitrate, and, by implication, manufactured inorganic nitrogen, as essentially natural and highlighted the contribution of other factors:

> 'Nature gives us nitrate. . . Without it nothing could grow . . . Unquestionably, it is one of life's essentials. Why then are so many people so concerned about it? . . . Nitrate is a naturally occurring substance, and fertilisers merely supplement sources in the soil.' (Fertiliser Manufacturers Association, 1989)

The FMA has argued forcefully that without the supplementation of natural sources, 'Food surpluses would become shortages. Prices would rise'.

National security and economic prosperity have demanded the increased output which inorganic fertilizers have allowed, and without current high yields world food requirements would not be met. Of course, such justifications are made more necessary at a time when the fertilizer manufacturers have their markets and now declining profits to defend. Their argument against being labelled as 'polluters' is heavily based on the claim that nitrate leaching is fundamentally the result of a natural process which it is difficult to control. Thus, they assert that a tax on inorganic nitrogen would be ineffective because, in their view, inorganic nitrogen is not in any way the cause of the problem.

The water industry

There is evidence of a certain difference in opinion between the water industry's two national experts on nitrates, Dr Andrew Skinner of the Severn Trent region and Dr Brian Croll of the Anglian region. Whilst Dr Croll has very much supported the evidence put forward by conventional agricultural scientists and agrees that inorganic nitrogen makes only a 'negligible' contribution to nitrate leaching (Croll and Hayes, 1988, p. 172), Dr Skinner has been more ready to place the blame for rising nitrate levels on the intensification of agriculture.

However, whilst the two experts emphasise different aspects of nitrate sources, there is a consensus within the water industry that agriculture bears the major responsibility for rising nitrate levels and that farmers have in the past been treated leniently in relation to water pollution. It is often pointed out that this special treatment was made legislatively explicit in Part II of the Control of Pollution Act, 1974. A clause in the Act, brought into force in 1986, deemed farmers exempt from prosecution for water pollution offences if they had been following 'good agricultural practice' (Howarth, 1989).

The water industry, of course, has good reason for emphasising the polluting nature of agriculture and the special treatment of farmers. Up until now, water suppliers, rather than farmers, have borne the cost of treating nitrate contaminated water and have been the frontline sector regulated under the EC Drinking Water Directive. As water treatment costs have increased alongside rising nitrate levels, the incentive for the water industry to identify farmers as nitrate polluters and to pass these costs onto them has grown. In particular, the stress which the water industry has placed upon agricultural practices has astutely avoided claims that nitrate leaching is a natural process. Such an admission would place responsibility for treatment firmly with water suppliers. In addition, it is also expedient for the water industry to place all the blame for nitrate pollution on agriculture when its own inefficient sewage treatment works have made a significant contribution to increased nitrate levels in surface waters.

The farming lobby

Whilst agreeing with government agricultural scientists and fertilizer manufacturers over the low levels of leaching from inorganic fertilizers, the farming lobby has been less inclined to stress the polluting potential of organic manures. For them to do so could result in restrictions in manure use which would, in turn, cause problems for many farmers over livestock waste disposal. Instead, they have been eager to point out the contribution that the ploughing of permanent pastures has made to nitrate leaching. They argue, in light of the time lag associated with nitrate contamination of groundwater, that the previous (rather than the current) generation of farmers may well have been responsible for the high rates of nitrate in water currently being pumped from aquifers (Bowman, 1988). These farmers were, of course, following government directives during the Second World War and the subsequent rationing period to cultivate permanent pastures. As such, the farming lobby argue, they were acting both out of patriotic duty to feed the besieged nation and under government duress. Both the NFU and the Country Landowners' Association (CLA) thus assert that the PPP should 'definitely not' be applied to farmers. Whilst the NFU does acknowledge that nitrate leaching problems 'are an unforeseen side effect of the national policy to expand agricultural production', it is unwilling to concede ground on its assertion that the government has been the main instigator of polluting practices.

Its water pollution consultant, Michael Payne, has, morever, emphasised:

> 'As the problem arises from Government policy adopted for the national benefit, and not from any bad practice by farmers, it seems equitable that the Government should pick up the bill.' (Association of Agriculture, 1988)

Although the war-time ploughing-up campaign must have released a surge of nitrates, to identify it as the prime cause of present problems is to stretch credibility, particularly given the WRc's estimates that the slowest percolation rates of surface water to aquifers (in chalk) are around 40 years, whereas some of the highest nitrate concentrations are found in limestone aquifers where the rate of percolation is estimated at less than ten years (DoE, 1988, p. 12). Similarly, rising nitrate concentration in surface waters points to more recent causes of nitrate leaching.

UK governments and the EC itself, through their post-War policies, have certainly played a key role in encouraging the intensification of agriculture which has led to nitrate pollution. Most notably, successive governments subsidized fertilizer use and the 'improvement' of permanent pastures (through ploughing and reseeding) up until the 1970s. It is, however, ingenuous of the farming lobby to present itself as an innocent instrument of state policy when it is clear that since the War the same lobby has been an active partner with government in shaping agricultural policy (Cox, Lowe and Winter, 1988b & 1989).

The UK government

The government has utilized the evidence produced by its agricultural scientists and the lack of consensus over the medical appropriateness of the EC standard, to legitimate its slow response to rising nitrate levels. Despite their awareness from the early 1970s that nitrate concentrations in some areas were over 50mg per litre and, moreover, that levels were rising at rates likely to threaten the 100mg limit by the late 1980s, successive governments have shown a lack of initiative and urgency in dealing with this issue. Thus, even after the 1985 deadline, the UK Government granted derogations allowing nitrate concentrations up to 80mg per litre until it was threatened with prosecution in the European Court in 1988 following the FoE report of a breach of the Directive in late 1986. Furthermore, up until 1987 the Government favoured a treatment response to the nitrate problem and failed to take a long-term view. Subsequently, it took two more years to introduce a pilot scheme for water protection zones, despite having the legislative capability since the passage of the Control of Pollution Act, 1974.

The lack of government action on the nitrate issue is partly to be explained in terms of the influence of agricultural and manufacturing lobbies within MAFF thwarting initiatives suggested by the DoE, the NCC and the newly constituted NRA. MAFF consistently failed to give any form or substance to the obligation contained in Section II of the 1968 Countryside Act to have regard to the natural beauty and amenity of the countryside, and only in 1986 was a clause written into the Agriculture Act which required MAFF to balance the needs of conservation, recreation and rural economy against those of agriculture, thereby indicating a reduction in the power of the productionist lobby.

Conclusion: the Developing Policy Agenda

The technical debate over the causes of increasing levels of nitrate in water and methods of meeting the EC Drinking Water Directive intersects with, and indeed is structured by, a political struggle over who is responsible for nitrate pollution and who should bear the costs of remedial measures. To the possible permutations of fertilizer manufacturers, farmers, taxpayers and water users, water privatization potentially added a fifth candidate - water investors. However, to ensure the success of its privatization plans for the water industry in a climate of growing uncertainty regarding increasing regulatory requirements, the Conservative Government agreed a formula whereby the newly privatized companies could pass on all of their costs in meeting such regulations to the water consumers. Arguments justifying such arrangements have been put forward by the farming lobby along the lines that although consumers are not polluters they have benefited greatly from the cheap food of which increased nitrate leaching has been a by-product and so should bear the cost. Theoretically, under interpretations of the PPP which effectively subvert its ethical impulse, all extra costs could be passed on to consumers anyway. Certainly, former Environment Minister, Nicholas Ridley, in a paper for the Centre for Policy Studies (1989), had no difficulty in transforming the PPP into 'the principle that the polluter, i.e. the polluter's customers, must pay'. Such an interpretation can easily carry weight in a situation where it is almost invariably impossible to assign responsibility to particular farms or farmers.

In this causally complex and politically delicate situation, a number of policy options are being canvassed. One, which has been favoured persistently by the EC, despite evidence of highly inelastic demand, is a tax on the inorganic nitrogen inputs which are seen as polluting. However, a recent study prepared for the EC's Directorate General for Agriculture, suggests that in order to reduce the economic optimum level of nitrogen use by 10 per cent, its price would have to be increased by between 50 and 100 per cent. The optimum level is simply not very sensitive to prices since expenditure on nitrogen is only about 10 per cent of the value of cereal output. An effective rate of tax would have, therefore, to be very high, and in view of the associated compensation, monitoring and administrative problems the report concludes that such a tax would be 'an inappropriate mechanism for restricting nitrogen use' (Commission of the European Communities, 1989).

An option favoured by the water industry to levy water treatment charges upon farmers, (or the fertilizer manufacturers or the government) - apart from being an extremely difficult task to implement fairly - has been weakened by the passage of the much discussed 1991 EC Nitrate Directive. This sets out to protect water used for public water supply abstraction, or susceptible to eutrophication, against diffuse nitrate pollution, and is sure to add a further dimension of complexity to the nitrate debate. It requires, within two years of its adoption, the establishment of 'vulnerable zones', not only where water which is to be extracted for human consumption has nitrate concentrations over or likely to exceed 50mg per litre, but also where water is eutrophic or in danger of becoming so. Within such zones, member states have a further two years to draw up measures to combat nitrate leaching and an additional four years to implement them. The version of the Directive agreed in June 1991 has, however, been significantly relaxed from earlier more stringent drafts, and it would appear that member states have been given a greater degree of flexibility in their choice of measures to address the nitrate problem as well as more time to develop and adopt them. Thus, as well as placing restrictions on nitrogen application and managing farming practice so as to minimise nitrate leaching, governments will be allowed to use some water industry measures to meet the Directive objectives (NFU, 1991, pp. 20-21). The involvement of farmers in the schemes would be compulsory but the Directive will probably follow early drafts which made some allowance for compensation to help farmers adapt their farming systems (House of Lords, 1988-89, pp. 7-9).

Any option in which the government **pays** farmers to farm in ways which conserve nitrogen in the soil and thus reduce leaching would appear to be problematic. Permanent payments to farmers would surely breach the PPP, and would seem to be tantamount to giving farmers a right to pollute. The current Nitrate Sensitive Areas (NSA) five year pilot scheme now instituted is of this type. It may well, however, be superceded by provisions drawn up under the EC Nitrate Directive. Another problem is that the NSA scheme is not comprehensive. Only ten areas covering about 15,000 hectares (ha) have been designated as NSAs and although groundwater supplies in all ten are above or in danger of exceeding the EC limit, some high nitrate aquifers have been left out of the scheme. An additional nine areas, representative of ground and surface water sources, have been chosen as Nitrate Advisory Areas (NAAs), and farmers within these have been subject to a twelve month intensive advisory campaign. These cover a further 23,000ha. Although the water industry was consulted over the areas to be covered by the NSA scheme, MAFF was given the responsibility for their designation and management (including policing) under the 1989 Water Act. In fact, MAFF expectations of the scheme differ considerably from those of the water industry. For the Ministry the scheme is a large-scale trial, the main objective of which is to learn about applying nitrate-conserving constraints on farmers. On the other hand, the water industry's priority is to reduce nitrate concentrations in aquifers to below 50mg per litre. MAFF regards this as only a secondary objective, a 'bonus' for the water industry, and as the Ministry is in charge of the scheme it can dictate the terms. The scheme, moreover, is only voluntary and its measures have been considerably weakened under pressure from the farming lobby which also succeeded in raising the rates of compensation on offer. The DoE, in contrast, was not in favour of the payment of compensation, whilst the NRA has been 'highly critical' of the voluntary approach which it reportedly feels is an "'insufficiently secure base on which to proceed'" (*The Guardian*, 2.8.89). The Authority has voiced concern that measures to cut nitrate leaching are not being implemented quickly enough and was 'disappointed' with take-up rates within the NSAs during the first year (National Rivers Authority, 1990, p. 3). Although 65 per cent of farmers within the ten NSAs joined the scheme, only 52 per cent of the agricultural land was covered. However, take-up has improved in the second year and now 87 per cent of the designated land has been entered into the scheme (MAFF, News Release 196, 1991).

The EC report and the Nitrate Directive favour only **interim** payments to enable farmers to shift from polluting to non-polluting practices. Such a policy would at least retain some vestige of the ethical merit of the PPP. Crucial to the success of any nitrate policy involving a shift in farming practices, however, is an advisory or education programme. Farmers must understand the sorts of practices which result in high nitrate leaching on their farms and be offered some practicable alternatives. It would be essential to such a policy that farmers see the point of the changes they are being encouraged to make. Government scepticism over the rationale of the EC nitrate pollution definition has in the past compromised its legitimacy. This uncertainty has been communicated to the agricultural industry and has hitherto greatly hampered farmer co-operation. The government should, therefore, place greater emphasis upon the 50mg per litre level as sensibly erring on the side of caution, both in light of the inconclusive evidence about stomach cancer and the detrimental ecological effects of high nitrate levels in water.

MAFF has taken some tentative steps in this direction by its production of a new Code of Good Agricultural Practice for the Protection of Water (MAFF, 1991). The guidelines laid out in the original Code of Good Agricultural Practice (CoGAP) (MAFF, 1985) are now known to have failed to contain nitrate leaching below polluting levels in certain regions, and the new Code has been drawn up partly to address this issue. The elements of the new Code which relate to the prevention of nitrate leaching in fact follow the principles developed within the basic scheme of the pilot NSAs. This attempt to promote such nitrate-conserving practices as the agricultural norm, if successful, would appear to obviate much of the compensation MAFF currently pays to farmers and, because of this, has aroused the concern of the farming organizations. In particular, the farming lobby has argued that the governments of other EC countries are paying the costs of either water treatment or changes in farming practice, and that it would put UK farmers at an unfair competitive disadvantage if the UK government did not likewise bear such costs.

More fundamentally, however, the productionist rationale of farming, which has been overwhelmingly in the ascendancy in the post-War period, must be modified through the sort of integration of agricultural and environmental policy which is presently only beginning to be seriously contemplated. Without such an integration, any policy geared towards the control of agricultural pollution is likely to cause confusion and frustration amongst farmers and regulators and be only fitful in its success.

References

Association of Agriculture (1988), *Studying an issue: nitrates in the water supply*, Association of Agriculture, London.

Baldock, D. (1988), *The nitrates issue: a case study of Anglian Water Authority, UK*, Institute for European Environmental Policy, London.

Bowers, J. (1988), 'Farm incomes and the benefits of environmental protection', in D. Collard, D. Pearce and D. Ulph (eds), *Economics, growth and sustainable environments*, Macmillan, London, pp. 161-70.

Bowers, J. (1990), *Economics of the environment: the conservationists' response to the Pearce Report*, British Association of Nature Conservationists, Telford, Shropshire.

Bowman, K. (1988), *Agricultural policy objectives and their implications for nitrate leaching into aquifers and the public water supply*, NFU Farming Information Centre.

British Geological Survey (1986), *The groundwater nitrate problem*, British Geological Survey, Wallingford.

Commission of the European Communities (1989), *Intensive farming and the impact on the environment and rural economy of restrictions on the use of chemical and animal fertilizers*, Office for Official Publications of the EC, Luxembourg.

Cox, G., Lowe, P. and Winter, M. (1988a), 'Private rights and public responsibilities: the prospects for agricultural and environmental controls', *Journal of Rural Studies*, vol. 4, no. 4, pp. 323-347.

Cox, G., Lowe, P. and Winter, M. (1988b), 'Agricultural regulation and the politics of milk production', in C. Crouch and R. Dore (eds), *Corporatism and accountability*, Clarendon Press, Oxford, pp. 169-99.

Cox, G., Lowe, P. and Winter, M. (1989), 'The farm crisis in Britain', in M. Redclift and D. Goodman (eds), *The international farm crisis*, Macmillan, London, pp 113-35.

Croll, B.T. and Hayes, C.R. (1988), 'Nitrate and water supplies in the United Kingdom', *Environmental Pollution*, vol. 50, pp. 163-187.

Department of the Environment (1988), *The nitrate issue: a study of the economic and other consequences of various local options for limiting nitrate concentrations in drinking water*, HMSO, London.

Department of the Environment, MAFF and Severn Trent Water Authority (1988), *The Hatton catchment nitrate study: a report of a joint investigation on the control of nitrate in water supplies*, Severn Trent Water Authority, Birmingham.

Dudley, N. (1990), *Nitrates: the threat to food and water*, Green Print, London.

Fertiliser Manufacturers Association (1989), *Briefing note: nitrate in water – an update*, Fertiliser Manufacturers Association, Peterborough.

Friends of the Earth (1988), *Briefing sheet: nitrates*, Friends of the Earth, London.

Haigh, N. (1989), *European environmental law*, 2nd revised edition, Longman, Harlow.

Hawkins, K. (1984), *Environment and enforcement: regulation and the social definition of pollution*, Clarendon Press, Oxford.

Hill, M., Aaronovitch, S. and Baldock, D. (1989), 'Non-decision making in pollution control in Britain: nitrate pollution, the EEC Drinking Water Directive and agriculture', *Policy and Politics*, vol. 17, no. 3, pp. 227-240.

House of Commons Select Committee on the Environment (1987), *River pollution*, HMSO, London.

House of Lords Select Committee on the European Communities (1988-89), *Nitrate in water*, HMSO, London.

Howarth, W. (1989), 'Water pollution: improving the legal controls', *Journal of Environmental Law*, vol. 1, no.1, pp. 25-37.

ICI (1986), *Nitrates and our environment*, ICI Fertilizers, Billingham.

Lowe, P. (1988), 'Environmental politics and agriculture in Western Europe', *Environnement et Societe*, (Fondation Universitaire Luxembourgeoise, Arlon, Belgium), vols 1 & 2, pp. 10-28.

Lowe, P. and Flynn, A. (1989), 'Environmental politics and policy in the 1980s', in J. Mohan (ed.), *The political geography of contemporary Britain*, Macmillan, London.

Lowe, P., Cox, G., Goodman, D., Munton, R. and Winter, M. (1990), 'Technological change, farm management and pollution regulation: the example of Britain', in P. Lowe, T. Marsden and S. Whatmore (eds), *Technological change and the rural environment*, David Fulton Publishers, London, pp. 53-80.

Macdonald, A.J., Poulson, D.S., Poulton, P.R. and Jenkinson, D.S. (1989), 'Unused fertiliser nitrogen in arable soils - its contribution to nitrate leaching', *Journal of Science, Food and Agriculture*, vol. 46, pp. 407-419.

MAFF (1985), *Code of good agricultural practice*, HMSO, London.

MAFF (1991), *Code of good agricultural practice for the protection of water*, HMSO, London.

National Farmers Union (1987), 'The nitrate in water debate', *Insight*, December, pp. 1-12.

National Farmers Union (1991), 'Compensation plea on nitrates', *The British Farmer*, August, pp. 20-21.

National Rivers Authority (1990), 'Pilot nitrate scheme', *The Water Guardians*, September, p. 3.

OECD (1989), *Agricultural and environmental policies: opportunities for integration*, OECD, Paris.

Pearce, D., Markandya, A. and Barbier, E.B. (1989), *Blueprint for a green economy*, Earthscan Publications, London.

Ridley, N. (1989), *Policies against pollution: the Conservative record - and principles*, Policy Study 107, Centre for Policy Studies, London.

Rothamsted Experimental Station (1988), *Keeping the balance: soil and fertiliser nitrogen*, Agriculture and Food Research Council, Rothamsted, Hertfordshire.

Sagoff, M. (1988), *The economy of the earth*, Cambridge University Press, Cambridge.

Vogel, D. (1983), 'Co-operative regulation: environmental protection in Great Britain', *The Public Interest*, vol. 72, pp. 88-106.

12 Water protection zones: A valid management strategy?

IAN FOSTER AND BRIAN ILBERY

Introduction

Nitrate levels in both surface and groundwaters throughout the European Community (EC) have been increasing for around 30 years (Roberts and Marsh, 1987). In a 1986 OECD report (OECD, 1986), the rate of increase in concentration in some public supply sources was found to be 2% per year. In the UK, increases in nitrate concentration are generally believed to reflect the rise in nitrogen fertiliser application rates, which doubled between 1969 and 1982 (Chalmers *et al*, 1990). However, the period 1983-87 saw a levelling off in total fertiliser usage and the first decline in application rates for three decades occurred in 1988 as shown in Figure 12.1. These general trends, however, belie considerable spatial variation in the application rate of fertilisers (Chalmers *et al*, 1990) and in both the concentration and total amount of nitrogen (as nitrate) transported in the surface waters of England and Wales (Walling and Webb, 1981; Betton *et al*, 1991). Spatial and temporal variations in nitrate concentration are a complex function of hydrometeorological, geological, and pedological conditions, as well as the pattern of intensive

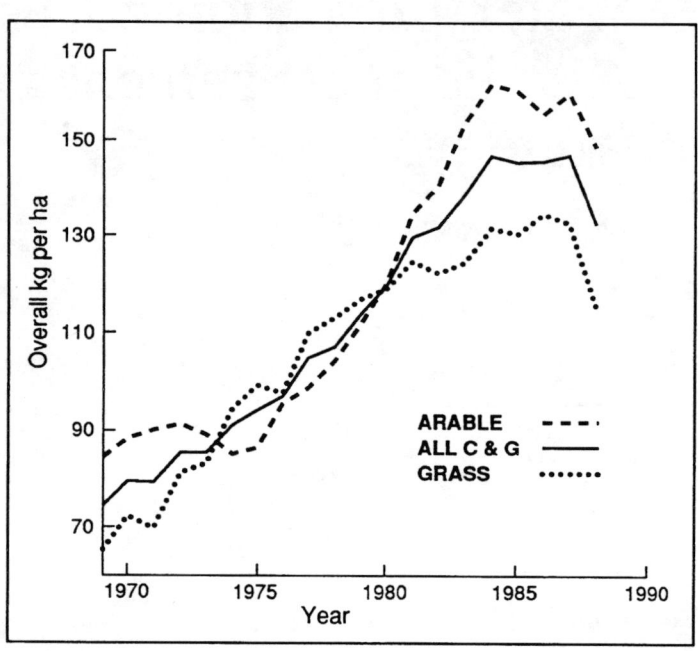

Figure 12.1 Post-1970 increases in average fertiliser application rates to arable land, grassland and all crops and grass (C & G) (after Chalmers *et al*, 1990)

fertiliser application and land management practices. The long term increase in nitrate concentration, although frequently ascribed to an increase in fertiliser usage, may also be associated with a significant shift in cultivation practice from spring to autumn sown cereals and the ploughing of permanent pastures. The latter gives rise to an increase in nitrate concentrations due to the mineralisation of organic matter. Pertebations to the long term increase in nitrate concentrations in UK surface waters have also been noted; for example, the 1976 UK drought produced a significant increase in nitrate levels in surface water supplies. This was a result of the flushing of unused inorganic fertilisers into water courses in subsequent storm events and the increase in rates of organic matter breakdown caused by higher soil temperatures (Walling and Foster, 1978; Burt *et al*, 1987).

Concern over high nitrate levels in water focuses primarily around their potential harmful effect on human health and the aquatic environment. Two specific medical conditions have been ascribed to excessive nitrate levels. First, Infantile Methaemoglobinaemia (Blue Baby Syndrome) and, second, stomach cancer (Nitrate Coordination Group (NCG) 1986). The Department of Health and Social Security, in a letter, however, to General Medical Practioners in 1985 (NCG, 1986), notes only 14 cases of the former in 35 years and, for many of these cases, argues that other environmental factors such as bacterial contamination may be equally important. The letter also concludes that the evidence examined up to that time gave no support to the suggestion that nitrate is a cause of cancer of the stomach. Furthermore, the World Health Organisation has recently stated that methaemoglobinaemia no longer exists in Western Europe (D. Hardwick, Personal Communication). In relation to the environment, the NCG (1986) concluded in its survey that there was no evidence of increasing nitrate levels in British coastal waters. Nevertheless, they accepted that high levels occurred in two specific cases examined in inland waters which could be the cause of changes to the ecological balance and the productivity of natural lakes. In one of these cases, however, other factors such as tourism and the clearing of banks may also have contributed.

Despite the equivocal evidence about the detrimental effects of nitrates on either human health or the aquatic environment, the EC Directive (EC, 1980) relating to the Quality of Water Intended for Human Consumption sets a maximum permissible level of 50 mg. of nitrate per litre of water (50 mg l^{-1} NO_3). This is equivalent to a concentration of 11.3 mg l^{-1} as NO_3-N with a recommended limit of half of this concentration. In some circumstances, especially at times of water shortage or if there are no public health hazards, member states are allowed to approve derogations. Despite this situation, the European Court is taking action against the UK Government for supplying drinking water with nitrate concentrations exceeding the maximum permissible threshold.

The aim of this discussion chapter is fourfold: first, to examine the general issue of farm pollution with special reference to the nitrate problem; second, to examine the measures recently adopted by the UK Government with regard to controlling the effect of fertiliser application on nitrate concentrations in surface and groundwaters; third, to assess, through a case study, the potential limitations and effectiveness of utilising land use controls as a management strategy; and fourth, to look at alternatives and improvements which might be adopted in the light of identified limitations.

Pollution in the rural environment

Fertilisers are not the only source of nitrogen entering water courses. Other sources of high nitrogen inputs to surface waters include outfalls from water reclamation and sewage treatment works and from inadequate management of farm slurries and yard waste waters. Farm pollution in general derives from two major sources: first, from point sources centred around the farmyard; and second, from diffuse, or non-point, sources associated with drainage and leaching from cultivated land.

The magnitude of the farm pollution problem is highlighted in the latest Government White Paper on the environment (DOE, 1990). This noted that the number of reported pollution incidents rose from 2367 in 1980 to 4141 in 1988, at which point in time they represented almost 50% of all serious water pollution incidents reported from all sources. Although the number of farm pollution incidents fell in 1989 to 2889 (National Rivers Authority (NRA), 1989), partly because of the dry weather, surveys also suggested that the scale of the farm pollution problem was much greater than the number of reported incidents would suggest.

Point source pollution, such as farm pollution, can be effectively tackled by legislative control over effluent discharges and monitoring at the point of input to water courses and the UK Government has indeed announced a number of strategies aimed at minimising the hazard posed by point source pollution in the rural environment. For example, since 1989, a Farm Conservation Grant, covering 50% of the cost of replacement of, or improvement to, facilities for the treatment and disposal of farm wastes, has been available. Also in 1989, the Government set up a joint NRA/MAFF committee to report on a survey of water pollution and farm waste, on the basis of which MAFF would prepare codes of practice and provide free initial advice on pollution control. In future, the Government intends to publish regulations setting minimum standards for the construction of silage and slurry stores, giving power to the NRA to enforce the legislation. The NRA, under its present powers, will be able to prosecute polluters and the level of fines has increased tenfold since 1988. There seems to be some limited evidence for an increase in the number of prosecutions by the NRA in the case of farm pollution. In 1988, 148 prosecutions were brought which represents 3.4% of the total number of incidents reported and 15.7% of those reported incidents considered to be 'serious'. In 1989, the number of prosecutions rose to 5.6% of the total number reported and 31.2% of those considered to be 'serious' (NRA, 1989; 1990).

The use of subsidies for farm improvements and the reduction in point source pollution, however, is not commensurate with the EC's 'Polluter Pays' principle, although the increase in the absolute number and proportion of incidents resulting in prosecution by the NRA in the latest survey may give cause for cautious optimism.

In contrast to the point source input of agricultural wastes, the leaching of excess fertilisers into ground and surface waters presents a significant number of problems in both regulating and/or controlling discharges and identifying the individual or organisation responsible. Such problems are implicitly recognised in the 1990 White Paper (DOE, 1990), since measures to combat the leaching of agrochemicals are based upon a substantially different set of principles from the control of point sources identified above.

Areas of environmental sensitivity

Although several options are available in order to minimise the impact of high nitrate concentrations in drinking water supplies, one favoured option has been to designate parts of the country as 'environmentally sensitive'. This began with the introduction of 8 Environmentally Sensitive Areas (ESAs) in 1986, the number of which had increased to 20 by 1989; 13 in England and Wales, 5 in Scotland and 2 in Northern Ireland as shown in Figure 12.2. Within these areas, farmers receive hectarage payments for voluntarily maintaining or introducing such environmentally beneficial farming practices as restrictions on drainage, fertiliser use, grazing levels and pesticides, and for the maintenance of hedges, woodland, barns and ponds. ESAs recognise the need, therefore, to support traditional systems and methods of farming in order to conserve the ecology and landscape of particular tracts of countryside (Potter, 1988; Baldock et al, 1990). They are not designated in order to control nitrates; if nitrate levels are reduced this is a beneficial side-effect.

In 1990, in a direct attempt to control nitrates, the UK Government introduced a pilot nitrate scheme to reduce leaching from inorganic and organic nitrogen fertilisers. The scheme has been concentrated in 10 Nitrate Sensitive Areas (NSAs) as shown in Figure 12.2, although there are also 9 Nitrate Advisory Areas (NAAs) where MAFF is conducting an intensive advisory campaign to encourage farmers to voluntarily reduce their application of fertilisers, without financial compensation. NSAs are defined as areas where nitrate concentrations in drinking water sources exceed or are at risk of exceeding the limit of 50 mg l^{-1} set by the 1980 EC Drinking Water Directive. Within such designated areas, farmers are financially compensated for complying with voluntary agricultural measures to reduce nitrate levels. Two types of scheme exist in the NSAs:

1. Basic Scheme, where farmers receive between £55 and £95 ha^{-1} per year for five years for restricting the use of nitrogenous fertilisers and animal manure; there is also a requirement to sow a crop or cover crop (e.g. rye, ryegrass and barley), to avoid bare land in the autumn, and to retain hedgerows and woodland.

2. Premium Scheme, where farmers receive up to £380 ha^{-1} per year for converting arable land to one or more of four forms of grassland: unfertilised, ungrazed; unfertilised; grassland with limited

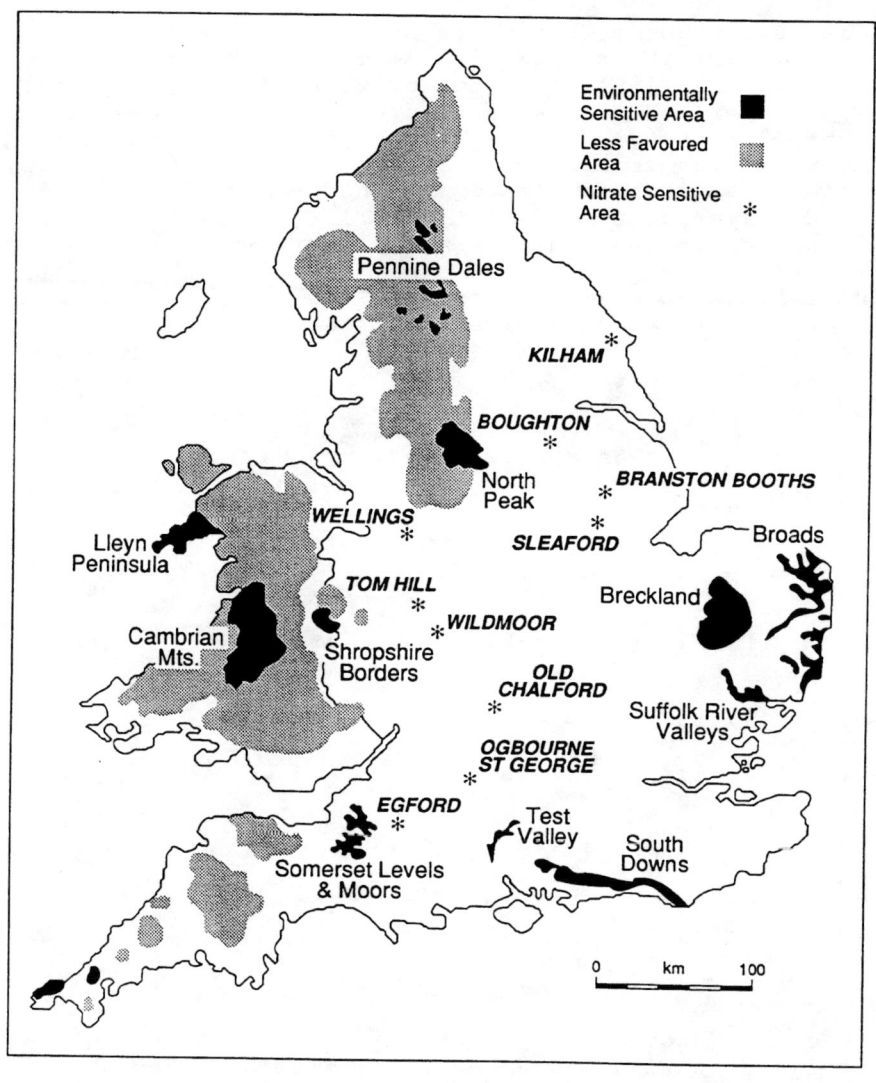

Figure 12.2 The distribution of Environmentally and Nitrate Sensitive Areas in England and Wales

fertiliser and optional grazing; and grass with woodland.

The uptake of both schemes has been variable during the first year as shown in table 12.1. By the closing date of May 1991, four out of every five farmers and just over 87% of NSA land were involved in the basic scheme. However, there is considerable variation between the ten areas (e.g. from just 38% of land in Kilham to 100% in Sleaford). The premium scheme has been disappointing, with only 14% of eligible land being converted. Farmers are clearly more willing to restrict the application of fertilisers than to convert arable land to pasture. While the NSAs are a step in the right direction, there is no general consensus that high levels of nitrate concentration in watercourses are the direct result of current

Table 12.1
NSA applications, by May 1991

NSA	Area (ha)	Basic Scheme % Agric' Area	Premium Scheme % Agric' Area	% NSA Farmers in Basic Scheme
	1991	1991	1991	1991
1	984	72	11	80
2	756	38	0	67
3	427	52	10	46
4	621	93	27	83
5	523	62	2	58
6	570	82	3	68
7	723	95	2	87
8	1652	99	1	95
9	2876	100	33	100
10	1592	100	13	96
ALL	10724	87	14	80

NSAs 1-Ogbourne St. George 2-Kilham 3-Egford 4-Old Chalford 5-Wellings 6-Tom Hill 7-Wildmoor 8-Boughton 9-Sleaford 10-Branston Booths

Source: MAFF News Release (June 1991) 'High Final Uptake for Pilot Nitrate Sensitive Areas Scheme', MAFF, London.

farming practices (Robinson, 1991); the problem may well have begun with the large scale conversion of grassland to arable activities during the 'dig for victory' campaign of the 1940s. As yet, results from surveys considering the effectiveness of uptake in NSA and NAA pilot scheme areas are inconclusive. In order to evaluate the potential success of such schemes in the UK, the following section considers the water resource and nitrate problem on the island of Jersey, where Water Pollution Safeguard areas were designated by the Island Development Committee in 1963. The problem of pollution control on Jersey is set within the context of water resource development in relation to both public supplies and the importance of agricultural production on the island.

The Jersey water resource and nitrate issue

The island of Jersey covers an area of 118 km² and is situated some 24 km from the west coast of the Cherbourg peninsula, France as shown in Figure 12.3. It is the largest of the Channel Islands and has a population of around 85,000, the majority of whom live in the main town of St Helier. The island is rectangular in shape, approximately 16.9 km long, west to east, and 10.9 km wide. The highest point on the north-west coast rises to 122 m above OD. The land surface dips gently from north to south. Geologically it comprises ancient sedimentary and volcanic rocks overlain by extensive loess deposits of Pleistocene age (Bishop and Keen, 1981). Mean daily air temperatures range from 6°C in January to 16.5°C in August. The 125 year annual rainfall average is 845.2 mm.

The water supply industry of Jersey has focussed on three major developments. In the rural northern half of the island, a large proportion of the community is served by groundwater supplies, often from privately owned boreholes. In both the south and the main urban centres, water supplies are provided by the Jersey New Waterworks Company (JNWC) which was established in 1882. Reservoir construction on the island began with the Millbrook reservoir in 1889 and by 1991, six major water supply reservoirs were operational as shown in Figure 12.3. Provision was made in 1970 for distillation of sea water capable of providing up to 1.5 million gallons per day, but at a cost well in

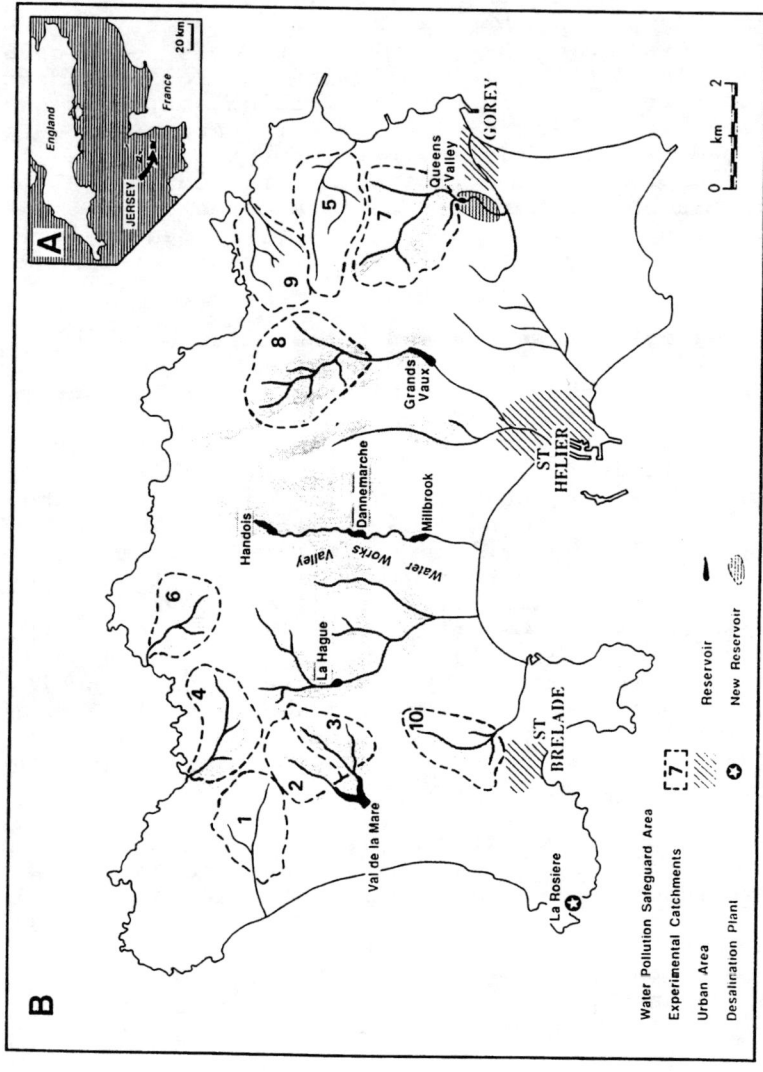

Figure 12.3 Jersey Location (A) and the distribution of WPSAs and reservoirs (B)

excess of water supplied from reservoir storage. This forms the third important source of water for the island (Clarke, 1988).

There are a number of problems in water supply which make Jersey unique. First, there are no remote areas of the island where water can be collected and stored and all of the major north to south flowing valleys of Jersey contain at least one storage reservoir. Since the valleys are generally not deeply incised or very wide and also provide important communication routes, water storage capacity of the reservoirs is generally small. Secondly, much of the collected water drains from intensively cultivated agricultural land which poses a number of potential pollution threats from both point and non-point sources. Furthermore, a number of 'unofficial' temporary dams are frequently constructed by farmers for irrigation. These dams are built on an *ad hoc* basis and frequently without the consent of the Department of Planning and Building Control. Although they are rarely more than several metres in width and length, they can rapidly reduce the discharge of the stream (Norman, 1990). Thirdly, Jersey has a strong seasonal demand for water for the support of an important tourist industry. In 1989, for example, the JNWC supplied 1301 million gallons of water, of which 11% was used in the month of May. In the last 10 years, however, peak demands have usually occurred in July and August at the height of the tourist influx (JNWC, 1989).

Development of Jersey's water supply has been a continuing cause for debate over the last two decades. The Fawcett Report (1976) and the Guthrie Report (1977) identified a significant increase in future demand for water. The latter report predicted a demand for water in 1990 of over 1800 million gallons, some 40% higher than current measured consumption. This was used as a basis for the JNWC to support its case for the construction of the Queens Valley Reservoir, which is now nearing completion. The Guthrie Report, however, recommended the development of other resources and improved water management strategies rather than the construction of a reservoir. Although the Jersey Public Works Committe accepted the need to manage demand and increase supply, a further suggestion in the Guthrie Report for the creation of an appropriate framework to control and plan water resource development was rejected in favour of giving such responsibilities to the JNWC under the guidance of a Water Advisory Panel comprising representatives from the Jersey States, the Public Works Committee and the JNWC.

The continuing and intense debate concerning water supply provision on the Island of Jersy may be one factor detracting from the implementation of coherent policies aimed at tackling the water quality problem. In an earlier paper, Foster *et al*, (1989) analysed the trends in nitrate levels in public supply and selected borehole sources. At worst, the EC (1980) maximum nitrate limit was exceeded for as much as 70% of the time. Analysis of weekly water samples from 10 catchments on the island indicated that mean nitrate levels were above or very close to the maximum EC standard for drinking water and that the concentrations were statistically related to the intensity of land use, expressed as the proportion of the catchment under intense cropping (potatoes and cauliflowers) as shown in Table 12.2. A more recent survey by Norman (1990) has suggested that rivers with low flow rates and with high nitrite levels (probably caused by denitrification of nitrate) have low ecological diversity. It is evident, therefore, that ecological deterioration may also be associated with water resource development and nitrate pollution on Jersey. The water quality issue was considered in the Fawcett Report (1976). It was concluded that runoff in the catchments was highly polluted at times, especially in spring after heavy rainfall, and that the high nitrate levels in both surface and groundwater supplies were due to the intensive agricultural use of the island. Despite this important identification of the water quality problem, the Island Development Plan (IDC, 1984a and b), the Guthrie Report (1978) and the Rural Planning Services (1983) Report make no direct reference to the issue of nitrates and agriculture. Furthermore, the Annual Report of the JNWC (1989) devotes only 7 lines of text to water quality and makes no information on quality available to its shareholders. The annual report concludes 'this process of daily and extensive sampling enables us to establish that our water is..... satisfactory for our consumers'. It makes no reference to quality objectives or criteria used to define the potability of water.

Table 12.2
Land use intensity and nitrate levels on Jersey

Site[1]	Area (ha)	% area in intensive cultivation[2]	Nitrate Concentration (NO_3-N) (mg l^{-1})		
			Minimum	Maximum	Mean
1	145	60	5	30	13
2	210	80	4	38	14
3	190	50	6	18	12
4	215	50	4.5	36	11.5
5	210	68	8	18	12
6	184	60	6.5	25	10
7	240	25	5.5	17	9
8	260	40	5	18	10
9	163	52	6	17	10.5
10	185	24	5	18	10

Site 1-L'Etacq 2-Val de la Mare 1 3-Val de la Mare 2 4-Greve de Lecq 5-St. Catherines 6-Les Mouries 7-Queens Valley 8-St. Saviour 9-Rozel Bay 10- St. Brelade

1 As shown in Figure 12.3
2 Potatoes and Cauliflowers

Source: Based on Foster *et al* (1989).

Within the Development Plan of the Island Development Committee (IDC, 1984b), the only reference to pollution control in agricultural areas is through the application of appropriate bye-laws defined within Water Pollution Safeguard Areas (WPSAs). These were established in the Jersey Development Plan approved by the States in 1963 and extended to cover larger catchment areas in 1975 as shown in Figure 12.3 (IDC, 1975). Within these areas, 'no person shall .... cause or permit to enter protected water any poisonous or noxious matter or any other matter likely to pollute water'. Policy SE3 (IDC, 1984b) states 'The Committee will continue to consult the Jersy New Waterworks Company before granting permission for development in WPSAs to ensure that the water catchment area is not put at risk of pollution'. The Water (Jersey) law of 1972 details the powers of pollution control within WPSAs granted to the JNWC, which is empowered under this act to define the area within which it deems it necessary to exercise control and prohibit or regulate the doing within that area of any act specified in the bye-laws. Fines for offences committed under the 1972 regulations were raised under the Water (Amendment) (Jersey) Law of 1990.

The JNWC and the Planning Department, in association with the Agricultural Department, have used these acts concerned with WPSAs to restrict nitrogen applications through information leaflets and leasing agreements (JNWC, 1985). In essence, therefore, Jersey has been utilising advisory control on the use of fertiliser nitrogen in WPSAs, the success or failure of which provides a useful analogy to the implementation of NAAs in the United Kingdom.

Foster *et al* (1989) have examined the attitude of farmers through questionnaire surveys on Jersey to the reduction in nitrogen application in these areas. The survey demonstrated, however, that only 9% of the sample population were aware of WPSAs and no farmer interviewed had reduced fertiliser applications within their boundary. Indeed, many exceeded recommended applications in such areas because of the high leaching losses on the steep cultivated slopes encompassed by WPSAs. It was also established in this study that the public were well aware of the nitrate pollution problem, although this awareness was conditioned by the media and public pressure groups rather than administrative authorites. Links between government institutions, the JNWC, farmers and the public were less clear cut. The public were not made aware by the Public Analyst or the JNWC of the nitrate problem which made the designation of WPSAs virtually ineffective as a pollution control strategy. There was no evidence from an analysis of seven years data on nitrate levels in public water supplies that substantial improvements had occurred in water quality. However, in some years lower nitrate levels were achieved during extreme water shortages because the desalination plant produced supplies which diluted surface waters contaminated with agrochemicals. The lack of public domain information is viewed as one of the more serious problems in the succesful use of WPSAs for pollution control. Despite the efforts on Jersey since 1963 to protect water supplies, the water quality problem has yet to be satisfactorily resolved.

Implications for UK pollution control

The attempts on Jersey to implement pollution control strategies focusing upon WPSAs have met with limited success in relation to the nitrate pollution problem, although prohibition of certain building activities through planning control has undoubtedly prevented serious contamination from other sources. Nevertheless, the strategy has clearly failed to resolve the nitrate problem and it is questionable whether the designation of NAAs or even NSAs in the UK will meet with any greater success given the variable and often low uptake on such schemes, as indicated above with the 'Premium Scheme'. Despite the 'Polluter Pays' principle being enshrined in Jersey law, no records of prosecution for over use of fertilisers are known to exist. This is similar to the UK mainland situation, where it is much easier to identify point source pollution and enforce quality criteria.

There is a clear need in managing nitrate release from agricultural areas to consider whether the problem is restricted to one of public health and domestic supply or whether wider environmental deterioration is recognised as a serious problem. According to the NCG (1986) 'increased nitrate concentration does not, by itself, adversely affect the ecological balance'. Other environmental scientists may well take a different view, but the physical problem is complex and may involve other nutrients, especially phosphorus, which behaves very differently from nitrogen in the aquatic environment and which in many lowland UK situations is the limiting nutrient. The development of protection policies may be unnecessary if the fundamental problem is one which can be dealt with through water treatment options prior to domestic supply. However, conventional water treatments do not remove large quantities of nitrate and the expense of further treatment installations may prove to be prohibitively expensive (NCG, 1986). An economic appraisal of various options undertaken by Laurence Gould Consultants Ltd (1985) concluded that it would be cheaper to treat water than to restrict nitrogen fertiliser usage in all situations but one, some of the Lincolnshire boreholes, where water protection zones might be a more viable alternative. The water treatment option, however, is also only viable if ecological deterioration is not of widespread concern.

Legislative control appears to be particularly ineffective in relation to non-point effluents, since the source of nitrates are difficult to trace and have accumulated in soils and groundwaters over a period of three decades in direct response to post war government initiatives to increase agricultural productivity. Agricultural management options through controls on the timing and amount of fertiliser application may offer an alternative solution (NCG, 1986), but require detailed consideration of an appropriate implementation mechanism. According to the NCG (1986), it is likely that the operation of protection zones would be technically feasible, but that 'this could only be achieved by major changes in land use which would make many farms uneconomic unless compensation were available'.

The identification of nitrate sensitive zones and the optional reduction in fertiliser application may not, despite the availability of subsidies and advice, bring about the desired reduction in nitrate levels for a number of reasons. First, evidence from Jersey suggests that despite designation of WPSAs since 1963, nitrate levels in public supplies have not shown substantial reductions. This is due to a range of factors determining farmers' attitudes towards the environment and a range of economic pressures controlling attempts to increase productivity (Foster et al, 1989). Secondly, relatively little is known about the attitudes of farmers on the UK mainland to the availability of subsidies. The economic disadvantages of lower productivity may not be sufficiently offset by farm subsidies through an optional scheme of nitrogen reductions. Thirdly, the ineffective application of the 'Polluter Pays' principle to this area of pollution control suggests that the UK Government is adopting a double standard. A more efficient way of reducing nitrogen application might be the imposition of a fertiliser tax, collected by the manufacturer and based on the nitrogen content of the fertiliser. The revenue raised in such a way might deter excessive applications, be consistent with the 'Polluter Pays' principle, and raise sufficient revenue to improve advisory and water treatment capabilities. Such an approach would not economically disadvantage farmers in nitrate sensitive areas and, where sensitive areas are designated by statute, may provide a source of revenue for improved subsidy for any necessary changes in farm operations.

References

Baldock, D., Cox, G., Lowe, P. and Winter, M. (1990), 'Environmentally Sensitive Areas: incrementalism or reform?' *Journal of Rural Studies* 6, pp 143-162.

Betton, C., Webb, B.W. and Walling, D.E. (1991), 'Recent trends in NO_3-N Concentration and Loads in British Rivers'. *International Association of Hydrological Sciences Publication.* 203, pp 169-180.

Bishop, A.C. and Keen, D.H. (1981) *Jersey Geologists' Association Guide.* No 41. 30pp. London.

Burt, T.P., Arkell, B.P., Trudgill, S.T. and Walling, D.E. (1987), 'Stream nitrate levels in a small catchment in South West England over a period of 15 years'. *Hydrol. Process.* 2, pp 267-284.

Chalmers, A., Kershaw, C. and Leech, P. (1990), 'Fertilizer use on farm crops in Great Britain'. *Outlook on Agriculture*, 19, pp 269-278.

Clarke, R.M. (1988), *A brief history of the Water Supply in Jersey.* Jersey New Waterworks Company. St. Helier

DOE (1990), *This Common Inheritance. Britain's Environmental Strategy.* HMSO, London.

EC (1980), *Directive relating to the quality of water intended for human consumption.* (80/778/EEC) and DOE circular 25/84 (18th Oct 1984). HMSO, London.

Fawcett Report (1976), *Report on Water Resources of Jersey.* Fawcett and Parners Consulting Engineers. London

Foster, I.D.L., Ilbery, B.W. and Hinton, M.A. (1989), 'Agriculture and Water Quality: a preliminary examination of the Jersey nitrate problem'. *Applied Geography.* 9, pp 95-114.

Guthrie Report (1977), *Jersey's Water; a new approach.* Report of the Water Inquiry Board (Chairman Sir Giles Guthrie) to the President of the Public Works Committee, States of Jersey. St Helier.

IDC (1975), *Report and Provision recommending the approval of revised water pollution safeguard areas.* States Greffe, St. Helier.

IDC (1984a), *Jersey Island Plan.* Volume 1. Survey and Issues. States Greffe, St. Helier.

IDC (1984b), *Jersey Island Plan.* Volume 2. Plan and Policies. States Greffe, St. Helier.
JNWC (1985), *Annual Report and Accounts.* The Jersey New Waterworks Company, St. Helier.
JNWC (1989), *Annual Report and Accounts.* The Jersey New Waterworks Company, St. Helier.
Laurence Gould Consultants Ltd (1985), *Reduction of nitrate in water supplies. An economic study of water treatment compared to with the effects of low fertiliser usage.* Laurence Gould, London.
NCG (1986), *Nitrates in Water.* A report by the Nitrate Coordination Group. DOE Pollution Paper 26. HMSO, London.
Norman, T.B. (1990), *An ecological survey of six streams on Jersey.* Unpublished MSc Dissertation in Conservation. University College London.
NRA (1989), *Water Pollution from farm waste in England and Wales.* National Rivers Authority, London.
NRA (1990), *Annual Report and Accounts 1989-90.* National Rivers Authority, London.
OECD (1986), *Diffuse sources of water pollution: agricultural activities - fertilisers and animal wastes.* OECD. Environmental Committee Water Management Policy Group Report, Paris, pp 1-114.
Potter, C. (1988), 'Environmentally sensitive areas in England and Wales: an experiment in countryside management'. *Land Use Policy*, 5, pp 301-313.
Roberts, G. and Marsh, T. (1987), 'The effects of agricultural practices on the nitrate concentrations in the surface water domestic supply sources of western Europe'. *International Association of Hydrological Sciences Public*ation. 164, pp 1-19.
Robinson, G. M. (1991), 'EC agricultural policy and the environment: land use implications in the UK'. *Land Use Policy* 8, pp 95-107.
Rural Planning Services (1983), *Jersey Island Plan.* Agricultural Survey; Technical Report. Rural Planning Services, Didcot, Oxon.
Walling, D.E and Foster, I.D.L. (1978), The 1976 drought and nitrate levels in the River Exe basin. *Proc. Institut. Water Engineers & Scientists*, 32, pp 341-352.
Walling, D.E. and Webb, B.W. (1981), 'Water Quality'. In Lewin, J. (ed) *British Rivers.* Allen and Unwin, London, pp 126-169.

13 Conservation, conversations and countryside change

KEN WILLIS

Introduction

The forces impinging on countryside change are many and complex. Figure 13.1 provides some indication of the broad range of agencies and issues involved. Within these general areas specific laws and policies operate, such as the Wildlife and Countryside Act 1981; Farm Woodland Grants; agricultural quotas; set aside; etc. This paper does not discuss these intervention processes in detail, but presents them to aid appreciation of the range of issues with which the valuation of countryside change has to deal. The object of this paper is to:
    (1) describe the methodological approach of the Countryside Change Unit (CCU) at Newcastle University to analysing changes in rural areas; and
    (2) present some empirical findings of the research to date.
But before doing this, it will be instructive to briefly contrast the approaches to analysing countryside change, between Newcastle University's Countryside Change Unit and University College London (UCL) Countryside Change Centre (CCC).

UCL Countryside Change Centre

Research in UCL's CCC concentrates on actors and agencies involved in countryside change, through interviews and discussions with respondents. From this wealth of empirical information and impressionistic evidence, intuitive rationalisation permits theoretical perspectives to be developed. The

FIGURE 13.1 Policy Instruments Classified by Policy Agency

Agency	Price support	Capital grants	Tax breaks	Extension	Infra-structure	Designation by: Orders	Designation by: Agreements	Designation by: Packages	Purchase	Full-Funding	Charging
MAFF	XXX	XX		XX	X	XX(LFA)		X(ESA)		(with EC)	X (extension)
Forestry Comission		XX	XX	X	X		X				X (services, recreation)
Countryside Commission		XX	X	X	X	X(access)	XX (access, NP)	(EXMOOR)	access areas ∧ + NPs		X (services)
NCC	(income)	XX	X	X		XX	XX	(X)			
Rural Development Comm.				XXX	XXX	XX			X		X
Education				XX	XX					XXXX	XX
Health				X	XX					XX	X
Industry		X	X	X	XX						
Transport					XXX					XX	?X?
Environment: General		X	X		X	X	X			XXX	
T&C Planning						XX	XX			XX	X

paper by Marsden and Murdoch (1990) on agriculture in retreat provides a nice example. From the case study information a cognitive continuum is developed of the agricultural cum diversification combination on farms, from the case of the farm family with no plans for diversification to the other extreme of a farmer whose objective is to hive off all his land and buildings into other uses. Between these two polar cases lies a plethora of pluriactivities [leisure, tourism, recreation, barn conversion, warehousing, horse livery, specialist agriculture (e.g. quail egg production), residential development, industrial units, etc] representing the physical manifestation of change in the countryside. More detail is provided by Munton (1991).

By contrast the Newcastle Countryside Change Unit (CCU), is based upon neo-classical economic theory, which uses markets as the principle conceptual vehicle of evaluation. System/data based aids, and quasi experiments, are also used to analyse data on rural markets and non-marketed goods. It is to this general area that discussion now turns.

Markets

When goods and services are exchanged in organised markets, it is easy to observe choices. The prices and quantities characterise how each person's values motivate them to respond to a market situation.

Most economists regard observed choice as the only dependable basis for understanding preferences. In support of this view the work of Needleman (1976) is instrumental, revealing the large discrepancy between what people say they will do and actual behaviour. In the case of kidney transplants the refusal rate for eligible parents was 88%, despite the media impression that such refusals are infrequent.

Of course the major problem in inferring valuations from behaviour is to interpret what is observed (Needleman, 1980). For example risky activities [such as farm work] typically vary in many respects apart from their riskiness, and it may be difficult to calculate what proportion, if any, of farm wages is payment for these other features, and what proportion is compensation purely for risk.

Non-Market Goods

Additional problems arise in valuing commodities which are exchanged outside markets, since such goods have no explicit value. However, there are three basic ways in which non-marketed goods can be evaluated, through: (1) observed choice in related private markets i.e. revealed preferences; (2) expressed preferences of individuals i.e. intentions to modify behaviour in the light of some proposed change; and (3) adaptations people make as they learn i.e. experience and learning affect people's values and also their behaviour and so changes in these values over time may provide a good indication of people's marginal valuation of specific attributes.

Observed Choice

In such cases, as non-priced open access recreation in the countryside, ways can be sought in which values might be revealed through observable choices. Using such choices in these circumstances requires some linkage between what can be observed and what needs to be valued. The amount people are willing to pay (WTP) in terms of the cost to travel to the recreation site is one such linkage; and the amount people are WTP for a house, to live in a particular landscape area such as the Lake District, over and above a similar house elsewhere, is another.

Despite problems, observed choice models feature strongly in the work of the Newcastle CCU. Hedonic house price models relating house prices to landscape types are based upon observed choice, where individuals purchase dwellings to enjoy environmental surroundings as well as house structure and locational services. Such choices are enumerated through building society records and documented data on environmental attributes. House prices were found to differ in a statistically significant way (by ANOVA and Kruskal-Wallis tests) in almost all regions according to the Institute of Terrestrial Ecology's landscape types (Garrod and Willis, 1991a). Hence landscape change will affect the value of rural resources such as housing. This work is continuing with a more detailed investigation into the impact of specific environmental and countryside attributes on observed choice in housing in the Forest of Dean and Gloucestershire areas using hedonic price models (Garrod and Willis, 1991b). Results indicate, for example, that while some neighbouring woodland seems to have a positive effect on house prices, homebuyers appear indifferent to the absolute level of cover, and woodland view actually detracts from house value. The presence of water has a strong and positive influence on value. The spatial arrangement of settlement also affects value, as does excessively steep land gradient.

Similarly, models of change in size distribution of agricultural holdings are based upon actual observed phenomenon/cases or a census/survey. In this way the number of large farms (>120 ha) has been observed as increasing despite the decline in the total number of farms. The pace of structural change in the size of agricultural holdings has been more rapid in the last 25 years than in the preceding 25 years, and this has been modelled through data based aids (Markov processes and the lognormal distribution)(Allanson, 1990).

Incidently, the neoclassical economic approach is not slavishly followed. Indeed, simple neoclassical theory fails to account for the skewed nature of the distribution of agricultural holdings: if all holdings face the same marginal cost and revenue curves then under perfect competition all holdings should be of identical size; which is clearly not the case. When these assumptions are relaxed then holding size will be indeterminate. Alternatively, each holding will have its own particular optimum size if there is no common production technology or if the opportunity costs differ between holdings due to specialised factors of production. In neither case does theory predict the specific nature of the distribution.

The difficulties of using observed phenomena is that of the:

(1) diverse influence of factors affecting an observed variable i.e. the difficulty of netting out all of the other influences except the one under consideration (the additionality problem).
(2) classification of variables (often arbitrary and with a changing definition over time) may affect the analysis.

Expressed Preferences

A second source of information arises through people's conversations (Smith, 1990). People's values affect their conversations. Conversation like choice is a form of social interaction, but does not require explicit actions. People evaluate things, even though no specific choices are involved: the weather, the environment, architecture, etc.. Much of this information relevant to estimating economic relationships and testing hypotheses is not normally recorded. But surveys have become a cost effective means of collecting such data. An interview is merely a structured conversation, and a survey a collection of conversations with a number of people defined by some sampling criteria.

The conversational approach is formally developed through surveys in terms of questionnaire design and statistical sampling. The conversational approach also features strongly in the work of the Newcastle CCU, and thus the difference in methodological approach between the Newcastle and London centres is not so great as might appear at first sight.

Using the 'conversational approach' we have completed a sample survey of residents and visitors to the Yorkshire Dales National Park to assess their preferences and values for conserving different landscapes (Willis and Garrod, 1991a). This approach not only documents the preferences for landscape types, but also reveals the differences between residents and visitors in terms of their preference for landscape characteristics and places a monetary value on different landscapes.

Researchers often use 'conversational surveys' completed by other organisations to investigated alternative issues than the one immediately at hand. In such a case someone else designs the survey and formulates the questions. Occasionally an existing survey completed by the researcher himself is used as data for the analysis on another issue. Both of these types of cases have arisen at Newcastle with the use of British Waterways and Forestry Commission data respectively, to value the environmental benefits of countryside recreation. Reliance on such surveys and data often necessitates constructing new estimators to try to compensate for the ways in which the questions were asked or answers coded.

Thus demand curves that are estimated based on surveys by the Forestry Commission and British Waterways of users conducted at recreation sites, provide no information on individuals who choose not to use the site. This implies that the measure of quantity demanded, the reported use of the site during the season (i.e. trips) will be truncated at one. This is an example of a case in which the data collection or reporting decisions differed from the behavioural decisions made by economic agents described. To overcome this problem a maximum likelihood model was employed to analyse recreational behaviour based upon stated (recalled) choice, when individuals were asked to recall previous visits during an occasion when they are actually visiting particular recreation sites such as canals, forests and inland waterways (Willis and Garrod, 1990a and 1991b). If the truncation bias is corrected by using a maximum likelihood method, the results will be more meaningful.

These 'conversational surveys' also revealed the preferences of respondents and their WTP from hypothetical questions such as "how much would you be willing to pay if .... occurred?" Although such a contingent valuation approach is open to biases, such biases can be minimised (Garrod and Willis, 1990). As long as the conversation process is controlled, it offers opportunities to substantially expand knowledge about economic decisions and improve on how conventional survey or census data is collected. To appreciate this point recall how individuals (and the researcher) respond to a conventional survey/census recording observed choice, by:

(1) remembering their behaviour during some earlier period;
(2) assigning a fraction of their time and money expenditure to the particular activity over a certain period;
(3) evaluating the condition or quality of some environmental criteria, availability of substitutes, health status, etc.; and
(4) reporting sensitive information such as income, wealth, employment status.

Data acquired by asking respondents recollections of 'environmental purchases' such as visits to particular sites, is often regarded as hard factual information; whereas that requiring involvement in developing ways to probe people's intended behaviour or responses to proposed programmes is not. In reality to categorize the 'truthfulness' of data by its method of acquisition is not satisfactory. Data based upon 'conversations' might be more accurate in many instances.

Results of the individual travel cost models (ITCM) of forest and inland waterways recreational activities have revealed that, in general, benefits accruing from these countryside activities just exceed the current recreational subsidy levels required to maintain them, although benefits do not always exceed the total subsidy level to the agency involved (Willis and Garrod, 1990a; Willis and Garrod, 1991b). The scale of benefits are such, however, that major extensions to these recreational provisions would not be justified. Some selected afforestation might be worthwhile in certain areas, depending upon location. However, there are examples of rural inland waterway routes where recreational benefits fail to cover running and maintenance costs (Willis and Garrod, 1990b), and a decision must be taken on whether it is 'economic' to conserve such facilities in the countryside.

Countryside Management

The need to incorporate environmental stocks and flows into national accounts has been stressed by Pearce et al (1989), to ensure welfare losses due to natural and environmental resource depletion, as well as environmental benefits, are taken into account in decision making. Adger and Whitby (1991a) have compiled such a set of environmental accounts for the agricultural and forest sector. Difficulties encountered were the paucity of data on the environmental costs and benefits of particular rural land uses and the difficulty of aggregating the data to the national situation. But results suggest that agriculture and forestry land uses provide major environmental benefits which might add 20 per cent to the net product of these industries. Most benefits accrue from green belt designation. There are some offsetting negative effects, but these costs appear to be small, but evidence is incomplete. Results should be judged against fully specified satellite accounts which indicate the physical magnitudes to be evaluated.

Research on the countryside begs the question as to how decisions will be made on particular projects and policies. Environmental impact assessment (EIA) and cost benefit analysis (CBA) are two commonly employed decision aids. But in a review of these, Adger and Whitby (1990) have reached the conclusion that both have important imperfections which lay them open to abuse and capture by individual agencies pursuing their narrower objectives. The only safeguard against such capture is greater transparency in the public sector: only full disclosure of calculations and assessments, guarantee better rural land use policy and planning decisions. EIA in the forestry sector does not appear to have contributed towards a more optimal mix of public and private goods, partly because of the nature of the proposed developments and the institutional arrangements for their implementation (Adger and Whitby, 1991b).

Conclusion

Considerable progress has been made in the first year of research on countryside change at Newcastle University. This will continue apace for the remainder of the programme. Projects in the next year of the programme are scheduled to investigate the amenity value of forestry in Great Britain using a hedonic price model, and the impact of forestry on the carbon balance and global warming. Other projects will complement those undertaken at UCL. Golf course development, for example, will be analysed from an actor and agency point of view by UCL, while Newcastle will undertake a quantitative study of the demand for golf.

Acknowledgements

The research reported here forms part of the ESRC Countryside Change Initiative. The views expressed are those of the author alone.

References

Adger N. and Whitby M. (1990), *Appraisal and the Public Good: Environmental Assessment and Cost Benefit Analysis. Countryside Change Working Paper Series WP7*, Department of Agricultural Economics and Food Marketing, University of Newcastle upon Tyne.

Adger N. and Whitby M. (1991a), *National Accounting for the Externalities of Agriculture and Forestry. Countryside Change Working Paper Series WP16*, Department of Agricultural Economics and Food Marketing, University of Newcastle upon Tyne.

Adger N. and Whitby M. (1991b), *Environmental assessment and the provision of public goods: the case of new afforestation*. Countryside Change Unit, Department of Agricultural Economics and Food Marketing, University of Newcastle upon Tyne. (forthcoming).

Allanson P. (1990) *The Evolution of the Size Distribution of Agricultural Holdings. Countryside Change Working Paper Series, WP11*, Department of Agricultural Economics and Food Marketing, University of Newcastle upon Tyne.

Garrod G.D. and Willis K.G. (1990), *Contingent Valuation Techniques: a review of their unbiasedness, efficiency and consistency. Countryside Change Working Paper Series, WP10*, Department of Agricultural Economics and Food Marketing, University of Newcastle upon Tyne.

Garrod G.D. and Willis K.G. (1991a). Assessing the Impacts and Values of Agricultural Landscapes: an application of non-parametric statistical methods. *Planning Outlook*, (forthcoming).

Garrod G.D. and Willis K.G. (1991b), *The Hedonic Price Method and the Valuation of Countryside Characteristics. Countryside Change Working Paper Series, WP14*, Department of Agricultural Economics and Food Marketing, University of Newcastle upon Tyne.

Marsden T. and Murdoch J. (1990), *Agriculture in Retreat: implications for the changing control and development of rural land. Countryside Change Working Paper Series, WP9*, Department of Agricultural Economics and Food Marketing, University of Newcastle upon Tyne.

Munton R. (1991), The Social and Economic Restructuring of Rural Britain, *Progress in Rural Policy and Planning*, 1, pp106-108.

Needleman L. (1976), Valuing Other People's Lives, *'The Manchester School'*, 44, pp309-342.

Needleman L. (1980), The Valuation of Chances in the Risk of Death by Those at Risk. The Manchester School, 48, pp229-254.

Pearce D., Markandya A. and Barbier E. (1989), Blue Print for a Green Economy. Earthscan, London.

Smith V.K. (1990), Can We Measure the Economic Value of Environmental Amenities. Southern Economic Journal, 56 (4), pp865-878.

Willis K.G. and Garrod G.D. (1990a). The Individual Travel Cost Method and the Value of Recreation: the case of the Montgomery and Lancaster Canals. Environment and Planning C, Government and Policy, 8, pp315-326.

Willis K.G and Garrod G.D. (1990b). Valuing open access recreation on inland waterways. Countryside Change Working Paper Series, WP12, Department of Agricultural Economics and Food Marketing, University of Newcastle upon Tyne.

Willis K.G and Garrod G.D. (1991a). Landscape Values: a contingent valuation approach and case study of the Yorkshire Dales National Park, Countryside Change Working Paper Series, WP21, Department of Agricultural Economics and Food Marketing, University of Newcastle upon Tyne.

Willis K.G. and Garrod G.D. (1991b). An individual travel-cost method of evaluating forest recreation. Journal of Agricultural Economics, 42, pp33-42.

14 Ecology and land use in Britain

R.G.H. BUNCE

Introduction

Statistics for the main land uses in Britain are available from the appropriate agencies, such as the Ministry of Agriculture. Since 1971, however, the Institute of Terrestrial Ecology (ITE) has been collecting data on the ecological component of land use and the changes which are taking place. This research is a response to increased public awareness of ecological factors, and an appreciation that not enough is known about the major changes have been taking place in the countryside. Local studies such as those summarised by Shoard (1980), have suggested that these changes involve a loss of landscape features and diversity, but no national or commonly based statistics were available for confirmation. Accordingly, the ITE approach uses quantitative procedures so that the information is as objective as possible and the results statistically reliable.

The ITE Merlewood land classification

ITE has developed a stratification procedure for sampling ecological factors throughout Great Britain, since the level of detail required to be measured in the field precludes a full field census. The procedure is initially based on dBk measurements of physical and other attributes for 1 km squares from published maps. These data are subjected to multivariate analysis (Bunce et al. 1981) in order to produce strata, termed land classes. These desk data thus provide great detail on the geographical distribution of the 32 land classes and a census of the relative proportions of different land classes throughout Great Britain. The land classes then provide a framework for selecting 1 km squares for field sampling and, in the first survey in 1978, eight squares were taken from each class, giving a total of 256 squares. The detailed ecological information on plant species, soil characteristics, landscape features, land cover and type of land use was analysed to produce the first national summaries of ecological characteristics (Bunce & Heal 1984). Once the sample had been validated as representative for Great Britain as a whole, a variety of studies used the sample to obtain estimates of national patterns, (Mitchell et al. 1987).

In 1984, a repeat survey concentrated on land use and landscape features. This developed the database further for future monitoring, and quantified the principal changes in such features as hedgerows, grassland, crops and woodlands (Barr et al. 1986). Other surveys, eg Huntings (1986) Technical Surveys Ltd. project on Monitoring of Landscape Change (MLC), were also carried out during this time, but were not concerned with the ecological factors behind the changes in landscape features. The need for information on the ecological consequences of land use change led the Department of the Environment (DoE) to contract ITE to coordinate the available information on the subject and to define the principal ecological changes which had taken place. This programme of work was completed in 1989. It identified the consequences of the intensification of agriculture in the lowlands, notably change in linear features such as hedgerows. In addition, it recognised the value of remotely sensed imagery to assess land cover and change, provided that the information obtained could be linked to detailed ecological data. The results also identified the future work that was required, and pinpointed the techniques for achieving statistically reliable results. The recommended methods were adopted in the Countryside Survey carried out in 1990 for the DoE. The survey was designed to measure ecological change since 1978, and to set a basis for future monitoring. The data collected during the survey are currently being analysed.

This chapter now presents some of the key applications using the ITE classification, for example, land availability for wood energy plantations and also describes the present status of the most recent survey.

The land availability study (LAS) for wood energy plantations

This study aimed to determine the amount of land which might become available for growing trees for energy under various economic assumptions. The resultant land availability model (LAM) provided a means of predicting a change in land use at the site-specific level (Mitchell et al. 1987). The core of the LAM lay in the ITE Land Classification System. The initial 256 squares surveyed in 1978 were used in the analysis to obtain estimates for Great Britain of the area of land under the various land cover categories. The potential land uses of different forest systems were overlaid upon the basic land cover patterns. We can assess the environmental impact of various practices because the areas under the different current and potential land uses can be overlaid and compared with each other. The criterion for predicting change in land use in the LAM was financial performance, ie that land use which achieved the highest net present value over 60 years at a given discount rate. The LAM enabled us to compare the relative financial performance of different actual and postulated land uses for the individual areas of land in the sample square, and provided estimates for Great Britain of, suitable areas, potential production levels, and the likely species, thus indicating possible future developments. In addition, the area and nature of displaced land use categories were given, enabling us to predict the implications of potential change in terms of associated habitats. The LAM also examined the effects of a wide range of economic assumptions on the area of land predicted as being available for forestry. One set of assumptions, for example, assumed the production of pipeline gas from wood, increased energy prices, constant timber and agricultural revenues, and a 5% discount rate. With this example, some 4.6 million hectares of land were predicted to change to forestry, with a potential annual production of some 38 million dry tonnes of wood for energy and 28 million cubic metres of timber. However, when the constraints in terms of designated areas for nature conservation or landscape were taken into account, some 1.8 million hectares of land were estimated to change to forestry, producing some 16 million dry tonnes of wood for energy and 11 million cubic meters of timber (Mitchell et al. 1987). The analyses also showed that the area of land was more sensible to the basic assumptions of energy prices and discount rate, compared with the absolute production potential.

This model system demonstrated the efficiency of the land classification in obtaining strata which could summarise the whole of Great Britain, but at the same time identify those regions most likely to be affected. In the present case, the marginal uplands had the largest area of potential forestry because of the balance of land uses present, and thus the area of greatest potential for change was identified. The model was successful in setting the scene for future work on wood energy plantations.

The Highland Region information system

The Highland Region is very large, over 25,000 km^2 in area, and generally upland in nature, with only small areas of lowland. The population numbers less than 200,000 and is predominantly rural. The remoteness of much of the land, combined with the many changes taking place, mean that the Planning Department (Highland Regional Council 1984) requires information on the rural environment, but no adequate data were available.

The requirements for a rural information system of the Highland Region were thus: first, to compile an inventory of rural statistics; second, to provide a broad regional description of resources; third, to monitor land use changes; fourth, to predict land use potential; and finally, to be able to compare policy options. The database had to be held within the Regional Office of the Highland Regional Council, rather than in a remote research laboratory, as it had been shown elsewhere that free access to a computer was essential. Accordingly, a inexpensive microcomputer was obtained which was able to carry out a wide range of mapping procedures, as well as to process other information for planning purposes at a regional level, such as school buildings. The land classification procedure for the whole of Britain was used to a 32-land class level, but the most abundant land classes were divided at a further stage, on the basis of their extent, to produce 24 classes for the Region, as opposed to the 16 original classes. The Highland Regional staff then surveyed eight squares drawn at random from each of the classes, using the standard approach for field recording developed by ITE. Preliminary assessments of validity were made; for example, the area of rough grazing in Highland Region was estimated from field survey at 1.86 million hectares, compared with the estimate of 1.89 million hectares supplied by the Department of Agriculture and Fisheries for Scotland. The database was expanded to cover the whole of the Region, and the validity and usefulness of treating the attributes separately in order to show their distribution was demonstrated. This was a major step forward in the development of the procedure - the necessity for complete cover had not previously been appreciated.

Another important development was in the integration of predictions from the field survey samples with the data held for each square. For example, a model was developed that enabled the competition between farming and forestry to be examined in financial terms for specific areas of sample squares drawn from the land classes. This model enables a combination of actual and potential area of forestry to be mapped at a regional level.

An extensive database was built up for the Highland Region from the simple data available for maps, and successfully used in a variety of planning exercises. A major advantage of the systems lies in its low cost in terms of the computing hardware required, and in the sampling procedure. It is, nonetheless, a powerful supplement to, rather than a replacement for, the traditional planning processes.

The importance of linear features

In the initial survey carried out in Cumbria (Bunce & Smith 1978) 16 random quadrats of 200 square were placed within representative 1 km squares. During the field survey, it was observed that quadrats placed in open country missed much of the variation that was apparent in linear features such as streamsides and roadside verges. Therefore, in 1978, when the land classification method was extended to cover the whole of Britain, data from three linear features were recorded. Since the analyses of these data, the importance of linear features has received wider recognition, with the incorporation of concepts relating to connectivity and corridors. This recognition is reflected in the wide range of literature now available on the subject, eg Schrieber (1988) and Bunce and Howard (1990). The linear features surveyed in 1988 (Bunce & Heal 1990) showed distinct ecological patterns. The hedges and verges contributed most diversity in the lowlands, whilst the streams were a more significant source of variation in the uplands. Diversity was greatest in the marginal uplands, where both upland and lowland habitats were present. In contrast, linear features were more diverse in the lowlands, but relatively uniform in the upland landscapes of northern Britain. There is, therefore, a marked contrast between the distribution of vegetation types in the lowlands and the uplands, the former showing most variation and the latter less strong contrasts. Whilst the general pattern is common overall, there is much local variation; for example, semi-natural vegetation on chalk and limestone is diverse in areas where it has not been replaced by intensive agriculture. Many of the linear features contain distinctive species not found in the open countryside. Thus, streamsides provide a habitat for wetland species and hedges for woodland species. However, many of the species found in hedgerows are also found in the open landscape. In the lowlands there are as many species present in the linear habitats - in fact, in many cases, more - as in the open landscape, although the former occupy less than 5% of the open area. In contrast, in upland areas, the majority of species are widely dispersed throughout the landscape, partly because most of the open habitats are less intensively managed, and partly because linear habitats are less common. In general, the lowland habitats are intrinsically richer in species than the uplands, but intensive management has meant that many plants and species are now restricted to small patches in the landscape, usually in linear situations. The results indicate the botanical significance of linear features, which is now emphasised by the paucity of undisturbed semi-natural vegetation in intensively farmed lowland landscapes.

Linear features are also important for their role in linking elements of the landscape, especially where semi-natural habitats are small and fragmented. In addition, they are also important as habitats and cover for many insects and other animal species. The role of many linear features as refuges for species that have not been able to survive in the fields is important in terms of the response of vegetation to potential changes in agricultural practice, such as set-aside. For example, a decline in the management of grasslands could lead to the expansion of species from field boundaries, as seen in derelict areas in the Pyrenees. Linear features still, therefore, retain much botanical capital that can be utilised to replace species lost from open landscapes. They need to be incorporated into the development of future landscape design in order to maintain and enhance ecological diversity.

Monitoring

Although some national agencies in Britain carry out regular assessments of the major land use categories, these figures do not contain information about the quality of the use or species composition. This is particularly important for grasslands, where a field may stay as permanent grass over many years, but change completely in its species composition. Only data from the 1978 and 1984 ITE surveys, described above, provide consistent coverage for the whole of Great Britain. The principal results are described by Barr *et al.* (1986) and are summarised below.

The main change in land cover during that period was a shift away from barley and grass production to wheat and oil seed rape. Other changes in land use were fragmentary, although they may be locally significant. However, analysis of the grassland quality data showed a consistent increase in agriculture intensity, as reflected by the species composition of the fields, with a loss of pastures containing many broadleaved species. These results indicate that the trends described by Fuller (1987) are still continuing, even within fields that had already shown some improvement previously. Although botanical data are the prime source of this information, many insect species will also be affected because of their direct relationship with plants as food material.

Another important change, this time in the marginal uplands, was the improvement in rough grazing, with species composition being modified mainly from rough grassland, containing species such as *Nardus* and *Molinia*, to improved grassland dominated by *Lolium* and associated agricultural species. The figures from the ITE survey for grassland thus support the generally accepted trend (Hopkins & Wainwright 1986), ie a shift away from reseeding towards the increased use of inorganic fertilizers for intensifying production. In comparison with the total area, the loss of semi-natural vegetation through practices such as grassland improvement was relatively small, and the core of unimproved upland vegetation remained relatively constant overall. However, forestry had expanded within the uplands, eg within the Flow country, as shown elsewhere by Forestry Commission statistics, leading to all the associated ecological impacts on species composition, for example, those described by Hill (1986).

The analysis also showed that hedgerows continued to be lost and that a variety of other changes, eg an increase in golf courses, were also taking place throughout the countryside.
As well as demonstrating the importance of the qualitative aspects covered in the DOE project on the Ecological Consequences of Land Use Change (Bunce & Heal 1990), the results from ITE surveys also underline the importance of obtaining detailed ecological data for the countryside as a whole. The DoE, therefore, contracted ITE to carry out a resurvey in 1990, and this is summarised below.

Countryside Survey 1990

The Countryside Survey 1990 (Barr 1990) differs in several ways from previous ITE land use surveys. It is co-funded by the DOE with support from the NCC, it links with freshwater biological research being undertaken at the NERC Institute of Freshwater Ecology, and it involves collaboration with a wider range of scientists and organisations than before. The field survey will be combined with a land cover map of Britain using satellite images, being developed at ITE's Monks Wood Experimental Station. Field recording detail has been increased to levels of individual plant species and many more samples of vegetation have been included in each 1 km square. In all, 508 squares have been visited, with all visits taking place between June and November. Each square may take up to 4 or 5 days to survey by a team of two people. Land cover is mapped in detail, to include agricultural crops, types of grassland and woodland, together with their dominant species, semi-natural and natural vegetation, recreation, and towns and villages. Each piece of land is mapped and coded. In addition, detailed vegetation plots are laid out in up to 27 locations within the square, and are marked permanently to allow relocation in future years. All vascular plant species within these plots are recorded. Samples of stream and pond animals are taken at 2 or 3 locations for later identification. The mapped land cover data are currently being converted into computer-readable format, and all the information will be entered on to a computer-based geographical information system, allowing automatic calculation of areas, lengths and numbers of features in the sample squares. The changes from 1984 and 1978 will also be recorded.

At a more detailed level, the species lists will be computerised, and analyses will determine the species numbers and composition in the sample squares. More complicated procedures will classify the plots according to their total species composition. Comparisons will be made with records from 1978 in order to assess: changes in extent; whether species are being lost from the landscape; which landscapes have the highest ecological diversity; and which are changing to the greatest degree.

The data analyses will not be completed for two years, but preliminary results will be produced by late 1991. One of the main objectives is to provide basic information on the wider countryside, as well as an overall context in which nature conservation policies and planning policies can be tested. In addition, a comparable survey in 1991 will be extended to Northern Ireland.

References

Barr, C.J., Benefield, C.B., Bunce, R.G.H., Risdale, H.A. & Whittaker, M. (1986), Landscape changes in Britain. Institute of Terrestrial Ecology, Abbots Ripton.

Barr, C.J. (1990), Mapping the changing face of Britain. *Geographical*, vol. LXII No. 9, pp. 44-47.

Bunce, R.G.H. & Smith, R.S. (1978), *An ecological survey of Cumbria. Structure Plan Working Paper No. 4.* Cumbria County Council, Kendal.

Bunce, R.G.H., Barr, C.J. & Whittaker, H.A. (1981). *The land classes of Great Britain: preliminary descriptions for users of the Merlewood method of land classification Merlewood Research and Development Paper No. 86.* Institute of Terrestrial Ecology, Grange-over-Sands.

Bunce, R.G.H. & Heal, O.W. (1984), 'Landscape evaluation and the impact of changing land use on the rural environment: the problem and an approach', in Roberts, R.D. & Roberts, T.M. (eds), *Planning and Ecology*, Chapman & Hall, London.

Bunce, R.G.H. & Heal, O.W. (1990). *Ecological Consequences of Land Use Change.* Annual Rept. Institute of Terrestrial Ecology 1989-1990, pp. 19-24.

Bunce, R.G.H. & Howard, D.C. (1990), *Species Dispersal in Agricultural Habitats*, Belhaven, London.

Fuller, R.M. (1987), 'The changing extent and conservation interest of lowland grasslands in England and Wales: areview of grassland surveys', *Biological Conservation*, vol. 40, pp. 281-300.

Highland Regional Council. (1984), *Highland Region/ITE Land Classification System.* Planning Department Information Paper No. 5, Highland Regional Council, Inverness.

Hill, M.O. (1986), *Ground Flora Success in Commercial Forests*, ITE Symposium No. 17, Huntingdon, pp. 71-78.

Hopkins, A. & Wainwright, J. (1989), 'Changes in botanical composition and agricultural management in enclosed grasslands in upland areas of England and Wales, 1970-86 and some conservation implications', *Biological Conservation*, vol. 47, pp. 219-235.

Hunting Surveys and Consultants Ltd. (1986), *Monitoring Landscape Change. Vol. I. The main report.* Huntings, Borelium wood.

Mitchell, C.P., Tranter, R.B., Downing, P., Brandon, O., Pearce, M.L., Bunce, R.G.H. & Barr, C.J. (1987), 'Growing wood for energy in Great Britain'. Report to the Energy Technology Support Unit.

Shoard, M. (1980), *The Theft of the Countryside.* Temple Smith, Hounslow.

Schrieber, K.F. (1988). 'Connectivity in Landscape Ecology'. *Proceedings of the 2nd International Seminar of the 'International Association for Landscape Ecology'.* Schöningh, Paderborn.